POLITENESS PHENOMENA IN
ENGLAND AND GREECE

POLITENESS PHENOMENA IN ENGLAND AND GREECE

A Cross-Cultural Perspective

MARIA SIFIANOU

CLARENDON PRESS · OXFORD
1992

Oxford University Press, Walton Street, Oxford OX2 6DP

Oxford New York Toronto
Delhi Bombay Calcutta Madras Karachi
Kuala Lumpur Singapore Hong Kong Tokyo
Nairobi Dar es Salaam Cape Town
Melbourne Auckland Madrid

and associated companies in
Berlin Ibadan

Oxford is a trade mark of Oxford University Press

Published in the United States
by Oxford University Press Inc., New York

British Library Cataloguing in Publication Data
Data available
ISBN 0-19-823972-6

Library of Congress Cataloging in Publication Data
Sifianou, Maria.
Politeness phenomena in England and Greece: a cross-cultural
perspective / Maria Sifianou.
Includes bibliographical references.
1. English language—Social aspects—England. 2. English
language—Grammar, Comparative—Greek. 3. Greek language—Grammar,
Comparative—English. 4. Grammar, Comparative and general—Deixis.
5. Greek language—Social aspects—Greece. 6. Social interaction—
England. 7. Social interaction—Greece. 8. Speech acts
(Linguistics) 9. Forms of address. 10. Courtesy. I. Title.
PE1074.75.S54 1992 306.4'4'09495—dc20 92-11078
ISBN 0-19-823972-6

Typeset by Hope Services (Abingdon) Ltd.
Printed in Great Britain
on acid-free paper by
Bookcraft (Bath) Ltd, Midsomer Norton, Avon

*To all those whose love and
support made this work possible*

ACKNOWLEDGEMENTS

Many people deserve my sincere thanks for helping me in various respects and at various stages of this work. Since this is a revised version of my Ph.D. thesis, I first of all wish to express my deep indebtedness to both my supervisors Prof. Peter Trudgill and Prof. Irene Philippaki-Warburton for having been constant sources of invaluable advice and support. Their continual guidance and encouragement made this work more of a stimulating challenge than the demanding burden I often felt it would be.

Similarly, my deep gratitude is also due to Dr Viv Edwards for the many stimulating discussions, her eager and expert guidance and support, to Dr Jenny Cheshire for the helpful discussions and her overall substantial support, and to Ms Jean Hannah for selflessly giving me so much of her time and providing detailed comments on various drafts of the whole work.

I should also record very special thanks to my colleagues Bessie Dendrinos, Sophia Papaefthymiou-Lytra, and Niovi Trlyfona-Antonopoulou for reading various parts of the draft and offering me their instructive and expert comments. Thanks are also due to many friends, students, and colleagues of the English Department of the University of Athens who kept rekindling my interest in politeness phenomena through stimulating discussions. Among those I should record specific thanks to my colleagues, Aliki Bacopoulou-Halls, Chryssoula Lascaratou, Sophia Marmaridou, Liana Sakelliou and, above all, to Eleni Antonopoulou who so willingly shared the burden of indexing and proof-reading.

I would like to express my deepest gratitude and indebtedness to Robert F. Halls, who so generously made the time to guide and assist me at various stages, especially with the most arduous final touches to the whole work.

Last but not least I would like to register my debt and gratitude to my family for their never-tiring love and generous support, without which the completion of this work would have proved doubly difficult.

I am grateful for permission to reproduce the following materials: modified forms of figures on pp. 33 and 35–6 from P. Brown and S. Levinson (1978), 'Universals in language usage: politeness phenomena', in E. N. Goody (ed.), *Questions and politeness: strategies in social interaction*, © Cambridge University Press, republished in P. Brown and S. Levinson (1987), *Politeness: some universals in language usage*, © Cambridge University Press; and Figure 2.1 modified from figure 1.4 of G. N. Leech (1983), *Principles of pragmatics*, published by Longman Group UK Ltd.

I would also like to record my thanks to the staff of Oxford University Press for their kindness and expert assistance.

If these acknowledgements sound too conventional it is only because I lack more appropriate words to express my real feelings. This book has benefited greatly from all those acknowledged here as well as from many others too numerous to mention, but of course all faults and inadequacies which remain are entirely my own.

CONTENTS

NOTE ON ABBREVIATIONS
AND SYMBOLS

The great majority of the examples employed in the text come from the data, and to facilitate the reader's tracing of their sources I have used the following notation: for plays, the initial(s) of the name of the author are given, followed by the number of the play (the details of which are found in Appendix I) and the page number. Thus, if what follows the example is [E.1: 40] it means that the example is taken from 'Efthemiades' first play, page 40'. Similarly, [Q.5: S.1] means 'questionnaire, number 5, situation 1' and [NB] means that the example is taken from my 'notebook'. The Greek examples are given in Latin characters. I have, however, used the Greek characters γ (velar voiced fricative), δ (interdental voiced fricative), θ (interdental voiceless fricative), and χ (voiceless velar fricative) which best render the equivalent Greek sounds. Greek examples are followed by a word-for-word or freer translation according to what was thought the best rendition of the case under discussion; all translations are mine. A few examples are invented, mostly in cases where a convenient illustration on the issue discussed was needed. These examples bear no label. An asterisk against a word or phrase indicates an ungrammatical or unacceptable form.

I

Introduction

1.1 CONTENT AND ORGANIZATION

Despite the great significance of 'politeness', it is only in recent years that this concept has become a major issue in linguistics. This is evidenced in the vast array of publications which followed Brown and Levinson's (1978) original extended essay on politeness phenomena, including both confirming and disconfirming findings for their theory. In fact, it was probably this wave of renewed interest which led to the republication in 1987 of the same essay, now accompanied by an extensive introduction. This introduction critically examines all relevant subsequent research, and concludes with Brown and Levinson's conviction that broadly speaking their initial findings still appear to be justified. Interestingly enough, this reissue coincided with the establishment of 2 October as 'National Courtesy Day' in England. This growing interest in and continuing development of the theory of politeness clearly point to the importance of the issue in human interaction and, consequently, in the study of language in its social context.

The research presented here has been motivated by a general concern for the study of the principles underlying interaction in cross-cultural contexts and has been inspired by the work of Brown and Levinson, exploring mainly their distinction between 'positive' and 'negative' politeness. It is this work, together with a brief review of the relevant literature on interaction and politeness, which is presented in Chapter 2.

Chapter 3 concentrates on the concept of politeness and discusses the extent to which it is universal. Examples from a variety of cultures are included which indicate that differences in the conceptualization of politeness are reflected in all levels of the linguistic code. Finally, this chapter focuses on social deixis and forms of address which perhaps constitute the most transparent indices of socio-cultural influence on language use. Chapter 4 examines various verbal and non-verbal aspects of politeness and attempts to define the concept itself and to investigate how it is visualized in Greek and English cultures.

Politeness phenomena are, however, inevitably reflected in language. Consequently, special emphasis has been given to the analysis and interpretation of the realization patterns of requests. Requests were chosen mainly because of their intrinsic reflection of the expression of politeness and their wide, everyday applicability to a variety of situations, thus offering grounds for an extensive analysis of the theory as it applies to specific languages. This analysis is what constitutes Chapters 5, 6, and 7 and is perhaps the main contribution of this study. Chapter 5 also includes an examination of indirectness and its relationship to politeness. Chapter 6 deals with request constructions, whereas Chapter 7 concentrates on their modification. The main hypothesis is that politeness is conceptualized differently and, thus, manifested differently in the two societies; more specifically that Greeks tend to use more positive politeness devices than the English, who prefer more negative politeness devices.

Although the study may appear to be exclusively concerned with the description and comparison of the Greek and the English cultural and linguistic systems, this analysis is intended to serve as an explicit illustration of and support for the more general claim that, despite popular stereotypes, no nation may be objectively verified as more or less polite than any other, but only polite in a different, culturally specific way.

Furthermore, this attempt to investigate the sources of stereotypic comments classifying societies according to degrees of politeness will, hopefully, be of value to all those involved in human interaction. These include not only scholars with particular interests in the study of language use in its socio-cultural context, but also foreign language educators, in fact, everybody who lives and interacts with others, whether native or non-native speakers. As cross-cultural communication continues to increase, it is crucial that native users of all languages become more sensitized to the fact that different languages, because they are integral parts of their respective socio-cultural systems, construct messages and express feelings in different ways which are not less logical than one's own. To this end, examples from a variety of cultures and subcultures are included. Chapter 8 discusses some applications of this work for language teaching and learning, and suggests some broader implications for further research.

The comparative approach in cross-cultural study is that advocated by Hymes (1972*c*: 36). Similarly, as Saville-Troike (1982: 4) quite rightly points out, one of the best ways of coming to an understanding of one's own 'ways of speaking' is by comparing and contrasting these ways with those of others; this process soon reveals that what we normally assume to be 'natural' or 'logical' communicative practices are just as unique and conventional to their particular culture as the language code itself. A comparative approach, then, to a subject such as politeness seems inevitable, and my concern here is both comparative and descriptive.

The main focus of the study is linguistic, though not in its narrow sense. It draws from areas such as pragmatics, sociolinguistics, discourse analysis, and the ethnography of speaking, mainly because a topic such as politeness cannot be adequately handled within a narrowly defined linguistic model. Politeness is a social as well as a linguistic phenomenon, and ignoring either of these two equally basic aspects cannot be justified.

Finally the question of methodology employed in the research requires some comment, but as we shall see, although the issues of data collection and their treatment are extremely controversial, there appears to be no strong evidence which singles out one method as superior to any other.

1.2 DATA FOR THE STUDY OF POLITENESS

1.2.1 *Introduction*

Data collection and analysis in sociolinguistics has been a highly controversial issue.[1] It is understandable and justifiable for scholars to adhere to varying and even contrasting methodologies in their investigation of language, due to their training and school of thought; but to condemn one approach entirely and present and support another as the only scientifically justifiable one is unrealistic. As Brown and Yule (1983: 270) maintain, 'there is a dangerous

[1] See, for instance, Labov (1972*a* and 1972*b*); Wolfson (1976); and Stubbs (1983); among others.

tendency, among established scholars as among students, to hope that a particular line of approach will yield "the truth" about a problem. It is very easy to make claims which are too general and too strong.'

For instance, Wolfson (1983: 95) claims that 'ethnographic fieldwork is the only reliable method of collecting data about the way speech acts function in interaction'. However, as Labov (1972b: 119) suggests, 'it is not necessary for everybody to use the same methods—indeed, it is far better if we do not'.

Another issue which arises is what constitutes natural speech. Wolfson (1976: 202), for instance, argues that no single, absolute entity answers to the notion of natural/casual speech, or as Stubbs (1983: 225) says: 'the hunt for pure, natural or authentic data is a chimera'. 'If speech is felt to be appropriate to a situation and the goal, then it is natural in that context' (Wolfson, 1976: 202). This is exactly what we want to study: what people regard as appropriate speech in different situations.

Linguists are, I suppose, lucky in that the object of their research is all around them, and perhaps unlucky in that this very advantage can become burdensome if they always have their minds switched on to record what happens verbally around them. Speech analysts cannot ignore this inundation of continuous, actual manifestations, but nor can they ignore either their own intuitions or those of other native speakers nor yet the data collected in experimental situations and/or from literary sources. Moreover, any corpus, no matter how long, may lack some cases which can be revealed by intuition. However, intuitive data also have limitations.[2]

The problems associated with recording and transcription of data are discussed in detail by Stubbs (1983), Chaika (1982), and Labov (1972b). These problems may vary from the time- and money-consuming procedures involved to the 'principle of formality', in which the participants tend to become more formal in their speech. These considerations, together with the possibility of shyness and embarrassment, introduce the question of what Labov (1972b: 113) calls the 'observer's paradox'—observing 'how people speak when they are not being observed'. Naturally, this last difficulty can be surpassed under certain circumstances by the use of hidden tape recorders and similar devices, provided, of course,

---

[2] See, for instance, Labov (1966); and Gumperz and Hymes (1972).

that participants are asked for their consent before such data are published (Tannen, 1984*a*).

Like Kramer (1975: 199), who argues for an increased sense of certitude based on several approaches, Wolfson (1976), Stubbs (1983), and Labov (1972*b*) also stress the advantages of a multiple-source approach. They maintain that data so acquired can, when properly interpreted and combined, be used 'to converge on right answers to hard questions'—Labov's (ibid. 119) 'principle of convergence' and Stubbs's (1983: 235) 'triangulation'.

In my own work I, too, have concluded that we can profit from the advantages of one method while overcoming the limitations of another, and have, therefore, attempted to collect data from a variety of sources. These include mainly literature, but also discourse completion tests, reports, and discussions with informants and friends. I also used my intuitions and personal experience as a life-time member of Greek society and a long-time participant in English society. Finally, following the ethnographic approach, I carefully wrote down occurrences of situations and patterns I found interesting, provoking discussions and interpretations from the people involved, wherever possible.

1.2.2 *Drama*

Here, the main source of my data has been literature, and plays in particular. Following the recommendations of a specialist in Greek and English literature, I chose a number of plays by ten English and ten Greek contemporary playwrights, both men and women (see Appendix I). Because of their varying lengths, I finally selected forty-four Greek plays but only twenty English ones. These I read carefully in an effort to collect a number of speech acts, including requests, compliments, apologies, and so on. In addition, because I felt that translations of these works in the languages under consideration might also prove useful sources of linguistic insights, I looked through all the translations available.

I firmly believe that literature, particularly plays, can be a valuable source of data for sociolinguistic research. Modern literature is a mirror of society and as such it reflects and portrays a great variety of people from different social backgrounds. Not only does it reveal their use of language in a variety of situations given in context, but also their attitudes and values about language itself.

This kind of extensive variation is very difficult to capture in any manageable corpus of fieldwork data.

It has been suggested by Vine (1975: 357) that in order fully to understand what goes on in face-to-face interaction, besides all the other factors involved, 'additional contextual factors, such as the histories of the interactors and their past encounters, their immediate and future goals, the cultural definition of the interaction situation' should be taken into consideration. Any observation and recording of particular speech situations will be inadequate in providing this sort of information, unless the researcher is an insider, whereas in a play this is often amply delineated.

Such a rich source of data has not been exploited very extensively so far, mainly because of prejudices against the practice of those linguists who relied heavily on their intuitions to unravel and explain the rules underlying the verbal behaviour of native speakers. This reaction seems to have led to the other extreme: rejection of any data which is not 'naturally occurring speech'. There are of course exceptions; for instance, Burton (1980: Chapter 5) argues strongly for literary data and also mentions others, notably Goffman, Webb *et al.*, Ray, and Brown and Gilman, who implicitly or explicitly share the view that literature can be used as a source of sociological and sociolinguistic data. Edwards, Trudgill, and Weltens (1984: 8) share the view that dialect literature is worthy of consideration in dialect studies.

Obviously, the chief characteristic of literature is that it is written, as opposed to actual spoken discourse. Therefore, two questions arise. First, can we draw a clear-cut distinction between the written and the oral modes of communication? And second, if such a clear distinction can be drawn, can plays be considered real representatives of the written mode? Although Hymes (1986: 50) provides an affirmative answer to the first, he does so with the reservation that such dichotomies should be relied on only with great discretion since they stem from prejudices and, thus, invite unfair evaluations. As far as the second question is concerned, a moment's reflection will reveal that plays are not really an example of the written mode, because they are obviously intended to be performed (spoken) rather than to be read. Many plays have never even been published, and the fact that many others have should not be misinterpreted. Their appearance in written form serves more or less the same purpose as transcriptions of recorded materials; that is, it facilitates the job of a few people who, for various reasons (i.e. being actors, stage managers, etc.), have to study them. If 'writing is parasitic upon speech in that it is simply a way of recording the spoken language in an enduring visual form' (Trudgill, 1975a: 20), then clearly plays are the best example of this. In any case, it should be clear to anybody slightly interested in and/or familiar with literature that there is literature which is meant to be read and literature which is meant to be heard, and plays definitely belong to the latter category.

Looking at plays historically, they seem to descend from Homer's oral tradition. Modern plays, whether published or not, share with speech something special in their structures and lexicon, which enables actors to memorize them. This is the same element which entertained people and helped them not only to memorize but also modify to suit their situations the long products of the ancient oral tradition. Generally speaking, major socio-political and cultural changes have contributed to the production of plays which are characterized by a language faithful to reality and far from the educated or pseudo-educated forms which were more valued at times when drama was addressed to an élite. Modern plays are concerned with everyday, human interaction and are realized by everyday, human dialogues. The communicative behaviour of the interactants in a play may embody some degree of exaggeration for emphasis, and the artist may have established a personal style to create the desired effects upon the audience, but a playwright who wants to be successful cannot take endless liberties. The feature that many modern playwrights have in common is that they make use of language which strikes us as genuine and natural. 'In German drama since about 1967 one can observe a realistic direction, the language of which, in its faithfulness to reality, seems to surpass all previous conceptions of realism and naturalism. Its origins are rooted in the general political and cultural climate of the time' (Betten, 1982: 1077).

Thus, I believe that a careful choice of a variety of modern plays by various playwrights who themselves claim that one of their aims is to represent actual speech, and who may have spent hours recording and listening to real interactions, can be a rich source of natural data and of powerful insights into everyday conversational structures. A careful examination of such materials will reveal that the characters converse and argue, describe events, and express

opinions on a variety of topics in ways comparable to what is seen
and heard in everyday interactions. Burton (1980: 69) contends
that 'Pinter is widely acclaimed by both the lay and the literary-
critical public as a notable writer of realistic-sounding dialogue'.
Armenis (1985: 594–5), a well-known Greek actor and playwright,
says that the speech in his plays is determined by his modern heroes.
He travels with them in their memories and lives the present with
them. He enters the places in which they move and speak. He hunts
and searches for their thoughts, what they say, where and why. The
precise moment, the exact situation and setting play a role of vital
importance in determining the speech. Armenis adds that the time
needed for this procedure is both exciting and agonizing.

On this issue of the relationship between ordinary and literary
language, Tannen (1984a: 153) suggests that 'literary language,
rather than being maximally different from ordinary conversation,
builds on and intensifies features that are spontaneous and
commonplace in ordinary conversation' and further adds that 'face
to face conversation, like literature, seeks primarily to MOVE an
audience by means of involvement'. She presents a number of
devices which have been recognized as features basic both to
literature and to spontaneous speech in ordinary conversation, for
instance redundant repetition, alliteration, and also a variety of
figures of speech, such as irony, metaphor, and synecdoche.

In this respect the products of artists who are usually gifted with
extremely sensitive ears and eyes can be an invaluable source of
linguistic data, and the linguist should not ignore the wealth of
knowledge the 'unsophisticated' native language user and the lay
observer of social behaviour may offer.

All this is not to say that literature is the only or the most
appropriate way of collecting data and gaining insights for
sociolinguistic analyses of speech behaviour, but simply that
literature, and plays in particular, cannot be discarded as an
inappropriate source of data, unless they are peculiar or highly
idiosyncratic. Each source has its advantages and limitations and
literature is no exception. Obviously it depends on what one needs
one's data for. To a great extent speech acts are fixed; consequently,
no matter how creative authors may want to be, they cannot
escape from the boundaries and limitations of their language and
culture. The only problem that I can see with the kind of literature I
have used is that it might not give easily comparable data for a

cross-cultural study. This, however, can be overcome by enriching the corpus of literature with naturally occurring data, and with data elicited by experimental procedures, and this is what I have endeavoured to do by the use of questionnaires.

1.2.3 Questionnaires

In addition to the data gathered from plays and from participant and non-participant observation, I also constructed three questionnaires in both Greek and English. The aim of the first one was to investigate the concept of politeness (see Appendix II/1), whereas that of the second was to elicit requests (see Appendix II/2) and that of the third to investigate the status of off-record indirectness (see Appendix II/3). I wrote the Greek and the English versions simultaneously and had each pilot-tested with ten informants. The final versions were distributed to a variety of people of both sexes and varying socio-educational backgrounds, ages, etc., but this information was filled in on a separate sheet. At the end additional space was provided for further comments if the informants so wished.

The first questionnaire asked informants, both Greek and English, to explain what the concept of politeness meant to them, to describe some of the attributes they thought a polite person should have, and to give examples of behaviour which impressed them as either polite or impolite. The idea behind this enquiry was that the concept of politeness itself might be construed differently in the two societies. Although I gave out 100 questionnaires, only 27 English and 27 Greek informants returned them appropriately completed. The results from these questionnaires are analysed and discussed in section 4.5.1.

The second questionnaire is a discourse completion test made up of a short description of six speech situations, each of which specifies the setting and the participants, followed by an incomplete dialogue. The task of the informants was to fill in the missing parts of the dialogue. Based on insights gained from the literary data and my personal experience, the situations were devised in order to elicit requests and were constructed in the hope that suspected differences would emerge. The situations and characters involved were so described as to capture variability in social distance and status between the interactants, and in the seriousness of the imposition of the request. Again, although I gave out 100 questionnaires in each case, only 60 Greek and 50 English informants returned them appropriately completed.

A common comment made by both Greek and English informants was that their responses were tightly controlled by what was given. This was an intentional limitation so that comparability of the data could be ensured. Other respondents were reticent to fill in these tests because they did not know what the tests were about and some said that they felt judgements would be made of their verbal behaviour. To ease this fear and thus maintain variability concerning social backgrounds, I had many of these questionnaires distributed by others. Again I was careful to avoid stating that I was doing research on politeness, because that, too, would have affected the validity of the results.

The third questionnaire is based on the following premiss: requests are closely related to indirectness, and although on-record indirectness is overtly marked and has been studied extensively, the situation regarding off-record indirectness is still highly problematic. In an attempt to investigate the position of off-record indirectness in the two societies I therefore constructed and distributed the questionnaire to 37 Greek and 37 English informants asking them to read short descriptions of four situations and to decide whether for them it sounded more natural for the speaker to be: (*a*) asking a simple question (direct reading) or (*b*) requesting something else beyond what was explicitly stated (indirect reading). The first and the last situations are real-life occurrences, which I observed, whereas the second is taken from Tannen (1982: 220) and the third from Gumperz (1982*a*: 135). The results of this questionnaire are discussed in section 5.2.2.

I do not underestimate the limitations of conducting sociolinguistic research through questionnaires. Nevertheless, I believe that they can offer an excellent source of supplementary data for cross-cultural comparisons.

Discourse analysis cannot ignore actual occurrences, but it would be a similar mistake to restrict study to actual occurrences, without using other data: intuitive and experimental, and participants' as well as analysts' accounts, in order to converge on a well corroborated descriptive statement. (Stubbs, 1983: 237–8).

Having collected these data from all sources, I started classifying requests according to their syntactic patterns. Next, I tried to ascertain to what extent these data would support my initial hypothesis, viz. that Greeks tend to use more positive politeness devices than the English, who prefer more negative politeness. Chapter 6 discusses this question in detail, naturally bearing in mind the distinction already made between positive and negative politeness and the strategies with which they are realized.

Thus, the purpose of this form of research has been to investigate the concept of politeness and to elicit requests in order to enrich my data and facilitate the investigation of politeness, with particular reference to the indirectness employed.

2

Politeness: Setting the Scene

2.1 INTRODUCTION

Recently it has become widely acknowledged that verbal communication is not simply a means of conveying information, but also an equally important means of establishing, maintaining, and even terminating social relationships with other people (Hymes, 1972b; Lyons, 1981a; Trudgill, 1974). For instance, strangers who, under certain circumstances, may exchange uninformative views about the weather or even apparently informative statements about their past experiences or future plans do not usually have any need for this information. Such exchanges are themselves courteous acts performed basically in order to satisfy the need for involvement (Hurford and Heasley, 1983: 5). Even scientific statements, whose main function is to inform, usually have as one of their aims to approach and influence people (Lyons, 1981a: 143).

The interrelationship of a culture of a society and its language has been repeatedly emphasized by various scholars (Greenberg, Osgood, and Jenkins, 1963; Nida, 1964). Consequently, linguistic theory cannot restrict its attention to the study of the linguistic code and ignore the general social communicative conduct, since they are closely interrelated (Hymes, 1972a and 1968a).

The rules of politeness, that is rules which determine appropriate behaviour, are one of the aspects of culture which are clearly reflected in language. The relationship of the interactants, their age, the specific situation, and so on, will directly affect their language use to degrees determined by the culture. We must understand non-linguistic social interaction before we can make generalizations about the degree of politeness of individual utterances, according to Lakoff (1972: 910). For Brown and Levinson (1987: 1) the significance of politeness phenomena goes even further, 'for they raise questions about the foundations of human social life and interaction'.

In the light of such observations, this book investigates the concept of politeness and the realization patterns of requests, and accounts for their similarities and differences in Greek and in English. Among the main aims of this undertaking is to establish some of the reasons which have contributed to a widespread impression that the Greeks are impolite or at least less polite than the English. To my knowledge, although there is no academic literature on the subject of Greek politeness, the claim that Greeks are impolite is a widely held view encountered in popular magazines and newspapers and heard frequently in discussions amongst both foreigners residing in Greece and Greeks themselves.

Similarly, Leech (1983: 84) states that 'I have been seriously told that "Poles/Russians/etc. are never polite", and it is commonly said that "the Chinese and the Japanese are very polite in comparison with Europeans", and so on.' Lakoff (1972: 908) also contends that English sounds "harsh" or "impolite" to the Japanese, while Blum-Kulka (1982: 31) points out that 'refusal is often expressed in Israel by a curt "No" . . . a habit that probably contributes to the popular view about Israelis' "lack of politeness"'. Thomas (1983: 97) mentions other such offensive stereotypings about "the abrasive Russian/German", "the obsequious Indian/Japanese", "the insincere American", and "the standoffish Briton".

Such views are obviously based on norms of behaviour, both verbal and non-verbal, which the people who make such judgements regard as appropriate in particular situations. These norms are assigned meaning and carry special significance so that evaluations concerning the intelligence and the social integrity of individuals are based on them. In what sense, though, can it be objectively verified that our practices are more or less polite than those of others or that people whose languages have highly elaborate honorific systems are more or less polite than others? What exactly is politeness? Is it a universal concept with identical connotations in every culture? Lakoff (1972: 911) wonders whether we can talk about universal conditions governing the use of politeness markers. If we could be sure that politeness was a single concept shared by all human beings, then judgements concerning degrees of politeness could be considered objective. Since this is not the case, the kinds of stereotypes referred to above are useful only in that they point to an interesting situation worthy of examination, or as Thomas (1983: 107) contends 'every instance of national or ethnic stereotyping should be seen as a reason for calling in the pragmaticist and discourse analyst!'

Moreover, the study of both intra-ethnic and inter-ethnic discourse deserves special attention, not only because it is an interesting and significant area of research, but also because industrialization and technological advancement have contributed to a greater need for and amount of communication among people inside and outside their nations: 'the fate of the earth depends upon negotiations among representatives of governments with different cultural assumptions and ways of communicating' (Tannen, 1985: 203). Therefore, the study of interaction becomes crucial because it unravels underlying principles people subconsciously follow when they communicate with others. The objective study of these principles devoid of value judgements will not exacerbate discrimination (ibid. 212) but will contribute instead to a better understanding of what the differences are and will offer a more secure basis for cross-cultural comparisons and generalizations. Sensitizing people to interactional similarities and differences in cross-cultural contexts may, consequently, contribute to the elimination of misunderstandings and negative stereotypings, provided that interactants are willing to attribute the same degree of rationality to their interlocutors as they do to themselves.

Thus, for the improvement of communication and the elimination of misunderstandings among individuals and nations a more precise understanding of the subconscious principles which lead to discriminatory stereotypes is needed.

2.2 THE CO-OPERATIVE PRINCIPLE AND THE MAXIMS OF CONVERSATION

An interesting attempt to investigate these underlying principles in everyday interaction is presented by Grice (1975). His work falls within what is usually referred to as the theory of conversation, and has been developed over the past fifteen years by philosophers, notably Austin, Searle, and Grice, rather than by linguists. This explains their basic preoccupation with philosophical issues such as meaning, sense, and reference and the truth or falseness of propositions. Their views have had a great impact on linguistics, however, especially in the development of pragmatics.

Grice proposes a framework for language use. According to him, the fact that conversation is usually coherent and continuous indicates that it is, to some extent at least, a co-operative effort of the interactants which is governed by 'a rough general principle which participants will be expected (ceteris paribus) to observe, namely: Make your conversational contribution such as is required, at the stage at which it occurs, by the accepted purpose or direction of the talk exchange in which you are engaged' (ibid. 45).

This is Grice's widely known 'co-operative principle' (CP). This principle is associated with four postulates, which, following Kant, he labels *quantity*, *quality*, *relation*, and *manner*. Each of these may consist of one or more specific maxims which govern appropriate conversational behaviour on the assumption that the co-operative principle is operational. These categories as outlined by Grice are given below.

A. Quantity:
   1. Make your contribution as informative as required (for the current purposes of the exchange).
   2. Do not make your contribution more informative than is required.
B. Quality: Supermaxim: Try to make your contribution one that is true.
   1. Do not say what you believe to be false.
   2. Do not say that for which you lack adequate evidence.
C. Relation:
   1. Be relevant.
D. Manner: Supermaxim: Be perspicuous.
   1. Avoid obscurity of expression.
   2. Avoid ambiguity.
   3. Be brief (avoid unnecessary prolixity).
   4. Be orderly.

Grice points out that the first three categories relate to what is said, whereas the fourth one relates to how something is said. These maxims should apply to all interactions irrespective of subject matter, vocabulary chosen, and type of speech act. Furthermore, he adds that the maxims he gives are not all of equal weight—for instance, undue prolixity is less serious than lying—and also that there might be other social, aesthetic, or moral maxims that participants observe in conversation.

Grice claims that interactants share implicit knowledge of these maxims, and thus conversational behaviour is governed by them.

He gives examples to illustrate a further claim that the maxims have their analogues in any co-operative, rational human activity, such as mending a car or helping to prepare a cake. Grice does not claim that his maxims can be applied to every conversation. On the contrary, he delineates various possible ways in which people might depart from the observance of such maxims. These departures, however, are not without consequences; they invite specific interpretations which he calls 'conversational implicature'. In other words, the addressee will have to search for the specific point that was intended by the speaker but was not explicitly stated. In fact, most of Grice's discussion revolves around the notion of implicatures which are generated when a maxim is flouted. His most frequently quoted example of violating the maxim of quantity refers to a recommendation letter written for a student who has applied for a philosophy job. This letter, which reads, 'Mr X's command of English is excellent, and his attendance at tutorials has been regular,' contains little and rather irrelevant information, unsatisfactory for the addressee's expectations. Consequently, it has to be inferred that the candidate is unsuitable for the post.

However insightful these principles of conversation may be, as Grice himself acknowledges, they are all rules which are grounded on efficiency and informativeness but which ignore the significance of the expressive aspect of language use. They sound more like rules prescribing what should happen in business encounters rather than those describing normal, everyday speech.

The problem is that a great deal of everyday language does not or does not only aim at a maximally effective exchange of information and, consequently, any adequate framework for a theory of language in use should encapsulate the variety of other purposes language use serves. Thanks and apologies, for instance, may be perfunctory or sincere, but they are usually effective because they fulfil social expectations rather than any conditions relative to truthfulness or brevity. In our daily interactions, purely informative speech is the exception rather than the rule. Consequently, a number of linguists have challenged Grice's maxims on a variety of grounds, especially as far as informativeness (maxim of quantity), truthfulness (maxim of quality), and their purported universality are concerned.

However, the question which I would like to consider concerning the Gricean conversational maxims is their alleged universality.

Grice himself and others have implied that his maxims are universal mainly on the assumption that they stem from rational behaviour, both verbal and non-verbal. Grice repeatedly states that observance of the co-operative principle and its subsequent maxims constitutes 'reasonable' and 'rational' behaviour. He does not, however, explain how he interprets these notions. Furthermore, when he says 'it is just a well-recognized empirical fact that people DO behave in these ways' (p. 48), he does not make explicit whether he is referring to conversational behaviour only in his own society. Hymes (1986) strongly objects to the idea of the universality of these maxims and states that only if they are reinterpreted as dimensions of behaviour can one legitimately claim their universality. 'It can reasonably be assumed that any community will have some orientation to the dimension of quality (truthfulness), of quantity (informativeness), of relevance, of manner (clarity)' (ibid. 73).

Keenan (1976) focuses on and argues against the universality of the maxim of quality based on the Malagasy language and conversational behaviour. She claims that Malagasy speakers, especially men, regularly violate this maxim. They are more reluctant to disclose information than Americans, because new information is rare and less easily accessible. Moreover, they are unwilling to commit themselves explicitly to information which might be proved to be false, especially information concerning future events. The language itself accommodates this need for indirectness by providing the circumstantial voice,[1] in addition to an active and passive, which enables its speakers to make any time, place, or instrument complement the subject of the sentence. Thus, 'it would be bizarre to postulate as basic to Malagasy verbal conduct and language acquisition an underlying maxim which the males at least consistently violate' (Hymes, 1986: 72).

All this does not imply that the maxim of quality never operates in Malagasy, but rather that its observance is constrained by social features related to the interaction, such as the significance of the information communicated, the interpersonal relationships, and the sex of the interlocutors. These constraints, Keenan suggests, are also present to a certain extent in Western societies. For instance, people in responsible positions take extra care not to reveal

---

[1] Examples of circumstantial voice can be rendered in English and in Greek, but the result will sound awkward, as in 'a stick was used by you to beat that child' (Brown and Levinson, 1987: 195).

confidential information. Even in everyday interactions people may feel that they should not disclose personal information, and for this reason they may become evasive.

In respect of the maxim of quantity, Eades (1982) has also come to the conclusion that the notion of informativeness is culturally dependent, in her study of conversational behaviour in information exchanges between middle class white Americans (MCWA) and South-East Queensland Aborigines (SEQAB).

It could, however, be argued that Grice accounts for such cases of underinformativeness, since he states that you should make your contribution as informative as is required for the current purposes of the exchange. Although this formulation might be seen as embracing such cases in his own society, it is more difficult to accept that it can also account for what happens in every culture. As has been repeatedly emphasized, language behaviour is a culture-dependent activity, and Grice's presentation may suffer from a certain degree of socio-cultural bias (cf. Lyons, 1981*b*: 217). In fact Hymes (1986: 72) concludes that the Malagasy example 'brings out the ethnocentric enormity of the maxims'. What is conceived of as the required degree of informativeness, sincerity, etc. may differ considerably from society to society.

Likewise Harris (1984: 191), in her study of Egyptian politeness and truth-telling behaviour, concludes that truthfulness is 'a sociolinguistic variable' and that, like phonological variables, it depends both on the relationship between the participants and on the socio-cultural groups to which they belong. Furthermore, Loveday (1983: 181) contends that the Gricean maxims are culturally relative even in academic work where one would expect greater uniformity among cultures. He cites the example of Japan, where the maxim of manner is rarely attended to because in most contexts clarity and explicitness could be easily interpreted as 'offensively self-assertive'. Similarly, in a very interesting article on the differences between English and Polish speech acts and their connection with different cultural norms and assumptions, Wierzbicka (1985*a*: 175) argues convincingly that the attested universality of the 'logic of conversation' seems ethnocentric. This stand is shared by Harris (1984: 189), who recognizes the necessity for the maxim of quality to be restated. The need for major revision of the theory is also propounded by Matsumoto (1989). She argues that since the principles of conversation are based on the propositional content of the utterances, they cannot satisfactorily account for salient characteristics of interaction in Japanese, in which the social context must be lexically encoded in any utterance. In other words, there is no neutral way in which even a simple construction such as *today is Saturday* could be appropriate in all situations.

All this evidence lends support to the objections raised concerning the generality and universality of Grice's maxims. If they are not outlined in such a way as to allow for both situational and cross-cultural variation, then we cannot accept claims for their universality, except in extremely broad terms. Qualities and values such as those included in the description of maxims are extremely difficult to determine and define even within the same culture, let alone across a variety of cultures. It is true that nobody has explicitly claimed that the maxims are always observed or that they govern every conversation (Harnish, 1976: 340), or that the CP applies identically to all societies (Leech, 1983: 80). Conversely, the reverse is not clarified either, so that the discussion on maxims, as it stands, may lead to misunderstanding. If we accept the assumption that conversational maxims are universal, then any participant from any society (provided that there is no language barrier) should be able to infer exactly the same or very nearly the same meaning from any given utterance most of the time. It is clear, however, that this is not the case. The growing literature on international miscommunication is amply suggestive.

It is important, however, not to underestimate the significance of Grice's work, one major asset of which is the flexibility to describe the violation and not just the observance of the postulates. None of the scholars who have criticized various aspects of his views fails to acknowledge his significant contribution to the study of conversation and utterance interpretation. Wilson and Sperber (1981: 155) say that 'we shall assume that the advantages of a Gricean approach are well enough known to need no further comment'. The generalizations Grice proposes provide us with useful insights and have had a considerable impact in achieving a better understanding of the mechanism of verbal behaviour. Furthermore, as Brown and Levinson (1987: 5) suggest, 'the assumption of cooperative behaviour is actually hard to undermine', at least until a more adequate formulation is provided.

However, what is perhaps more to the point is that Grice also maintains that 'be polite' is yet another maxim participants observe in interactions, and although he does not expand on this issue of politeness, he has provided a strong incentive for others to do so. Consequently, whether in supporting or contesting his views, scholars such as Lakoff, Leech, and Brown and Levinson have been encouraged to produce a great deal of interesting work on the subject of politeness.

2.3 THE RULES OF POLITENESS

In her article 'The logic of politeness; or, minding your p's and q's', Lakoff (1973) expands on Grice's views in her attempt to account for politeness phenomena. Unlike Grice, she begins by considering the inadequacy of grammars based solely on grammatical rules and argues that some kind of pragmatic rules should also be incorporated. Such rules will enable us to detect and determine deviant utterances which pose neither syntactic nor semantic problems. She proposes the following two basic rules which she calls rules of pragmatic competence.

1. Be clear.
2. Be polite.

As Lakoff says, if the main concern is the message to be communicated, the speaker will concentrate on the clarity of the utterance; whereas, if consideration of the status of the interlocutors and/or the situation is involved, then the main concern will be the expression of politeness. She points out that although sometimes clarity is politeness, very often the two are incompatible. In most cases in which they are in conflict, then, it is clarity which is sacrificed. In informal, everyday encounters it is more important not to offend than to be clear because in such cases we are usually interested in establishing or maintaining social relationships rather than conveying accurate information, and so clarity can take a secondary position.

Lakoff (ibid. 297) argues that all Grice's conversational postulates fall under her rule 1—'be clear'—expressed as 'we are lucky in our work that the rules of clarity have been formulated . . . in Grice's work' and she is right because Grice's maxims do relate mainly to clarity and orderliness in conversation. Lakoff further argues that communication strictly adhering to such postulates would be boring and extremely formal, and consequently they are violated in everyday interactions. In her words, 'the rules of conversation are apparently more honored in the breach than in the observance'.

Lakoff's second pragmatic rule—'be polite'—comprises three rules of politeness. These are:

R1. Don't impose.
R2. Give options.
R3. Make *A* feel good—be friendly.

The first rule, 'don't impose', is associated with distance and formality. Her second rule, 'give options', is associated with deference and accounts for cases in which the linguistic manifestations of politeness appear to leave the choice of conforming or not to the addressee, for instance by employing hedges or other markers of hesitation. Her third rule, 'be friendly', accounts for the cases in which the speaker employs devices which will make the addressee feel liked and wanted.

Lakoff (1975: 65) subsequently reformulates, or rather rephrases, the rules of politeness as follows:

1. Formality: keep aloof.
2. Deference: give options.
3. Camaraderie: show sympathy.

In this reformulation she has chosen more positive terms. She says that at least these three rules are needed and that collapsing them into one would be at the expense of the ability to make predictions. It could be argued, however, that politeness is something even broader and more complex than the sum of these rules and is difficult to capture in its entirety by any number of rules of the type Lakoff proposes.

Brown and Levinson (1978: 287), in their discussion of the advantages of analysing in terms of strategies rather than in terms of rules, maintain that although a 'rule-based analysis works very well for well-bounded ritualized speech events like greetings,' it appears problematic with less ritualized episodes. Elsewhere, Brown (1976: 246) contends that, although Lakoff seeks to present an analysis which is both non-rigid and non-arbitrary, her definition of politeness, consisting as it does of three kinds of rules, rigidifies her account and is her major weakness. In fact, as Tannen (1984a: 13) reports, Lakoff, in her later work, talks about 'points on a continuum of stylistic preferences' rather than rules of rapport.

This view is shared by Tannen (1986: 36) who points out that these are not actually rules, but are senses we have of the 'natural' way to speak.

Another equally important issue is that Lakoff does not define the terms she uses. Formality does not necessarily equate with politeness, nor is 'aloofness' always polite. At least in Greek society, an aloof, very distant person is not usually regarded as polite. The same seems to be true for Americans who, according to Tannen (1986: 37), try to balance the rules, or senses of politeness so as 'to be appropriately friendly without imposing, to keep appropriate distance without appearing aloof'. Moreover, deference does not necessarily mean giving options, and in any case, giving options is usually conventional and culture-dependent to a great extent. Camaraderie does not only mean showing sympathy. One may show sympathy to somebody who is in a difficult position, implying the presence of pity, which is not usually associated with camaraderie or even politeness. Thus, it appears that the notions Lakoff uses to formulate her rules are not defined rigorously enough and thus are susceptible to misinterpretation.[2] Consequently, her analysis seems to suffer from the same weakness that she pinpointed as a problem in Grice's work on the rules of conversation.

At the beginning of her 1973 article, Lakoff claims that Grice's maxims fall under her first pragmatic rule, 'be clear'. Later on, however, she subsumes 'clarity' under her first rule of politeness, 'don't impose'. In other words, she proposes that the rules of conversation can be interpreted as one kind of rule of politeness, thus hoping to achieve 'an interesting generalization'. Lakoff (1973: 303) claims that, 'we can look at the rules of conversation as subcases of Rule 1 [don't impose]: their purpose is to get the message communicated in the shortest time with the least difficulty: that is, to avoid imposition on the addressee (by wasting his time with meandering or trivia, or confusing him and making him look bad).'

Elsewhere (1975: 74) she claims that 'women will tend to speak with reference to the rules of politeness, conversational implicature, and interpersonal exploration; men will tend to speak with reference to the rules of conversation and straight factual communi-

---

[2] For instance, Fraser (1990: 224) interprets the 'give options' rule as obeyed when informal politeness is required.

cation,' a statement which seems to be drawing the original differentiation between clarity and politeness. To subsume all conversational rules under politeness is, I believe, perhaps wishful thinking. For instance, the teacher, the lawyer, the doctor, and so on, in their daily attempts to explain things and/or impart information, are mainly concerned with rather neutral functions as far as politeness is concerned. Leech (1983: 105) says that competitive (i.e. demanding, begging, etc.) and convivial (i.e. greeting, thanking, etc.) functions are the ones which mainly involve politeness; whereas with collaborative functions (i.e. announcing, reporting, etc.) politeness is not usually involved, and with conflictive functions (i.e. threatening, etc.) politeness is out of the question. For Goffman (1981: 17) politeness closely refers to matters of ceremonial rather than substantive import. Thus, it can be argued that politeness is not always present in every interaction.

Furthermore, it is very difficult to understand in what sense Grice's rules of conversation do not operate in R3 situations, as Lakoff (1973: 303) claims when she says that 'the rules of conversation are in effect in non-R3 situations: that is, R1 situations, cases of formality'. The function of her third rule, as Lakoff (ibid. 301) maintains, is to produce a sense of camaraderie between speaker and addressee, in other words to make the addressee feel good because he or she is liked and approved of by the speaker. Do people in such situations become more ambiguous (violation of the maxim of manner) or irrelevant (violation of the maxim of relevance), and so on? Obviously they do not. Rules of conversation may be violated in R3 situations, as can also happen in R1 situations. But if their purpose, as mentioned earlier, is to get the message communicated quickly and effectively, then clearly 'shut the window' fulfils that purpose better than, say, 'would you mind shutting the window, please' or 'it's cold in here'.

Lakoff (ibid. 304) states, and it is generally true, that hedging sometimes serves to enhance the politeness of an utterance and sometimes works in the opposite direction. One of the examples she employs to clarify her claim is 'for the last time, I'm telling you to take the chewing gum out of your mouth'. This is undoubtedly rude, she says because it 'imposes on the addressee' (thus, it violates her R1), secondly, it 'destroys his options' (thus, it violates her R2), and thirdly 'treats him not as a friend' (thus, it violates her R3). However, she then states that here we have violation only of rules 2 and 3, because the speaker's intention is absolutely clear. Although it is true that the speaker's intention is unambiguously clear, her first rule of politeness is 'don't impose', not 'be clear', which is only a subcase; and the fact that the message is absolutely clear does not imply at all that it is not an imposition, even in a parent–child exchange. She goes on further to claim that since we tend to favour politeness when we have to make a choice between politeness and clarity, sentences like the aforementioned are not true exceptions but simply serve to show that our rules are generally correct; i.e. because politeness may be waived for a variety of reasons, such rules simply help us to deal with apparent exceptions and show why they exist.

Summing up, it can be said that the main problems with Lakoff's analysis are that, on the one hand, she tries to account for the diverse and complex notion of politeness in terms of rules, and on the other, that she attempts to subsume the rules of conversation under her first rule of politeness. Conversation and politeness are intricately interrelated, but not in the way Lakoff proposes.

The other charge against Lakoff's rules which I would like to discuss here is their purported universality. As Brown and Levinson (1978: 91) quite rightly point out, 'to posit highly specific and diverse universal rules is to invent a problem to be explained, rather than to explain it'. One source of the problem seems to lie with the terms used to formulate such rules. The apparently culturally specific connotations of the terms 'aloof' and 'aloofness' have already been pointed out. One could even argue that notions such as 'formality' and 'informality' are culture-specific (Duranti, 1985: 222). Thus, if the notions used for the formulation of the rules cannot be claimed to have identical universal connotations, then it is rather unlikely that the rules themselves will be universal. Tannen (1984a: 11) notes that these terms are part of Lakoff's system and do not necessarily have the same connotations as in popular use. Without a thorough and in-depth examination of how the concept of politeness is perceived by a particular group, and without working definitions of what it is to be polite, aloof, formal, etc., we cannot make any claims for universality.

Lakoff, however, claims that the rules she proposed are universal, the only difference among cultures lying in the order of precedence of these rules. She cites the example of belching, which in a Chinese context is the polite thing for guests to do after a meal, but which is quite impolite in an American context. Can we conclude, then, that in Chinese society Rule 3 (camaraderie) takes precedence over Rule 1 (formality) in all circumstances, and that the Chinese in general are an R3 society, or in Brown and Levinson's terms a 'positive-politeness' society? Or, conversely, if this is true of belching only, could it be suggested that we will have to reorder the rules of politeness for every single, simple verbal and non-verbal action? The most plausible interpretation seems to be that the Chinese are an R3 society in general.

There are, however, certain problems here. First of all, Lakoff does not make clear which Chinese society (i.e. mainland China, or the Hong Kong Chinese society) she is talking about, although this inexplicitness is common in the literature concerned. China has often been regarded as a typical deference politeness society (Young, 1982: 80), whose formality and elaboration is rather incompatible with Lakoff's R3, camaraderie rule. In any case, Chinese society is a society undergoing social change and any claims about their norms of politeness should take this into consideration. Is this then an example of ordering the rules differently or rather a matter of differing interpretations of the politeness involved in each particular action or utterance? I believe it is a matter of differing interpretations: belching, for instance, is regarded as an imposition and thus inappropriate in one culture, while in another it is the appropriate expression of gratitude after a meal.

This point becomes even more explicit with Lakoff's example of 'non-free goods'—that is, those which cannot be obtained without someone making a specific request. A case in point is the asking of questions concerning personal finances. What constitutes free and non-free goods—in this case what kinds of questions you can ask and of whom—is a matter largely determined by culture. Consequently, it is not a matter of ordering the rules differently for every single action in different societies, but rather a case of assigning different definitions to the different actions and entities which determine what type each society is. Lakoff also claims that the order of precedence of the rules may not only vary between different cultures, but also 'dialectally'.

For Brown (1976: 246) the major weakness in Lakoff's analysis is that 'she offers no integrating theory which places these rules of politeness in a framework that makes them nonarbitrary, that explains their form in terms of social relationships and expectations about humans as interactants'.

Politeness phenomena, therefore, can be adequately explained neither by adding another maxim such as 'be polite' to the list, as Grice appears to have implied, nor by inventing arbitrary rules and subsuming all rules of conversation under politeness, as Lakoff proposes. Despite their limitations and a certain degree of inexplicitness, Lakoff's rules of politeness should not be condemned as 'common sense platitudes' (Arndt and Janney, 1985: 281), for she has extended the range of the study of politeness, only hinted at by Grice.

2.4   THE MAXIMS OF POLITENESS

Like Lakoff, Leech (1983) expands and elaborates on Grice's views. In his *Principles of Pragmatics*, he develops his previous work (*Language and Tact* in 1980), and presents a thorough and detailed analysis of politeness in terms of maxims, within a more general pragmatic framework, where politeness features are a very important pragmatic factor regulating interaction. His pragmatic framework comprises two main parts, which he calls, after Halliday, 'textual rhetoric' and 'interpersonal rhetoric', each of which is realized with a number of principles. Grice's co-operative principle (CP), his 'politeness principle' (PP), and his 'irony principle' (IP) fall under interpersonal rhetoric. He adopts Grice's CP, with its four maxims—*quality, quantity, relation,* and *manner*—intact. Similarly, his politeness principle consists of a set of maxims: *tact, generosity, approbation, modesty, agreement,* and *sympathy*. Figure 2.1 is a slightly modified illustration taken from Leech (1983: 16).

Leech says that in communication, Grice's co-operative principle interacts with his proposed politeness principle. Similar to Grice and Lakoff, Leech claims that his maxims hold for both verbal and non-verbal behaviour. He justifies the need for the politeness principle as a necessary complement, not just as an addition to the co-operative principle, by discussing apparent exceptions which cannot be handled satisfactorily solely in terms of the co-operative principle.

In line with both Grice and Lakoff, he recognizes the possibility of conflict between the co-operative and politeness principles.

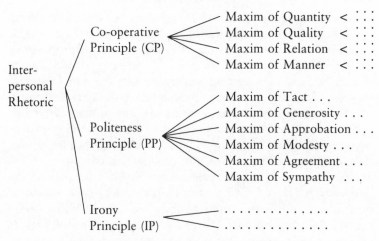

FIG. 2.1 *Principles and maxims of interaction*
Source: Leech, 1983: 16.

When a tension between them arises, participants are faced with a dilemma as to which one to sacrifice. By sacrificing the politeness principle, one risks the equilibrium of peaceful and harmonious human relationships, which is a necessary prerequisite for co-operative behaviour, thus further justifying the complementarity of the two principles. Brown and Levinson (1987: 5), however, argue that Grice's co-operative principle and Leech's politeness principle have different status mainly on the grounds that no violation of Grice's maxims occurs without a reason, whereas Leech's politeness maxims constitute such reasons for violations.

Leech elaborates further on his maxims and suggests that there are pragmatic scales associated with them. He identifies three such scales which have 'a bearing on the degree of tact appropriate to a given speech situation' (1983: 123).

1. The 'cost/benefit' scale which specifies how much the proposed action is judged by the speaker to be of cost or benefit to the speaker or to the addressee.

2. The 'optionality' scale which specifies to what extent the proposed action is at the choice of the addressee.

3. The 'indirectness' scale which specifies how much inference is involved in the proposed action.

Besides these three scales, there are another two which are relevant to politeness: 'authority' and 'social distance', which are roughly equivalent to 'power' and 'solidarity', respectively, as proposed by Brown and Gilman (1960). Thus, if speakers judge that the cost to the addressees, their relative authority, and the social distance increase, they will attempt to provide the addressees with more options and will formulate their utterances with greater indirectness.

The maxims of politeness proposed by Leech are the *generosity maxim*, which forms a pair on a bipolar scale with the *tact maxim*; the *approbation maxim* and the *modesty maxim*, which form another pair on a bipolar scale; and the *agreement maxim* and *sympathy maxim*, which form unipolar scales. Each maxim is distinct from the others, although there are various links between the scales. Furthermore, like Grice, Leech notes that not all of them are of equal importance. For instance, the tact maxim is assumed to be more powerful than the generosity maxim. If this is true, Leech claims, then it reflects a general law that politeness is focused more strongly on the other person than on the self. However, what is unclear in this assumption is the sense in which the tact maxim focuses on the other more than the generosity maxim. Leech acknowledges the possibility of cross-cultural variability when he says that certain observations indicate that different cultures tend to place more value on different maxims, and mentions, for instance, that Mediterranean cultures place a higher value on the generosity maxim than on the tact maxim, which is valued more in English-speaking societies. This observation appears to be valid, at least as far as Greeks are concerned. Greek norms of politeness appear to emphasize the importance of generosity, thus maximizing the benefit to the other. Evidence of this might be the abundance of offers and the relative ease with which requests are exchanged, both in number and in form. Sometimes even a sincere compliment may result in the recipient sincerely offering the item concerned as a gift to the person who expressed admiration. Durrell (1978) describes this gift-giving generosity of Cretans very vividly. He says that, 'it is dangerous to express admiration for something, for you will certainly find it in your baggage as a farewell gift when you leave. You cannot refuse. They are adamant. I knew a lady who got a baby this way' (ibid. 60).

Leech further points out that each of his maxims includes two submaxims. For instance, the tact maxim consists of the two submaxims, (*a*) *minimize cost to other*, and (*b*) *maximize benefit to other*. The submaxims of the generosity maxim are (*a*) *minimize benefit to self* and (*b*) *maximize cost to self*, and so on and so forth. Leech says that the second submaxims are less important than the first, and this illustrates the more general law that negative politeness (avoidance of discord) is more important than positive politeness (seeking concord). However, as is the case with the maxims themselves, cultures will differ in the importance they assign to each of the submaxims.

Leech (1983: 83) proposes an interesting distinction between 'absolute' and 'relative' politeness. The former can be analysed as a scale with a positive and a negative pole in that some acts are intrinsically polite (e.g. offers) and some others intrinsically impolite (e.g. orders). Within this framework, negative politeness is viewed as minimizing the impoliteness of impolite illocutions, and positive politeness as maximizing the politeness of polite illocutions. Relative politeness depends on the context and the situation, because it is clear that the 'Co-operative Principle and the Politeness Principle operate variably in different cultures or language communities, in different social situations, among different social classes, etc.' (ibid. 10). General pragmatics, being more abstract in that it studies 'the general conditions of the communicative use of language' (ibid.), can deal with absolute politeness, which is thus assumed to be universal. Socio-pragmatics, on the other hand, being less abstract in that it studies 'more specific "local" conditions on language use' can deal with relative politeness. In general, when we talk about politeness, what we have in mind is relative politeness, based on what we think is appropriate behaviour in particular situations. These norms, however, vary from culture to culture, leading to stereotypic comments of the type that a certain nationality is polite or impolite.

I wonder, however, whether Leech, in his attempt to account for cross-cultural variation with respect to politeness, has drawn an interesting but nevertheless arbitrary distinction between 'absolute' and 'relative' politeness. How are we going to define an intrinsically impolite action, for instance, outside its cultural and even situational context? In what sense are orders always intrinsically impolite? Can they be considered impolite in a military or even an educational context? What about belching, mentioned earlier on in Lakoff's example—is it intrinsically polite or impolite?

The maxims of politeness are not offered by Leech as absolute rules but rather as rules that are observed 'up to a point'. Thus conflict is not always avoided and inaction (see below) does not always result. He discusses an interesting phenomenon which he calls the 'politeness paradox'. He suggests that in ideally polite situations, where both participants would be determined to be absolutely polite, we would have an infinite series of polite exchanges which could lead to inaction. For instance, two people wishing to go through a doorway might stand there endlessly, politely offering each other the opportunity to go through first and politely refusing the other's offer. Leech (ibid. 112) says that 'it is just as well that in practice, no one is ideally polite,' because these 'paradoxes of politeness function as an antidote to a more dangerous kind of paradox'. In the above situation, for instance, this could lead to a collision in the doorway if both attempted to go through first at the same time.

It is true that in practice nobody is ideally polite, but this does not seem to me to be the solution to this politeness paradox. Society has prescribed rules for most cases so that these paradoxes rarely arise. Status, sex, or age, for instance, are usually the determining parameters of who should accept the offer to go first through the doorway. Acting against these determining parameters is impolite or indicates a specific motive, rather than being not ideally polite as Leech puts it. There are cases in which status is not obvious or relevant and sex or age are not determining factors. In such cases, some societies have provided other solutions, such as queuing. Members of societies with such norms will judge others as impolite partly because they do not share the specific rules for the avoidance of the paradox.

Another reason why such paradoxes do not usually arise is that politeness would come into direct conflict with sincerity. To refuse endlessly a polite offer might be interpreted as suspicion of the speaker's sincerity. People tend to accept offers, thanks, apologies, etc., unless they have a specific reason for not doing so, mainly for the sake of the balance between politeness and sincerity.

The question of whether politeness may be categorized as 'absolute', paradoxically or otherwise, and defined in terms of maxims followed in interactions universally, is extremely doubtful. Only by considering a model for strategic interaction shall we be able to address these and other problems of politeness more

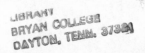

adequately, mainly because it concentrates on choices interactants make in actual contexts and allows for cross-cultural variability. It is basically for these reasons that I have chosen to focus upon Brown and Levinson's detailed and influential work, which is discussed in the following section.

2.5 A MODEL FOR STRATEGIC INTERACTION

In their extensive essay 'Universals in language usage: politeness phenomena' Brown and Levinson present their theory of politeness. The main difference between Leech's approach and that of Brown and Levinson is that, whereas Leech develops his theory of politeness within a more general pragmatic theory, Brown and Levinson present a cohesive and comprehensive theory of politeness in which linguistic devices are realizations of specific politeness strategies. Although they make references to non-verbal behaviour, their main concern is linguistic. The different extents to which each theory derives from actual interaction render the former a more abstract, rather normative model and the latter a more functional one.

Following Goffman's views on politeness or deference in behaviour in general, Brown and Levinson have proposed a linguistic theory in which the concept of 'face' is central. They assume 'that all competent adult members of a society have (and know each other to have) "face",' which they define as 'the public self-image that every member wants to claim for himself' (1978: 66). The concept of 'face' is the kernel element in folk notions of politeness in both cultures, Greek and English, and perhaps in many more. Although a person's 'social face can be his most personal possession and the center of his security and pleasure, it is only on loan to him from society; it will be withdrawn unless he conducts himself in a way that is worthy of it' (Goffman, 1972: 322).

For Brown and Levinson (1978: 66), too, 'face is something that is emotionally invested, and that can be lost, maintained, or enhanced, and must be constantly attended to in interaction'. Since face is so sensitive, it is in the mutual interest of both participants in interactions to try to maintain each other's face. This is reflected in Goffman's (1972: 323) claim that 'the combined effect of the rule of self-respect and the rule of considerateness is that the person tends to conduct himself during an encounter so as to maintain both his own face and the face of the other participants,' and thus face-saving has both a defensive and a protective orientation. The motivation to preserve everyone's face is very strong and ultimately underlies the preservation of orderly communication, although 'maintenance of face is a condition of interaction, not its objective' (ibid.). Participants, it appears, need not be concerned so much with finding ways of expressing themselves as with ensuring that the extensive resources by which interactions are expressed do not, by chance, convey unintended or improper messages (Goffman, 1981: 19). 'To study face-saving is to study the traffic rules of social interaction' (Goffman, 1972: 323).

Brown and Levinson (1978: 67) distinguish two components of face, 'positive face' and 'negative face', which are two related aspects of the same entity and refer to two basic desires or 'wants' of any individual in any interaction: 'negative face' refers to 'the want of every "competent adult member" that his actions be unimpeded by others'; 'positive face' refers to 'the want of every member that his wants be desirable to at least some others'.

According to Brown and Levinson (ibid. 66), all competent adult members of a society also have, besides face, 'certain rational capacities, in particular consistent modes of reasoning from ends to means that will achieve those ends'. They claim that both (i) 'face, describable as two kinds of wants' and (ii) 'rational action devoted to satisfying others' face wants' are universal human properties, as well as 'the mutual knowledge between interactants of (i) and (ii)' (ibid. 249). The universality of 'face' is also pointed out by Arndt and Janney (1985: 293), who state that 'the desire to maintain face, and the fear of losing it, are interpersonal universals transcending all sociocultural, ethnic, sexual, educational, economic, geographical and historical boundaries'.

Many communicative activities entail imposition on the face of both or either of the participants: that is, they are intrinsically face-threatening activities (FTAs).[3] Face-threatening activities are 'those

[3] Brown and Levinson (1978: 238) clarify the delicate point that 'FTAs do not necessarily inhere in single acts' and propose the term 'face-threatening intention' as a better label to describe the concept of face-threatening activities. This leads to a subsequent expansion of some politeness strategies which 'are describable only in terms of sequences of acts or utterances, strung together as outputs of hierarchical plans'. They illustrate this with offers, which in many cultures may have to be made

acts that by their nature run contrary to the face wants of the addressee and/or of the speaker' (Brown and Levinson, 1978: 70). Acts that appear to impede the addressees' independence of movement and freedom of action threaten their negative face, whereas those which appear as disapproving of their wants threaten their positive face. Examples of the former include orders and requests, suggestions, advice, and so on, whereas examples of the latter might be expressions of disapproval or disagreement, and so on. Thanks, acceptance of thanks, or offers, and so forth threaten the speakers' negative face in that they accept a debt and humble their own face. Apologies (i.e. regretting a prior FTA), acceptance of compliments, and so on threaten the speakers' positive face in that they may feel that such activities have to be played down or reciprocated in kind. Because they are able to reason from ends to means, participants in an interaction usually select from a set of strategies those which will enable them to either avoid or minimize such face-threatening activities, in other words, they use politeness, or tact.

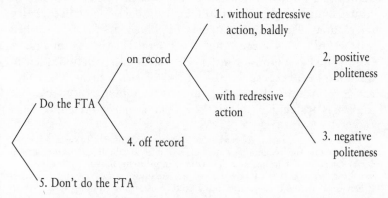

FIG. 2.2 Possible strategies for doing FTAs
Source: Brown and Levinson, 1978: 74.

The five strategies that Brown and Levinson identify (see Figure 2.2) are claimed to be dependent on the extent to which risk of loss of face is involved. This risk factor increases as one moves up the scale

and refused repeatedly before they are finally accepted or rejected. This presents some recognition of the shortcomings of a sentence-based analysis, which has been one of the critiques of the theory.

of strategies from 1 to 5, that is, the greater the risk, the more polite the strategy.

The degree of this risk or weight of imposition is determined by the cumulative effect of three universal social variables which, according to Brown and Levinson (1978: 79) are:[4]

(i) the social distance (D) between the participants
(ii) the relative 'power' (P) between them
(iii) the absolute ranking (R) of impositions in the particular culture.

At the two extremes (i.e. 1 and 5) politeness is rather irrelevant. Their first category of strategies is what they call 'bald on record', which is employed when there is no risk involved. Redressive action is not necessary because such strategies are either performed by interactants who are on intimate terms or because other demands for efficiency override face concerns (ibid. 103). The second and third categories—'positive' and 'negative' politeness strategies, respectively—involve redressive action and attempt to satisfy the addressee's positive or negative face wants.[5] These two sets of strategies include the majority of linguistic devices used in everyday interactions. Their fourth category of politeness strategies is called 'off record'. This means that the utterance used is ambiguous (formulated as a hint, for instance), and its interpretation is left to the addressee, because the risk of loss of face is great. Their fifth category includes those cases in which nothing is said because the risk is prohibitively great. Brown and Levinson present detailed

[4] More recent research (see references in Brown and Gilman, 1989; and Kasper, 1990) supports the assumption that these variables are the basic determinants in social interaction, but suggests that their treatment by Brown and Levinson is simplistic because lack of power does not necessarily elicit greater politeness (Cherry, 1988), and because 'distance' has to be distinguished from 'affect', which appears to be a more powerful variable (Baxter, 1984).

[5] It is worth noting here that Scollon and Scollon (1981: 175 and 1983: 167) say that they prefer to call the positive politeness system 'solidarity politeness', because of its emphasis on the common ground between the participants, and to call the negative politeness system 'deference politeness', because of its emphasis on deference and formality, and in order to avoid possible negative connotations in using the word 'negative'. A similar view is held by Tannen (1981: 385 and 1984a: 15), who prefers to use the more neutral and more descriptive terms 'community' and 'independence' in place of 'positive' and 'negative' in order to avoid value judgements. Although there is some validity to their arguments (especially since the term 'negative' will most probably invoke unpleasant connotations), it is possible to argue strongly against the idea of inventing new terms for already well-established concepts in the literature, because this can very easily lead to confusion.

descriptions of the specific manifestations that each of their main strategies can take. Examples are given from three unrelated languages, English, Tamil (a Dravidian language of South India), and Tzeltal (a Mayan language of Mexico), in an attempt to substantiate their claims to universality. I have selected illustrations from their charts of positive and negative politeness manifestations, because these two sets of strategies are the ones most central to my work:

Positive Politeness   (from Brown and Levinson, 1978: 107)
   Claim 'common ground'
     1. Notice, attend to H (his interests, wants, needs, goods)
     2. Exaggerate (interest, approval, sympathy with H)
     3. Intensify interest to H
     4. Use in-group identity markers
     5. Seek agreement
     6. Avoid disagreement
     7. Presuppose/raise/assert common ground
     8. Joke
   Convey that S and H are co-operators
     9. Assert or presuppose S's knowledge of and concern for H's wants
    10. Offer, promise
    11. Be optimistic
    12. Include both S and H in the activity
    13. Give (or ask for) reasons
    14. Assume or assert reciprocity
   Fulfil H's want (for some X)
    15. Give gifts to H (goods, sympathy, understanding, co-operation).

Negative Politeness   (from Brown and Levinson, 1978: 136)
   Be direct
     1. Be conventionally indirect
   Don't presume/assume
     2. Question, hedge
   Don't coerce H (where x involves H doing A)
   (both (1) and (2) are included here, too)

3. Be pessimistic
4. Minimize the imposition
5. Give deference

Communicate *S*'s want to not impinge on *H*

6. Apologize
7. Impersonalize *S* and *H*: Avoid the pronouns *I* and *you*
8. State the FTA as a general rule
9. Nominalize

Redress other wants of *H*'s, derivative from negative face

10. Go on record as incurring a debt, or as not indebting *H*.

Besides Goffman, another source of inspiration for Brown and Levinson is the work of Lakoff and Grice. Although they reject a rule-based approach like Lakoff's to the analysis of politeness phenomena (1978: 286–7), they acknowledge their debt to Lakoff's work because it enabled them 'to promote the view that social functions are a prime candidate for the motivation of the great mass of superficial derivational machinery that characterizes a particular language' (ibid. 262).

Their debt to Grice's work is perhaps even greater in that it runs through their whole analysis. This fact is encapsulated in the statement that 'the whole thrust of this paper is that one powerful and pervasive motive for *not* talking Maxim-wise is the desire to give some attention to face', a statement which they subsequently clarify by adding that 'even in such departures from the Maxims, they remain in operation at a deeper level' (ibid. 100). Their bald-on-record strategy is an exception in that it fully conforms to Grice's maxims (ibid. 99), whereas their off-record strategy is based on provoking conversational implicature of the kinds manifested by violating all of Grice's maxims. The relationship between the maxims and redressed on-record utterances is more complex. Positive politeness, with the element of insincerity in exaggerated expressions of interest or approval (ibid. 106, 108), can be seen as a violation of the maxim of quality; and negative politeness, with its emphasis on indirectness and elaboration, can be seen as a violation of the maxim of quantity.

The positive/negative politeness distinction is closely related to two of the main forms inherent in Goffman's (1956: 481) 'deference', i.e. 'avoidance rituals' and 'presentational rituals'.

Avoidance rituals are 'forms of deference which lead the actor to keep at a distance from the recipient'. Presentational rituals encompass 'acts through which the individual makes specific attestations to recipients concerning how he regards them and how he will treat them in the on-coming interaction' (ibid. 485). Thus, showing involvement and keeping distance present the two main ways of being polite to other people. These are universal, conflicting needs which all human beings share, but which, according to Brown and Levinson, are mutually exclusive, whereas for Goffman they are not. For Brown and Levinson (1978: 75), 'positive politeness is approach-based; it "anoints" the face of the addressee by indicating that in some respects, S wants H's wants (e.g. by treating him as a member of an ingroup, a friend, a person whose wants and personality traits are known and liked)'. By contrast, 'negative politeness . . . is essentially avoidance-based . . . [and] is characterized by self-effacement, formality and restraint, with attention to very restricted aspects of H's self-image, centring on his want to be unimpeded'. Positive politeness is less obvious, because when we talk or think of politeness, what immediately springs to mind is negative politeness, which is our familiar formal politeness (ibid. 67).

The assumption that negative politeness is a more serious consideration than positive politeness is directly voiced by Leech (1983: 133). Although the terms 'positive' and 'negative' politeness as used by Brown and Levinson and Leech are not strictly speaking equivalent, they share the elements of 'presentation' and 'avoidance' respectively. Brown and Levinson do not make any such explicit claims, but their hierarchy invites such implications along with the fact that they devote three times as much space in their essay to the consideration of negative politeness strategies as they do to positive politeness.

Scollon and Scollon (1981) argue for the different nature of these two strategies and Brown and Gilman (1989: 165) actually propose the collapse of the two into one redressive superstrategy, since linguistic realizations appear to be frequently mixed in interactions. Furthermore, as Craig, Tracy, and Spisak (1986: 452) observe, certain strategies cannot only be mixed but may also be multifunctional. Thus, if there is such divergence of opinion concerning English, one could argue that there will be greater dissent in examining cross-cultural data.

Both Leech (1983) and Brown and Levinson (1978) recognize the possibility of cultural differences, but are more interested in what is perceived as universal. The many similarities detected by Brown and Levinson in their study of politeness phenomena in three unrelated languages do point to a certain degree of universality, but they do not preclude major differences which were not detailed so extensively in their study. Furthermore, surface similarities may conceal significant differences as regards underlying motivations. As Hymes points out,

> The universal presence of such [linguistic] forms is worth knowing, but one needs to know as well the ways in which such forms are selected and grouped together with others in cultural practices. . . . Clearly the occurrence of parallel forms of utterance is not enough to provide the basis for a universal theory. One has to know the social structure in which the forms of utterance occur and the cultural values which inform that structure. (1986: 79–80)

In spite of the valid objections by Hymes and others concerning claims to universality Brown and Levinson's work still remains an invaluable and comprehensive source for the concept of politeness. They do allow for a certain degree of cross-cultural variation, which they call 'ethos' and define as 'the affective quality of interaction characteristic of members of a society' (1978: 248). Their distinction between positive and negative politeness strategies, whether mixed and multifunctional or not, and the subsequent differentiation between positive and negative politeness societies, even with its 'immense crudity', as they put it, can shed very considerable light on differences between cultures and provide a secure basis for their investigation. However, Brown and Levinson claim that:

> we cannot account for cultural differences in terms, say, of greater desire for positive-face satisfaction than negative-face satisfaction in some society (in the U.S.A. compared with England, for example). Note that if we allowed extrinsic weighting of face wants, then cultural (emic) explanations of cross-cultural differences would supersede explanation in terms of universal (etic) social dimensions like D [distance] and P [power]. (1978: 249)

Their justification, however, does not appear to be adequate. If emic explanations can account better for the phenomena under investigation, why should we discard them in favour of etic explanations? The 'greater desire' for the satisfaction of a particular aspect of face cannot be a superficial preference, but a choice deeply ingrained in the specific system of values predominant in the particular society. Moreover, social dimensions like vertical and horizontal distance and rate of imposition may be universal, but they are variably defined interculturally and intraculturally, deriving their weight from basic cultural values.

As Triandis and Triandis (1970: 178) point out, every society has established norms which determine the social distance that is seen as 'correct' towards various classes of people. Moreover, as Brown and Levinson (1978: 253) themselves recognize 'the actual factors that go into assessing the size of these three social variables are of course culturally specific (with even some leeway for idiosyncratic variation)'. If these variables are culturally specific, as is the content of face itself, then all these considerations determine to a great extent the type of politeness that will prevail in that society.

I am not implying here either that *all* societies or that societies *as a whole* can be clearly categorized as being either positively or negatively polite. It may be true that the theory is in need of modification (Matsumoto, 1988) in order to become a model of universal applicability, as it is also clear that no society is likely to be completely uniform in its politeness (cf. Harris, 1984: 175). It is obviously true, as Brown and Levinson (1978: 25) point out, that complex, stratified societies will exhibit both kinds of politeness, with perhaps upper classes having a negative politeness ethos and lower classes a positive politeness ethos. On similar lines, Goffman (1956: 481) claims that, 'not only are some of the tokens different [between social classes] through which consideration for the privacy of others is expressed, but also, apparently, the higher the class the more extensive and elaborate are the taboos against contact'.

Similarly, it is widely reported that women tend to value positive politeness strategies and informality more than men.[6] On this issue Brown and Levinson (1978: 251) maintain that: 'this distinction between positive- and negative-politeness emphases not only marks class from class in hierarchical societies, but also marks different kinds of social roles from one another. Thus, we suspect that, in

---

[6] See, for instance, Lakoff (1975), Harris (1984) on speech patterns in an Egyptian village, and Keenan (1974) in Malagasy. The issue, however, concerning women's politeness is controversial and I shall not go into its details, but see Trudgill (1974: ch. 4), Trudgill (1975*b*), and Brown (1980), among others.

most cultures, women among women have a tendency to use more elaborated positive-politeness strategies than do men among men.'

Nevertheless, we can distinguish societies according to the ethos predominant in daily interactions, both verbal and non-verbal. In this sense then, it is true to say that these societies, for which the distinction is applicable, cannot be distinguished as either absolutely positive or absolutely negative, but rather as relatively more positive or relatively more negative, according to the type of ethos which is given more play. And this is what I mean when I talk of positive and negative politeness societies.

Brown and Levinson (1978: 248) themselves maintain that: 'to the extent that types of social relationship are repetitive throughout a society—that there is a constancy, a stability, in such relationships —it is possible to generalize about the kinds of relationships that prevail in that society . . . [and thus] it is possible to generalize about the kinds of politeness that typically, in public, are employed by members of that society.'

It should be added here, however, that since this politeness orientation is relative rather than absolute, it follows that even two societies which may be characterized as having the same politeness orientation will not exhibit identical preferences of strategies. The interactional needs of participants which derive from specific underlying values and determine the choice of strategies will vary even within the same system, let alone cross-culturally. Given these caveats, in our cross-cultural comparison between Greek and English we will attempt to substantiate the intuitive conviction that the two societies differ in relation to the way in which each views face, a difference which leads to the varying politeness orientations.

2.5.1 *Greek culture and the notion of face*

Brown and Levinson (1978: 66–7) say that, although the notion is universal, the exact content of face will differ in different cultures, and they elaborate on this by saying that there will be differences as to the exact limits to personal territories, and to the publicly relevant content of personality. Notions of face are closely related to some of 'the most fundamental cultural ideas about the nature of the social persona, honour and virtue, shame and redemption and thus to religious concepts' (Brown and Levinson, 1987: 13).

The notion of face, consisting of the aspects of approval and non-imposition, seems to account for the motivation of politeness phenomena in Greek and to explain the differences between Greek and English. I suggest that a fundamental difference between the two politeness systems can be explained in terms of differences in the significance attached to the two components of face. The English seem to place a higher value on privacy and individuality, i.e. the negative aspect of face, whereas the Greeks seem to emphasize involvement and in-group relations, i.e. the positive aspect. For Greeks the limits to personal territories seem to be looser among the individuals who belong to the same in-group. The barriers which will have to be removed to establish social relations are not so high and for this reason territorial intrusion is measured on a different basis. Furthermore, the notion of face among Greeks seems to include not only the desire of a person to be appreciated, liked, and approved of by at least some others, but also a strong desire that closely related associates are also appreciated, liked, and approved of by the same. The actions of every member of the in-group are most strongly reflected in the others' face. Very often the individual's needs, desires, expectations, and even actions are determined by considering those of the other members of the in-group. Face is not lost, maintained, or enhanced solely on the basis of how each individual behaves. The behaviour of other closely related members of the in-group contributes greatly to the overall picture of every individual's face.

These speculations are supported by the results of an interesting and extensive study of the Greek national character carried out by Triandis and Vassiliou (1972). They discuss the great importance which the in-group–out-group distinction plays in Greece. They define the 'in-group' as one's 'family, relatives, friends, and friends of friends'. They add that guests and people who are thought of as '"showing concern for me" are seen as members of the ingroup' (ibid. 305). In contrast to the in-group, the 'out-group' consists of anyone who is not regarded as an acquaintance or as someone concerned with one's welfare. Acquaintances are classified more frequently in the in-group than in the out-group. The importance of this distinction for Greek society is also discussed by Campbell (1975) and Herzfeld (1980, 1983, and 1984), who observes that 'the implications of the *ksenos–dhikos* (outsider–insider) opposition were extremely interesting' (1983: 162). This distinction strongly influences the way in which Greeks behave towards other people both verbally and non-verbally. 'Within the ingroup the appropriate behaviors are characterized by cooperation, protection and help. . . . Relations with members of the outgroup are essentially competitive' (Triandis and Vassiliou, 1972: 305).

Members of the same in-group will most often employ informality and positive politeness strategies and they will save formality and negative politeness (or no politeness at all) for members of the out-group, depending on their status. Towards their in-group, Greeks behave with spontaneity and enthusiasm and tend to express their feelings overtly. Members of the same in-group see it as their duty to help and support each other, both morally and financially, so they find no obvious reason for thanking or apologizing, unless for something they conceive of as being very serious or beyond the normal duties of the performer of the action, since the appropriate response is similar behaviour from everybody when the occasion arises. On the verbal level, their requests and wishes, advice and suggestions are expressed structurally more directly than in English because they are not perceived as impositions to the same extent. They prefer those patterns which involve what Brown and Levinson (1978: 320) have called interactional 'optimism', such as imperatives and indicatives. In England, on the other hand, cultural norms demand a more distant system of behaviour, where helping each other is seen more as depending on the individual's discretion rather than as conforming to a more general duty. Thus, requests are comparatively more sparingly employed, since they are perceived as impositions to a greater extent and they are preferably expressed more elaborately and indirectly. Verbalizations of thanks and apologies are imperative even for minor relevant situations and among members belonging to the same in-group. This is, I believe, a major source of misinterpretation and misjudgements which have led to negative stereotypic comments such as 'the Greeks are impolite' or 'the English are hypocritical' and many others of a similar sort concerning the degrees of politeness.

It may be the case that in societies where people depend on each other more and rely on their personal experience of those others, explicit expression of needs and feelings is expected and overt manifestations of fixed politeness formulas become less necessary than in societies where greater emphasis is placed on the individual. Other expectations, such as the obligation to behave in a similar way, may supersede expectations for overt verbal realizations of politeness. Consequently, an adequate account of linguistic behaviour should not ignore the nature and quality of relationships and the values predominant in the culture under study. They seem to play a determining role as to what constitutes appropriate behaviour, perhaps to a greater extent than Brown and Levinson (ibid. 91) would like to accept.

Summing up, it could be suggested that although positive and negative politeness interact in intricate ways, Greeks tend to use more positive politeness devices, especially to their in-group members, as opposed to the English who seem to prefer more negative politeness devices. As Brown and Levinson (1978: 135) contend 'in our culture, negative politeness is the most elaborate and the most conventionalized set of linguistic strategies for FTA redress; it is the stuff that fills the etiquette books'.

More generally, there is evidence that societies which have been stereotyped as less polite most probably correspond to positive politeness societies (see Wierzbicka, 1985*a* on Polish; Blum-Kulka, 1987 on Israeli; and Bentahila and Davies, 1989 on Moroccan). Those which have been stereotyped as more polite most probably exhibit a more negative politeness orientation. There are, however, cultures which have been stereotyped as even more polite than the latter. Such oriental, high deference cultures have been described either as exhibiting a negative politeness orientation (Brown and Levinson, 1978; Young, 1982; Hwang, 1990) or as not entirely fitting into the existing system of politeness (Matsumoto, 1988; Gu, 1990), thus challenging its alleged universality.

It is important to acknowledge and study this socio-cultural relativity in discourse activity but it is equally important not to exaggerate such differences. There must be universal principles of communication, because otherwise meaningful contact between people from different ethnic backgrounds may prove impossible. Undoubtedly, however, a great deal more data from different cultures is needed before one can reach any definitive answers to the thorny and controversial issue of what is universal and what is culturally specific, an issue which is discussed in the following chapter.

3
Politeness: Cross-cultural Perspectives

3.1 THE QUESTION OF UNIVERSALITY IN LANGUAGE

One of Brown and Levinson's concerns has been the search for universals in language usage. Extensive parallels across unrelated languages have convinced them that, in spite of cultural peculiarities, there are universal linguistic properties. The issue of universality in language is quite controversial and seems to be related to earlier considerations concerning the relationship of language, thought, and culture. Sapir and Whorf strongly advocated this interrelationship and the uniqueness and distinctiveness of each language on which the 'real world' or culture is built. This thesis came to be widely known as the 'Sapir–Whorf hypothesis', or 'linguistic relativity'.[1] Hymes (1966: 116) presents a different version of 'linguistic relativity' when he says that 'cultural values and beliefs are in part constitutive of linguistic relativity,' whereas for Whorf it was the structure of language which in part determined thought and culture.

The subject of 'linguistic relativity' is no longer so intensely discussed as it used to be in the 1950s, and it has now been partly superseded by a controversy between universalistic versus non-universalistic approaches to language theories. It has been claimed by many linguists that languages share a universal deeper level and differ only on a more surface level. What exactly this deeper level includes is far from clear, but it is seen as being determined by the interaction of genetically transmitted biological factors, cognitive constraints, and social needs, and by the natural world in a broad sense. The surface level is determined in part by particular cultural needs and values and, therefore, varies across languages.

---

[1] However, it should be noted that this question has a much longer linguistic history (Janney and Arndt, 1993).

Differences between the structures of particular languages seem to correspond to a great extent to distinctions exhibited in the cultures in which those languages are used. As has become quite evident from the various studies of diverse languages, the more diverse two cultural systems are the more distinct their languages will be. As Lyons (1981*a*: 312) maintains, 'there are . . . many differences of both grammatical and lexical structure which can be correlated with differences in the cultures with which particular languages are associated'. Such considerations do not mean that we should not seek for more general universals in language. Similarities in language structures exist because there are similarities in cultures, a kind of cultural overlap, due to common cultural heritage and/or contact. On this issue Lyons (1968: 433) observes that 'there will be a greater or less degree of *cultural overlap* between any two societies; and it may be the case that certain features will be present in the culture of all societies'.

In fact, Wierzbicka (1979: 314) observes that different languages may incorporate different philosophies, but that the philosophies themselves have much in common and can, therefore, be compared.

Clearly, this issue of universality is quite delicate and controversial, and many researchers have been criticized because they have tended to ascribe universality to communicative patterns and principles which operate in their society, based mainly on analyses of their intuitions as native speakers of English. Hymes illustrates this point quite eloquently when he states that:

There is a particular tendency today to seek the satisfaction of universal frameworks without realizing the empirical inadequacy of them. Our sense of historical and cultural relativism and diversity seems attenuated, if not lost. The appeal of universal grounding tends to overcome any fear of ethnocentric origin, yet differences of social structure, ecology, class, religion, historically derived character give rise to very distinctive cuts of cloth, grounded in fundamental concerns and motives of different kinds. (1986: 47)

3.2 UNIVERSALITY OF POLITENESS

The issue of whether or not politeness is a universal value features prominently in sociolinguistic discussions. House and Kasper (1981: 157) say that 'we don't know whether politeness is a universal phenomenon,' whereas Lakoff claims that her rules of politeness are universal, a claim, however, which has been challenged (see section 2.3). What seems to have been taken for granted in such accounts is that the connotations of terms for politeness are the same in all cultures and, consequently, its manifestations are expected to be very similar, if not identical. Wierzbicka (1985*a*: 145) has shown that certain features of the English language which have been attributed to universal principles of politeness are language-specific and culture-specific rather than universal. For Hymes (1986) neither the maxims of conversation nor the rules of politeness are justified candidates for universality, unless they are seen as dimensions.

It seems reasonable to assume that the concept of 'politeness', which represents an abstract, social value is most probably universal in some form or other, even though the way in which this concept is visualized and thus defined and how it is realized verbally and non-verbally will most probably be culture-specific. Evidence for this lies in the study of very diverse language communities which all exhibit some form of this phenomenon (Brown and Levinson, 1978; Leech, 1983). This claim becomes stronger if we accept observations that some form of politeness is even evidenced in animal interaction. 'A great deal of animal communication involves agonistic displays, signals regulating aggression, submission and appeasement' (Bates, 1976: 316).

Brown and Levinson (1978: 260) claim that the concept of 'face' because of which politeness is exhibited will most probably be universal, but what its exact content will be is culturally specific.[2] They argue that not only 'face' but also the emanating strategies of face redress are universal and, furthermore, that they are 'a

---

[2] The extent of cultural variability allowed by Brown and Levinson's theory is shown to be inadequate for satisfactory predictions of politeness phenomena in Japanese (Matsumoto, 1988) and Chinese (Gu, 1990). They both observe that, although the notion of 'face' may be universal, the two components attributed to it by the theory cannot be universal because neither the positive nor the negative aspects of it can account satisfactorily for politeness phenomena in these cultures. They argued that this conceptualization derives from the great significance attached to individualism in European and American culture. On similar lines, Ide (1989: 241) argues that it is not the content of face which crucially differs between Western and non-Western societies, but the weight of face itself.

powerful functional pressure on any linguistic system'. They contend that there are universal principles of politeness, but that different languages select the strategies and forms most appropriate to their needs. This sounds like a plausible candidate for universality, because it can better accommodate, on the one hand, the existence of a diversity of structures for expressing politeness even within the same community, and on the other, the existence of striking similarities between entirely diverse language communities. More generally, Scollon and Scollon (1981: 169) argue that 'productive systems of cultural behavior are the result of the interaction of human universals and the culturally specific input of a particular group'.

There are, however, scholars who believe that a more realistic approach to the examination of sociolinguistic behaviour can be based on non-universalistic claims. (See for instance, Janney and Arndt, 1993; Blum-Kulka, 1983; Olshtain and Cohen, 1983.) It is true, as some argue, that although the same form, for example a question or an imperative, might be utilized in two languages to perform a request, the resulting illocutionary force might be different. This, however, can also be true even within the same language community. For instance 'Are you going to the University tomorrow?' might simply be a request for information or a conventionalized request for action, i.e. the speaker is requesting a lift. It is also true that forms which are apparently equivalent might have different functions and the same function can be realized with different forms.

However, such facts do not invalidate the hypothesis of a certain universal repository of possible structures. The fact that two languages can utilize interrogative and imperative forms to function as requests does not necessarily mean that these languages must conventionalize the same form. It does not imply that languages cannot make finer distinctions among types of imperatives or interrogatives, it does not suggest that one or the other may not be avoided as a request form, nor does it signify that there are no language-specific constructions to convey politeness. So a distinction should be drawn here between 'utilized', 'utilizable', and 'conventionalized' forms and strategies. By 'utilized' forms I mean the ones which could be used but are not very common, and by 'utilizable' those which are possible but are never used. An example of the former could be the imperative construction to perform a request in

English, which is possible but rare. An example of the latter could be the present indicative to perform direct requests. It would be possible, but never used in English, whereas it is very common in Italian, Spanish, and Greek; for example, *mu δinis to molivi su?* 'do you give me your pencil?' in Greek, and in Italian *mi dai un dolce?* 'do you give me a sweet?' By 'conventionalized' forms I mean both fixed, formulaic expressions and those which are highly preferred by the majority of native speakers. The crucial point here is to realize that the forms each language will select, modulate, and conventionalize are motivated to a great extent by its cultural norms and values.

Considering the question of universality, Goody similarly asserts that

> what seems to happen is that different societies select different basic signals to elaborate and institutionalize. These then become special strategic forms and are subject to learning just as are other aspects of culture. And, indeed, occasionally a culture assigns to one of these basic signals a meaning which is different from or even opposite to its apparent natural meaning.
>
> (1978*b*: 7)

Furthermore, it should be noted that such choices for conventionalization are not static but undergo change just as other aspects of language do. An interesting illustration of this is offered by Brown and Gilman (1989: 181) who state that the common, conventionalized subjunctive interrogative request forms in modern English were completely absent from Shakespeare's tragedies.

The distinction drawn earlier is, I believe, important, because people tend to think that the patterns their language has conventionalized are the only natural and logical ones, which inherently somehow express, for instance, politeness or impoliteness, and so on. However, the observation that these are the most problematic ones for foreign learners to master and use appropriately (unless conventionalized in their own languages) indicates that this is an illusion. Nevertheless, such observations do not indicate that there are no universals and areas where cultures overlap. But these similarities tend to go unnoticed because they do not cause problems. Even within the same culture this kind of distinction appears to be valid for explaining individual differences. From the culturally available repository, individuals choose and use most frequently those forms and strategies which better express their ideology, age, sex, mood of the moment, and so on.

In identifying universal human needs which motivate communication, Tannen (1986: 30–1) also reflects Goffman's (1956: 488) views when she says that they are 'the needs to be connected to others and to be left alone. Trying to honor these conflicting needs puts us in a double bind,' and adds that 'the linguistic concept of politeness accounts for the way we serve these needs and react to the double bind'. This choice, however, is not entirely free, since it is informed by the individual's cultural knowledge.

Interactants, in order to be successful, must be conversant with the culturally specific norms for balancing these conflicting needs of involvement and independence. It is then that it becomes effortless behaviour and stems from a desire for balanced relations and/or a dislike for friction which undermines equilibrium. The meaning and importance of politeness, sometimes expressed with trite, fixed formulas, become conspicuous when such formulas are absent or not properly realized according to the norms of the society in which one finds oneself.

We can, therefore, conclude that rules for appropriate, polite speech behaviour may vary from one society to another, but if there were nothing shared and universal about politeness, then learning a foreign language as well as translation from one language to another would be almost impossible tasks. What exactly it is which is universal may still be obscure and in need of further investigation, but the fact that there is the possibility of translation and of comparative study is, I believe, indicative of the fact that there is some common ground on which studies of politeness may be based. For this purpose, therefore, I would like to address some of the differences exhibited in politeness across cultures, since this will eventually help us discover the extent of the similarities.

3.3 POLITENESS ACROSS CULTURES

The fact that the concept of politeness is most probably universal and that what differs from culture to culture is its specific connotations and manifestations, is probably best exemplified from a variety of cultures which illustrate the fact that different socio-cultural norms and values are reflected in all levels of the linguistic code.

Japanese and Hindi speakers tend to develop their topics in a spiral way which is the reverse of the more linear direction of development which is used by many Westerners. (Smith, 1987*b*: 2; Kachru, 1987: 90). The problems which can arise from this kind of difference are obvious. Such speakers will include in their accounts all those points which they regard as relevant and necessary for the issue under discussion, only to be perceived as illogical, irrelevant, and circumlocutionary by their non-native addressees.

However, this roundabout form of discourse organization, does not seem to be an exclusively Japanese or Hindi feature, it is also found in many other Oriental cultures (Clyne, 1987*a*). Young (1982) observes that the preferred sentence structure in Chinese is 'topic-comment', exemplified as old–new information, and illustrates the fact that the same is true of discourse organization as a whole. In other words, the Chinese tend first to delineate all relevant details, chiefly old, known information, which naturally leads to the main point, the new information. The common tendency in English to start with a clear and precise statement of what will be discussed—a 'subject-prominent' language—is in sharp contrast with and almost inconceivable in Chinese—a 'topic-prominent' language. The Chinese believe that if a request is stated immediately, it may make demands or impose views on the requestee. Thus, in providing the rationale behind the request before making the request itself, they perceive their discourse style of making requests as one which respects the other person. Consequently, the Chinese regard as boring, inconsiderate, or even rude any style that does not conform to their expectations. In contrast, their style is seen as simultaneously saving the speaker's face in case of rejection of the request.

The Chinese are thought of as people who value harmony in social relationships and appear to operate on the basis of extreme indirectness, a characteristic which Young (ibid. 80) interprets as a manifestation of negative politeness. Interestingly enough, this is clear in both their social and discourse behaviour. However, outsiders who are unaware of different discourse organization preferences may condemn the Chinese discourse style as 'imprecise, unwieldy and downright inept' (ibid. 81).

Differences in discourse organization are observed not only when one investigates preferred patterns in cultures as distinct as the Far East and the West. Although the English and the French seem to follow a more linear pattern for the development of their argumentation, the Germans, Italians, and Russians tend towards a more spiral type of argumentation (Clyne, 1987*a*: 76). It could be added here that Greeks also follow this latter practice. This type of organization is perceived by Anglo-Saxons as digressive, whereas for those who use them such digressions do not indicate bad organization but have a specific function, as they lead to conclusions based on broader perspectives.

These digressions are not without more general consequences as they contribute to a greater asymmetry in both textual and propositional balance and allow for more repetition because of the need for recapitulation. What deserves attention here is that such culture-specific patterns are also found in academic writing where greater uniformity would be expected (Clyne, 1987*b*). Furthermore, the interactions between writers and readers in academic texts involve positive and negative politeness devices (Meyers, 1989). It is easy to predict what is likely to happen when speakers or writers who are not conversant with such norms for circularity and digression or who do not place the same emphasis on the same type of politeness strategies have to interact with others who have internalized and, therefore, follow different principles. The consequences can be dramatic and/or traumatic because difficulties in comprehending the other will not be attributed just to differences in discourse organization and/or to the politeness of the individuals concerned but, even worse, to their intellectual abilities.

Attributions of inherent features of politeness to certain patterns can also be found at a different level of discourse organization, that of turn-taking. An example of this is telephone call openings, which exhibit interesting cross-cultural variation. For instance, overt self-identification is the preferred and thus appropriate and polite strategy of achieving recognition on the telephone in some cultures, but the dispreferred one in some others (Schegloff, 1979: 50). Such differences are discussed in more detail later (see section 8.1). A number of other cross-cultural differences at this level, such as the amount of overlapping appropriate, have been detected (Tannen, 1984*a*).

'There is [also] no reason to assume that speech acts are the same everywhere' (Ervin-Tripp, 1972*b*: 242). Even the names used for speech acts can reveal differences in the functions performed. Apologies and thanks are a clear case in point. As Coulmas (1981*b*:

89) points out, although thanks and apologies are activities which may be found across cultures, their incidence of use is culturally defined. Similarly, apologies in Japan are not only performed to express admission of fault, which is usually the case, but also serve as a social lubricant, in cases in which both participants accept responsibility for a problematic interchange (Smith, 1987*b*: 1).

Wierzbicka (1986: 365) suggests that the absence of verbs for thanking and apologizing, and the presence of many verbs referring to attitudes based on kinship in Australian Aboriginal languages reveal certain aspects of those cultures. They reflect different conceptions of what the function of thanks and apologies really is and to whom and by whom these speech acts may be expressed. Thus, in societies where such kinship-based relationships prevail and so determine clearly the rights and obligations of the individuals concerned, even favours done and received are interpreted within the framework of kinship duties and are consequently not seen as acts based on the free will of the individuals. Further supportive evidence can be found in languages from South Asia, where speakers do not verbalize their gratitude or indebtedness to family members because helping each other in this context is perceived only as compliance with one's duties, so that this form of verbalization is considered inappropriate and even insulting (Coulmas, 1981*b*: 81). It follows, then, that the norms which determine what kinds of behaviour demand thanks and apologies differ from society to society; consequently, we need to consult the values of each society before determining what is appropriate and polite for each specific situation.

Such variation is also true of the ways people perform other social functions through language. Manes and Wolfson (1981) and Wolfson (1983) have demonstrated this in their interesting and extensive study of the multifunctionality of compliments and the responses to them. The kinds of things which elicit compliments, their frequency, and the ways in which they are accepted or deflected clearly reveal the system of values of the particular community under study. Paying compliments is a common and frequent way in which middle class Americans express approval in an attempt to achieve and maintain successful social relationships with others. By contrast, Indonesian and Malaysian students are puzzled by what they perceive as the high frequency of compliments in American English (Wolfson, 1981). Compare this with the fact that Americans offer a lot more compliments than South Africans do, most of which, however, they tend to ignore or reject. These rejections seem to compel addressees to offer more compliments, which in turn will be rejected, and so on. South Africans, on the other hand, offer compliments more sparingly but tend to accept most of them. Consequently, in intercultural encounters, South Africans will be judged by Americans as impolite, accepting self-praise through agreeing with most compliments, whereas the American relative excess of offering compliments will also be judged by South Africans as impolite and insincere (Herbert and Straight, 1989).

Similar misinterpretations can arise with invitations which can be categorized as ambiguous and unambiguous (Wolfson, D'Amico-Reisner, and Huber, 1983). Since unambiguous invitations request a response after specifying the time and/or place of the activity, they do not usually pose problems to interlocutors. However, invitations are often not so clearly unambiguous and, therefore, require negotiations which are determined to a great extent by the degree of intimacy between interactants, a factor which requires adequate socio-cultural knowledge for one to proceed appropriately. Thus, an ambiguous utterance, such as 'Let's get together for lunch sometime', may be perceived as an invitation by a non-native speaker who, misinterpreting the speaker's intention, may then feel hurt by what he or she considers to be the interlocutor's insincerity.

The degree of directness required for the successful performance of speech acts is a major area in cross-cultural communication and will be discussed in detail later (section 5.2.2). Examples of this abound: for instance, requests and complaints in German versus English (House and Kasper, 1981) and requests in Russian versus those in English (Thomas, 1983). In both cases the former languages use more direct constructions, thus appearing to be less polite.

Japanese, like other oriental languages, permits one to tell a higher-status addressee what one assumes the addressee would like to hear rather than the true facts (LoCastro, 1987). Again, direct straightforward answers are considered to be impolite, a practice which contrasts with that of South-East Queensland Aboriginal society, in which direct questions to elicit information are unnecessary and addressees are under no social obligation to respond and/or give information (Eades, 1982). Moreover, the Warm Spring

Indians may even reserve their answers till days later (Philips, 1976).

For the Ilongots of the Philippines the main distinction should be drawn between commands (directives) and all other speech acts: 'whereas most modern theorists think of language as a tool designed primarily to "express" or to "refer", Ilongots think of language first in terms of action' (Rosaldo, 1982: 203); understanding how this works needs 'some appreciation of the distinctive conceptual and relational shape of Ilongot society' (ibid. 230). Thus, it is clear that there is considerable variation across cultures as regards speech acts.

Differences between cultures, however, are not restricted to higher-level linguistic phenomena, such as discourse organization and the function of speech acts, but permeate the minutiae of the language, and can be observed in lower-level linguistic phenomena as well.

In Japanese, for instance, it would be considered assertive and impolite for the addressee not to use back-channel cues, such as 'uh', 'huh' and 'yeah', as their use indicates that one is attending to what the speaker is saying, irrespective of whether or not one agrees with the content. Such cues, however, could create the impression of agreement for non-natives and thus cause minor or serious misunderstandings (LoCastro, 1987). Comparing also Japanese and English, Hatch and Long (1980: 31) conclude that 'back-channelling styles differ for different social, cultural and linguistic groups'. Whereas Japanese students smile and nod, lean forward and murmur 'yesss' at the appropriate places only to indicate that they are attentive, English students do so to show that they have understood.

Interestingly enough, this insertion of minimal responses in an interchange is seen as a characteristic of female style in Western cultures (Maltz and Borker, 1982). Wetzel (1988) notes a number of features shared by Japanese and Western female styles of communication and argues that these similarities are not indicative of feminine, 'powerless' elements in Japanese style, but rather reveal cultural differences in the notion of 'power'.

For an extensive account illustrating the interrelationship of language and culture, see Loveday (1983). This interrelationship, however, should not be thought of as direct and clear, nor as static. Societal changes influence the language and language changes can bring about changes in society. Saville-Troike (1982) reports that since the communist revolution in Cuba, a former non-standard variety of Spanish has become prestigious, whereas the previously prestigious variety has been devalued. The Greek situation of 'diglossia' is also similar, in that it had for years been closely linked to socio-political views and changes. *Demotiki* (the people's language) was favoured by more liberal governments and people, but was almost forbidden by conservatives, who favoured *katharevousa* (the purified language). In the more recent past, the military junta established *katharevousa*, but in 1974, the restoration of democracy and freedom gave an impetus to a conscious preference for the spoken language (i.e. *demotiki*), which was later accepted as the official national language. In other words, 'linguistic innovations which go hand in hand with historical and cultural changes will have a good claim to being a reflection and an expression of sociocultural phenomena' (Wierzbicka, 1986: 351).

Wierzbicka (1986: 350) contends that although this interrelationship of language and culture is more evident in lexical items since 'lexicon tends to change more quickly than grammar in response to changes in the "social reality",' this relationship is, nevertheless, true for grammar in its broadest sense. Not all areas of grammar can legitimately be thought of as reflecting culture, but 'optional grammatical categories are likely to be more revealing of the ongoing culture than obligatory ones', for instance, diminutives. Furthermore, 'those parts of language, including grammar in the narrow sense of the term, which have to do with the relationship between the speaker and the addressee, are . . . among those most likely to reflect the living, ongoing culture,' for instance, second person pronouns (ibid. 351). It is true that pronominal systems and systems of address, in general, are particularly sensitive to social changes and appear to reflect the underlying cultural system.

Pronominal systems and systems of address are markers which reflect the relationship between speaker and addressee directly, and which are part of what has been called *social deixis*; in contrast to this, *strategies of language use* reveal the same relationship, but indirectly, and refer to particular choices from among the possible alternatives appropriate in the specific context (Brown and Levinson, 1979).

This distinction is similar to that of politeness as *social indexing* ('discernment') and *strategic politeness* ('volition'), discussed in more recent studies (see Kasper, 1990). Hill *et al.* (1986) argue that the former refers to the almost automatic observance of and passive submission to social rules (e.g. honorifics), whereas the latter allows for more free, active choice according to the speaker's intentions. Both groups of social markers operate in all systems of politeness and differences can be evidenced in the extent to which the one or the other may be obligatory and/or prominent. For example, in a Japanese context, overwhelming importance is attached to discernment, whereas in Western languages volition appears to be predominant. The question of strategic politeness is clearly an almost inexhaustible subject, and although I propose to limit its treatment by using requests as examples, without addressing politeness as social indexing, that is, social deixis and forms of address, we cannot begin to appreciate the subtleties inherent in the requests themselves.

3.4   SOCIAL DEIXIS

Deixis is a word borrowed from the Greek verb meaning 'point' or 'indicate'. In linguistics 'deixis' is a term used to denote a word or phrase which directly and categorically refers to temporal, locational, or personal characteristics of a communicative event and its participants. Examples are *here/there*, *now/then former/latter*, and *I/you*. These are referred to as 'place deixis', 'time deixis' and 'discourse deixis', respectively.[3] Similarly, there exist features of communicative events which mark the social identity of the speaker or addressee, and the social relationship which holds between them. Examples are the T/V (singular/plural to single addressees) alternates, forms of address, honorifics, and so on, which are ways of communicating politeness and formality, or intimacy and informality.

Brown and Levinson (1978: 281) define honorifics as 'direct grammatical encodings of relative social status between participants, or between participants and persons or things referred to in the communicative event'. Within the honorific system three categories are distinguished: 'addressee honorifics', 'referent honorifics' (Brown

---

[3] For a detailed discussion of deixis, see Levinson (1983).

and Levinson, 1979; Neustupný, 1978), and 'bystander' or 'audience honorifics' (Levinson, 1983).

Addressee honorifics convey respect to the addressees by the choice of specific linguistic items or forms, without directly referring to them. In some addressee honorific cultures 'it is possible to say a sentence like *The soup is hot* and by choice of lexical item convey deference or the reverse to the addressee' (Brown and Levinson, 1979: 318). Similarly, Donaldson (1984: 195) drawing upon Stevens, says that in Madurese there are eleven different ways of saying *I'm going to your house*.

Referent honorifics convey respect to things or persons actually referred to. Levinson (1983: 90) says that the familiar T/V distinction is a referent honorific system, though the referent and the addressee are the same in this case. Elsewhere, Brown and Levinson (1978: 281) point out that there is considerable overlap between these two systems, and that 'referent honorifics are basic and—at least as encoded in address forms—universal'. They (1987: 23) also claim that diachronically addressee honorifics developed out of referent honorifics.

Bystander honorifics include those cases in which a different vocabulary is used in the presence of certain relatives. An interesting example of this is provided by almost all Australian Aboriginal communities. There is a special 'avoidance' speech style, often called 'mother-in-law language', which is employed by everybody when the presence of certain relatives requires special verbal and non-verbal behaviour (Dixon, 1980). This could be roughly equated to avoiding certain expressions and/or resorting to more formal language in the presence of certain people in European cultures.

This categorization of honorific systems is important because it is reflected differently in the grammars of languages of the world. As Brown and Levinson state:

Referent honorifics are necessarily confined to referring expressions, and morphological agreements with them, and empirically they tend to turn up in titles of address, verb endings, words for persons and their body parts and belongings. Addressee honorifics, on the other hand, could theoretically turn up in any part of the linguistic system, and empirically tend to be found in lexical alternates for common words (including function words, auxiliary verbs, and so on), aspects of morphology, special particles that are otherwise without meaning, and aspects of prosodics and paralinguistics. (1979: 318)

In addition to these three types of socially deictic information which Levinson (1983: 91) calls 'relational', there is a fourth which, he claims, points to the relationship between speaker and setting and which he calls 'absolute' socially deictic information. Following Fillmore, he distinguishes between 'authorized speakers' and 'authorized recipients'. Authorized speakers are those who are entitled to use certain forms and authorized recipients those who are entitled to receive certain forms.

A very elaborate honorific system can be found in Japanese and closely related systems exist in Chinese, Madurese, Javanese, and other South-East Asian languages.[4] European languages exhibit 'remnants' of such elaborate systems, English being particularly restricted. However, Lakoff (1972) argues that there are configurations in English whose force is very close to that of honorifics, but whose function is less explicit so that they are not so readily recognizable. In European languages, addressee honorifics are restricted to rare polite intonations, whereas referent honorifics can account for different titles and second or third person pronominal alternates. In most cases, pronoun alternatives are restricted to the second person (i.e. the addressee): French *tu/vous*, German *Du/Sie*, Russian *ty/vy*, Greek *esi/esis*, and so on. Levinson (1978: 12) points out that out of 38 languages, '25 have V pronouns derived only from second person plural pronouns, 5 derived only from third person singular or plural, and 8 have two V pronouns (or more) derived from both sources'.

The choice between one or the other of these forms tends to be reciprocal and determined by the degree of intimacy. This is obviously not a categorical rule because cases of non-reciprocity are found and are determined by power and status differences. There are various stories explaining the origin of this distinction to mark something more than the singular/plural distinction. Brown and Gilman (1960) suggest that the singular/plural differentiation historically originates in the dual emperors of the Roman Empire (but see Levinson, 1978, for objections).

---

[4] For detailed descriptions of these honorific systems, see Geertz (1968) on Javanese, Neustupný (1968 and 1978), and Yamanashi (1974) on Japanese.

What is clear, however, is that in medieval and early modern European languages, honorific systems were more elaborate. Societies were more clearly stratified then, and people consciously and conscientiously followed the patterns of language which supported class divisions. English had a T/V distinction as follows: *thou* and *ye* for the second person nominative singular and plural, and *thee* and *you* for the second person accusative singular and plural, respectively. The plural *you* was then generalized as nominative for both singular and plural. It was promoted to cover both usages, thus enhancing the distance between the interlocutors and keeping class boundaries where they should be. Nowadays, *you* does not have the same distancing connotations for English speakers. This establishment of the plural *you* as the only second person pronoun in English is said to have originated as a reaction to the Quakers, who favoured the establishment of the more egalitarian, singular *thou* (Brown and Gilman, 1960; Haugen, 1975).

The seminal study of second person pronouns of address is the article 'The pronouns of power and solidarity' by Brown and Gilman (1960), which instigated much research on the modes of address in European and in Asian languages. They introduced the familiar T/V notation for the distinction between singular or 'familiar' T (from the Latin *tu*) and plural or 'polite' V (from the Latin *vos*) second person pronouns in any language. They then tried to clarify the close association of these pronouns 'with two dimensions fundamental to the analysis of all social life—the dimensions of power and solidarity' (ibid. 252).

Very briefly, what they found was that when interactants were closely related, they could use T pronouns reciprocally. If they were of the same power, but not close they would exchange V pronouns reciprocally. In both cases the relationship is symmetrical. Levinson (1978: 11) contends that 'there seems . . . to be some general way in which, as status increases, reciprocal T usage diminishes'. Elsewhere, Brown and Levinson (1979: 323) offer the explanation that high-status groups 'do not rely on each other for support or services . . . with the consequence that relations between these units tend to be socially distant, and appropriately symbolized by V-exchange'. If the relationship is based only on power, there is also an asymmetrical possibility of non-reciprocal T/V use with T pronouns used downwards, towards the person of lower status, and V pronouns upwards, towards the person of higher status. Levinson (1978: 11) maintains that 'the same association of V-giving and status occurs in many unrelated cultures and therefore does not seem to be arbitrary'. Generally speaking, the use of V form is linked with differences between interactants (Brown and Gilman, 1960). Thus, through the choice of pronominal forms, a variety of attitudes concerning the relationship of the interlocutors can be revealed. As Wardhaugh (1986: 267) points out, this choice can indicate 'our feelings towards others—solidarity, power, distance, respect, intimacy, and so on—and our awareness of social customs'.

The Greek language includes a pronominal system similar to those of many other European languages. The second person plural *esis* can be used towards a single addressee as a means of indicating formality and/or politeness, either because of social distance or status differences between the participants in an encounter.[5] The pronoun itself is not necessarily stated, because Greek has a rich verb inflectional system which indicates person as well as number, rendering personal pronouns redundant. Thus, formality and/or politeness versus informality (but not necessarily impoliteness) are determined by the choice of the number and person of the verb. In other words, the second person plural form of the verb is used to denote formality and perhaps politeness towards a single addressee, seen as somebody distant. Mackridge states that

The polite plural is not used as frequently in MG [Modern Greek] as it is in French, but is regularly found in the conversation of educated adults. Children hardly use it, and young people tend to avoid it except when being especially polite (e.g. to a teacher). Middle-class adults, on the other hand, use it regularly among themselves unless and until they have passed beyond a threshold of familiarity, which may happen at any time (even during their first meeting), or not at all. (1985: 77)

Mackridge's observations might be linked to the conclusions drawn by Brown and Gilman (1960: 264–5) concerning Germans, French, and Italians. Germans preferred more informal forms than French among family members, whereas the reverse was true outside the

---

[5] It should be noted that in most discussions of pronominal systems, second person plural forms directed to a single addressee are referred to as 'polite plurals', a label which ignores the difference between 'formality' and 'politeness' (see section 4.3).

family among people sharing similar interests. Italians seemed to prefer more solidarity forms on both levels. Thus Greeks appear to be more similar to Italians than to French and Germans in this respect.

It should be borne in mind that although structurally this T/V distinction is rather simple, being simply the second person plural used to a single addressee, when it comes to actual use, decisions are rather delicate. Appropriate use requires a certain degree of formal education, and inconsistencies and inappropriateness are not rare as one moves down the educational ladder. Education, of course, is not the only factor determining choice, because individual views may also be reflected. A certain degree of fluctuation and inconsistency may also be observed before a relationship is mutually established as either intimate or formal.

There is a tendency, however, for the plural to be avoided as society becomes more egalitarian and relationships more informal. 'The general trend is towards the retrenchment of the polite plural as relations among people in middle-class Greek society become more informal' (Mackridge, 1985: 78). These egalitarian views, however, seem to have led to an interesting paradox—a reversal in the use of pronouns, which has also been observed in Italian by Bates and Benigni (1975). They found that young lower class informants used more formal forms than upper class young informants, and older informants fell in between. They also pointed out that 'some of our peers have approached a virtual mirror-image of the old address system, using *tu* [informal] with professors and employers, and *Lei* [polite/formal] with sales-clerks, waiters, and the family maid' (ibid. 287). What is more interesting is that such changes in the address system are not restricted to Italian, but are also found in some form or other in countries with diverse social systems such as Sweden (Paulston, 1976) and China, where it is reported that 'for some young people *shī·fu*, which is traditionally used to address workers, has become an honorific form for any person regardless of his job status' (Scotton and Wanjin, 1983: 494). Makri-Tsilipakou (1983) also observed a similar kind of reversal in the use of singular/plural second person pronouns in Greek. She contends that in Modern Greek the singular forms of address are mainly employed by working class people and those who share left-wing ideologies, whereas plural forms are generally cherished by the conservative bourgeoisie. Recently, however, due to societal changes, especially after the downfall of the junta, this picture has started changing. Bourgeois youth tend to favour T-forms and working class people tend to exploit, so to speak, their right of access to the V-forms. For a tendency to use plural forms and polite expressions towards people thought of as lower ranking in Greek, see section 7.3.2.4.

It should be noted, however, that this change is not an attempt to distance speakers from lower class people, but rather to give them due respect. It could be seen as a reaction against the most prevalent pattern of non-reciprocal address towards lower-ranking people. This subject is, of course, very delicate. Levinson (1978: 19) argues very tentatively that such changes are not simply a matter of changing fashions in pronominal usage, but rather a reflection of more asymmetrical T/V usage within rural families, which is the pattern extended to a wider circle outside the family. Although it may be true that there is an element of authoritarianism in rural families, such an explanation runs contrary to the widely reported move towards more egalitarian relationships in general. In any case, authoritarian attitudes must have always existed and do not constitute a recent development within rural families. Furthermore, and perhaps more importantly, Levinson's explanation does not account for the reversal. In other words, although it may sound plausible to say that the greater V-giving of the lower class is due to the more asymmetrical T/V usage in rural families, this does not explain the adoption of more T usage in upper class exchanges.

In Greek, polite plurals are used only in direct address, and cannot refer to other persons that are spoken of. The polite plural system is restricted to the use of the second plural verb form towards a single addressee. The only exception appears to be the use of 'royal plural' (see section 5.2.1), the use of which, however, is not directly related to politeness or formality. There is also an extremely limited possibility of using the third person singular when directly addressing somebody unknown, indicating formality. For instance, *ti θa iθele o kirios?* 'what would the gentleman want?'

Another feature of the Greek polite plurals is that plurality is confined to verbs and to pronominal subjects, if overt, but does not extend to other predicates of the verb, whether nominal or adjectival constructions. For example:

ipate (2nd pl.)	oti isaste (2nd pl.)	aδjaθetos (sing.)?
did you say	that you are	ill (not feeling well)?

As Levinson (1983: 92) states, 'nominal predicates tend to agree with actual number and person, finite verbs with the morphological person and number encoded in the polite form of the pronoun, with language-specific decisions on predicates of intermediate kind'. (For variations among European languages, see Comrie, 1975).

This facility, though structurally rather simple, appears to be socially very important because it enables speakers to make distinctions and indicate formality that would otherwise require a different, perhaps more elaborate system to express. This, then, is an important difference between Greek and English, which partly explains the need for elaboration and indirectness in English to express formality, politeness, and social distance. Even the simplest grammatical construction, the imperative, which in English would be condemned as impolite in most cases, exhibits in Greek a gradation of more or less acceptability partly due to the availability of the singular/plural distinction. It would not be unreasonable to suggest that at the time that the singular *thou* gave way to the more distancing *you* in general use, a degree of formality and elaboration in the language was also adopted, expressing the same mentality and serving the same purpose as the abolition of the singular *thou*, or perhaps in order to counterbalance the need for the expression of the distinction between formality and informality.

Therefore, in 'social deixis' we can observe the different choices open to a speaker according to the status of and degree of familiarity with the addressee. These same parameters determine choices among the various forms of address.

3.5   FORMS OF ADDRESS

In my discussion of forms of address in Greek and in English, I have referred extensively to Brown and Ford's (1964) article 'Address in American English'. In this work they extend the association of the power and solidarity dimensions of pronouns to cover the choice between terms of address.[6] These dimensions are seen as basic in

---

[6] Examples of other studies on the forms of address clearly influenced by the intellectual wealth of the articles by Brown and Gilman (1960) and Brown and Ford (1964) are: Ervin-Tripp (1972*a* and 1972*b*) for American English, Bates and Benigni (1975) for Italian, Kempf (1985) for German, Paulston (1976) for Swedish, Friedrich (1966 and 1972) for the Russian of the nineteenth century, Makri-Tsilipakou (1983) for Greek, Keshavarz (1988) for Iranian Persian, Hinds (1976) for

social behaviour, but the terms 'power' and 'solidarity' have been replaced by 'status' and 'intimacy', respectively. Robinson (1972) points out that since the unqualified use of 'status' is value-laden, it would be better to use 'power'.

Nevertheless, I will not go into great detail, since my intention is to concentrate solely on those differences which are indicative of differences in the type of social relationships prevailing in everyday encounters. Forms of address function in ways parallel to T/V pronominal systems, as has already been mentioned. Modern English, which has reduced the binary T/V distinction into a single V pronominal system, has also reduced the basic tertiary distinction, first name (FN), title plus first name (TFN), and title plus last name (TLN) into a binary FN/TLN distinction. Other possibilities are also available, including last name only (LN), title (T), and of course a variety of more individual, intimate address expressions, which Brown and Ford call multiple naming (MN), plus no naming at all (NN).

Greek includes a T/V pronominal system and a more elaborate system of address, in that besides the address possibilities encountered in modern English, it also includes the title plus first name (TFN) possibility which existed in older English.[7] This is not only just as acceptable as FN and TLN, but it also appears to bridge the gap between the very intimate FN and the very formal TLN. I suspect that this TFN is the most common construction in everyday Greek interactions. Children are usually taught to use this pattern as being more appropriate with people with whom their parents are on first name terms, and sometimes with their teachers, especially the younger ones. TFN usage appears to be a welcome solution to the conflict between the extremes of status and familiarity which often arises, hence its widespread use.

Number choice in Greek is concomitant with the choice of the term of address. Singular number is always employed with the first name of the addressee, and plural with a title or title plus last name. This picture, however, is not always so simple, because the intermediate possibility—that of title plus first name (TFN)—can be followed by either singular or plural. Adults tend to use TFN

Japanese, Howell (1965) and Kim (1968) for Korean, Scotton and Wanjin (1983) for Chinese.

[7] See, for instance, Jane Austen's *Pride and Prejudice*, which is full of title plus first name (TFN) terms of address.

with equals with whom they are not very well acquainted or with people who are thought of as lower-ranking, such as porters, plumbers, and cleaning ladies. In the former case, the TFN followed by plural tends to be reciprocally used, whereas in the latter, the accompanying number will most probably be different, with the higher-ranking people employing TFN plus singular and the lower-ranking ones TFN plus plural, or title plus last name.

Besides the common *kirios* 'Mr' (vocative *kirie*), *kiria*[8] 'Mrs', and *δespinis* 'Miss',[9] titles which are the most distancing and impersonal forms of address include those of occupation or position and respect. Examples of respect titles are *sevazmiotate* (vocative of the superlative degree of the adjective *sevazmios* 'respected')—reserved for the clergy—*aksiotime* (vocative of the adjective *aksiotimos* 'worthy of honour'), and so on. Examples of occupational or positional (PT) titles are *jatre* (vocative of *jatros* 'doctor'), *δikiγore* (vocative of *δikiγoros* 'lawyer'), *kaθijita* (vocative of *kaθijitis* 'professor' and 'high school teacher') and others.[10] There is no equivalent for 'Dr' (referring to doctorate holder) used as a direct form of address. *δiδaktor* is used only indirectly to refer to somebody who has a doctorate.[11]

It appears to be the case in both English and Greek that occupational titles function in the same way as TLN, and are not usually followed by a name in direct address, although they are in indirect use. In Greek some of the occupational titles are preceded by *kirie* (but not by *kiria* and *δespinis*), whereas others are not (see below), and still others oscillate between the two. Respect titles are never preceded by other titles, as is also the case in English. In Greek one can say *kirie kaθijita* 'Mr Professor' and *kirie δikasta* 'Mr Judge', but not **kirie jatre* 'Mr doctor', the latter being ungrammatical, while *δimarχe* 'mayor' could be used with or without *kirie*

---

[8] In slang use, the masculine nominative *kirios* and the feminine *kira* could be used as terms of address with deprecatory connotations when there is social distance. For example: *ja pjon me perases kirios?* 'who do you think I am, sir?'; *ti mas les kira mu?* 'what are you telling us, madam?'

[9] The marital status discrimination for women is as important in Greek as it is in English. On the subject of sexism in the English address system, see Lakoff (1975), Hook (1974), Kramer (1975), and Wolfson and Manes (1980), among many others.

[10] Some of these vocatives are *katharevousa* forms still used in *demotiki*. See Ferguson's (1959) pioneering work on diglossia. Nowadays, although the established language for use at all levels is *demotiki*, there are still *katharevousa* forms in it.

[11] The borrowed word *δoktor* is sometimes used by uneducated people to address medical doctors in order to express familiarity and respect.

'Mr'. The first of the two titles is always omitted when the name of the person follows and this is more frequently used indirectly rather than directly as a form of address. The only cases in English where a positional title is preceded by 'Mr' is 'Mr President', and this only in the United States. 'Mr Justice', 'Mr Ambassador', and 'Mr Chairman' are also encountered. This construction is more prevalent in Greek perhaps because it is believed that occupational titles do not necessarily imply gentlemanliness.

Another explanation may be that the use of two titles in Greek represents an attempt to distance the interlocutors. Since this combination of the two titles is never followed by the name of the addressee, it may imply that the first title (*kirie*) functions as a proper title and the occupational one (e.g. *δikasta*) functions as a name, a kind of distinguishing characteristic, but this combination sounds more impersonal and distant than TLN. The tension which is created by the possibility of having two titles of address plus a last name as a term of address is resolved in Greek by omitting the name of the addressee, whereas in English it is done by omitting the first title 'Mr'. Thus, in English the appropriate term of address for a professor is 'Professor X', whereas in Greek it is *kirie kaθijita* 'Mr Professor'. Moreover, this is why in English a professor may well be called 'Professor X' and not 'Mr X' in activities outside the university, such as when booking tickets, whereas in Greek, he will be addressed or referred to as 'Mr X'.

Table 3.1, though not comprehensive, indicates the major differences between Greek and English basic forms of address. In Greek higher status occupational titles tend to require the use of *kirie* before them; this restricts the possibility of a name being used after the occupational title, and so appears to increase the formality and distance between interactants. Sometimes, however, as with doctors, because people feel dependent on or emotionally involved with them and/or their profession, they tend to seek more intimacy and warmth, avoid the title *kirie* and simply use the form *jatre*. There is, however, an even more intimate possibility available—*jatre mu* 'my doctor'—although the interaction which follows in both cases will most probably be in the formal plural, indicating that the interactants observe the existing distance.

The situation with *kaθijitis* 'professor' seems to be exactly the opposite. The use of *kirie* 'Mr' before *kaθijita* 'professor' is obligatory. The explanation might be that most professors adhere

TABLE 3.1 *Differences between Greek and English forms of address*

Greek	English
T (*kirie, kiria, δespinis*)	T (*Mr, Mrs, Miss, Ms, Dr*)
FN	FN
T + FN	—
LN	LN
T + LN	T + LN
T + PT	—
MN	MN
NN	NN

Note: The initials used are borrowed from Brown and Ford and have already been explained. 'PT' is suggested here to mean 'positional title' including occupational, political, and military ones. This kind of address seems to be restricted to male addressees.

more stringently to distancing norms, or it may be an age difference involved between interactants. Especially in the past, professors were older people who instigated or even demanded distance and respect from their students, and although the situation has now changed to a great extent, it seems that this pattern (i.e. 'Mr professor') is so strongly fixed that it is resistant to change. More generally perhaps, the feeling of dependency on doctors enhances an emotional bond which is absent in the case of teachers.

The common practice in English universities for postgraduate students and teachers to be on first name terms is rather exceptional in Greek. Many Greek teachers still feel it is inappropriate, and many students still feel uncomfortable about using first name terms even if they have been so encouraged. What is more frequent is an asymmetrical usage, with the students using the formal *kirie* or *kiria* plus last name or *kirie* plus title and plural and the teachers using first name and singular. In some cases, symmetrical formal usage can be found, especially with older, more conservative teachers. An explanation of this phenomenon may also be the larger numbers of students in Greek universities, which prohibits teachers from knowing all of them personally.[12] Generally speaking, in Greek, when there are obvious or assumed status differences, the

---

[12] For a more extensive discussion on this, see Makri-Tsilipakou (1983).

asymmetrical usage is preferred. People can more easily employ symmetrical informal usage in cases where familiarity is absent, but they are more reluctant to do so in cases of status difference.

Lower status occupations do not provide titles for their practitioners in either language and consequently combinations like *kirie taksidzi* 'Mr taxi-driver' are non-existent.[13] However, there are cases in which the occupation, or more commonly a substitute related to the occupation, might be used, but this is understood as an attention-getter rather than as a form of address—for instance *manavi* 'greengrocer' or *fotoγrafe* 'photographer', and so on, with the most common being *taksi* to a taxi-driver. However, *kirie* 'sir' or 'Mr' and *kiria* 'madame' or 'Mrs', not followed by anything, or a different attention-getting device, are more frequently used.

The situation concerning women's titles, i.e. *kiria* 'Mrs' and *δespinis* 'Miss', before occupational titles is entirely different—such double titles are hardly ever encountered. The reason appears to be obvious. Higher-status occupations with which double titles can be used were once the prerogative of men. Although nowadays, women have been accepted as equals in these formerly male domains, they have not been accommodated by the language, which still fails to provide female equivalent forms; consequently, **kiria* (fem.) *δikiγore* (male) 'Mrs lawyer' is unacceptable. This extends even to professions for which a female designation is available, for example, *kiria* (fem.) *kaθijitria* (fem.) 'Mrs Professor', which sounds extremely odd.[14] Thus, women professionals tend to be addressed by their marital status title plus their last name on formal occasions.

More generally, however, it has been reported that women in general tend to receive more intimate, first name, and singular forms, even in situations where that would not be the case for a male.[15] According to Lakoff (1975: 37), 'although, in our society, naming conventions for men and women are essentially equal (both have first and last names, and both may have additional names, of lesser importance), the social conventions governing the choice of form of address is not parallel in both sexes'. Similarly, Kramer

---

[13] This point has also been made by Makri-Tsilipakou (1983).

[14] For the problems involved with Greek female occupational terms, see Pavlidou (1984).

[15] See Lakoff (1975); Ervin-Tripp (1972a); and Makri-Tsilipakou (1983) among others.

(1975) has observed that men and women address and are addressed in different ways. She cites works which indicate that this is true in other cultures as well, such as Japanese and Korean.

A difference between Greek and English titles is that Greek does not provide different words for *Mr*, *sir*, or even *gentleman* or for *Mrs*, *lady*, or *madam*. *Kirios* covers all three male titles and *kiria* all three female titles. Sometimes *madam*, borrowed from French, and *dzentleman*, borrowed from English, are used rather informally in Greek, the latter only to refer to rather than to address somebody.[16] The reason for this lack of Greek terms is that the social positions requiring titles such as *Sir* or *Lady* were non-existent in Greek social structure and, therefore, no such titles were available for use in everyday interactions among 'common' folk, as they were in England. This is reflected in the Greek Constitution (1975), where in paragraph 7 of article 4 on individual and social rights, it is clearly stated that 'titles of nobility or distinction are neither conferred upon nor recognized in Greek citizens'.

Endearment forms (such as *duck*, *love*, and *dear*) that are encountered in English, mainly in service encounters, do not occur in Greek among strangers. The forms which are rarely and idiosyncratically used, mainly by older, effusive women when addressing younger girls, are *ayapi mu* 'my love', *pulaki mu* 'my birdie', or *matja mu* 'my eyes'. These are related to endearment forms used among intimates. Languages differ as to the entities they utilize to express intimacy and endearment, and as such these forms are extremely language-specific. Thus, the choice of specific birds in English will sound odd to Greek ears, just as Greek references to vital organs of the body will sound odd to English ears. Attempts to translate such terms into other languages can only sound ridiculous because these references will be deprived of the emotional connotations and values they have acquired in the language of origin.

Terms of intimate address tend to be used more frequently in Greek than in everyday English encounters in cases where they are unnecessary from a semantic point of view. Such terms include first names in either their full form or in a variety of diminutive forms:

kosta mu . . . akuse me . . . kost*aki* mu . . . [KE 3: 72]
my Kostas . . . listen to me . . . my Kostas-*dim*. . . .

[16] *dzentleman* in predicative position means that the person referred to behaves

Garnica (1977: 161) says that 'the use of a diminutive form usually marks a dependency relationship between the user and the person being referred to'. It also marks a strong emotional bond between interactants, because diminutives of names, unless established as nicknames, cannot be freely used by everybody.

Similarly, terms such as *karδja mu* 'my heart' and *psixi mu* 'my soul', can also be used in their diminutive forms, in which case the sense of intimacy and endearment is enhanced.

> mi θimonis   matja mu . . .   [KE 3: 76]
> don't get upset   my eyes . . .
>
> po, po, po! . . .   mi   karδula mu
> po, po, po! [exclamation] . . . don't [shout] my heart-*dim*.
>
>   [KE 2: 104]

Kinship terms are also used as terms of address, alone or accompanied by a first name, although they are on the decline, especially among younger people, who tend to prefer first names. For example:

> ase me   na χaris,
> leave me [alone]   in order for you to be happy,
> barba taso   [AN 1: 9]
> uncle Taso

These can be used even in cases in which there is no relevant affiliation. Thus, older people can be called 'uncles' and 'aunts', though not usually with their diminutive forms unless there is an actual relationship. 'Grandfather' and 'grandmother' can be more freely used in the diminutive, even in the absence of such a relationship.

The form *manula mu* 'my mother-*dim*.' can be used even among male friends. More common is *peδi mu* 'my child' addressed to younger people, which is also used among friends of approximately the same age. The plural *peδja* 'children' can also refer to close friends or relatives. For example:

> [husband to wife]
> ande   manula mu,   to taksi perimeni   [KA 2: 114]
> come on   my mother-*dim*., the taxi is waiting

---

appropriately and gallantly. In this use *kirios* tends to be more frequent. The feminine *kiria* also has such connotations.

[among family members]
ti ora   θarθun   ta peδja?   [NB]
what time will come the children?

All these, I believe, are indicative of a closeness in relationships among members of the same in-group. Combinations of FN and intimate address forms are also possible. For example:

[lady to her maid]
. . . marina aγapi mu,   mi mas feris akomi kafe . . .
. . . Marina my love,   don't bring us the coffee yet . . .
                                                        [KA 3: 208]
[mother to son]   [MN 1: 51]
. . . staθi,   ja ela δo,   peδi mu!
. . . Stathi, come here,   my child!

Terms of address can also be used in successive turns in an encounter. They are obviously semantically unnecessary, in most cases, but serve as expressions of strong emotion and solidarity.

Additionally, other affectionate terms of address can also be found in both languages, such as *angele mu* 'my angel', or 'angel'; *moro mu* 'my baby', or 'baby'; *kukla mu* 'my doll', or 'doll'; *fos mu* 'my light', and so on. The list could be extended to cover all sorts of endearment forms used in very intimate relationships, but this would be beyond the scope of this work.

In Greek there are also some, usually meaningless, lexical items which can be used before intimate terms of address or in isolation to emphasize familiarity. The most common ones are *vre*, *re*, and *more*,[17] which cannot be translated into English. These may also be used pejoratively in association with deprecatory lexical items, and tend to be used more frequently by men. For example:

vre   ti mas les   [NB]
(vre)   what are you telling us

re   file mi fevjis ke si tora   [AN 1: 40]
(re)   friend don't leave and you now (please)

---

[17] *more*, which is a vocative, originates from the ancient Greek adjective for 'stupid', and when used in the feminine form, *mori*, it is insulting.

It seems that *more* is a kind of extremely informal variant of 'please', because it exhibits a similar positional flexibility. For example:

> (more) ton pernis (more) tilefono se parakalo (more)?   [NB]
> could you ring him please?

The possessive pronoun *mu* 'my' can also be used with all intimate terms of address. Such usage obviously has nothing to do with possession, but rather emphasizes closeness and intimacy and perhaps dependency, as we observed in the expression *jatre mu*. For example:

> klisto   pavlo mu   klisto!   [AN 1: 105]
> turn it off   my Pavlo   turn it off!

The possessive pronoun is also used in English, but it appears to be restricted to certain fixed expressions, such as *my dear* and *my love*.

Another interesting use of the plural possessive pronoun in Greek is exhibited in indirect reference. Thus *i maria mas* meaning 'our Maria' is used among friends and/or relatives to differentiate between the member of the in-group and an outsider with the same name, although this differentiation is very often redundant because of the context.

Thus, the Greek system of address, besides being more elaborate than the English in that it provides the TFN and TPT possibilities, appears to provide a wider range of address terms which could be characterized as in-group markers. The flexibility which diminutives offer with first names, kinship terms, and other endearment forms is extensive. This, along with the use of the possessive *mu* where no possession is involved or implied, points to a solidary view of the whole encounter and of the relationship in general. Using any of the innumerable ways to convey in-group membership is one of the characteristics of positive politeness through which the speaker can implicitly claim common ground with the addressee (Brown and Levinson, 1978: 112).

Moreover, as has already been mentioned, systems of address are particularly sensitive to social changes. An example of this is found in modern China (Fang and Heng, 1983; Scotton and Wanjin, 1983), where the Communist party attempted to replace most terms of address with *tóngzhì* 'comrade' in an effort to emphasize social and economic equality. Similarly, the forms of address which are preferred in post-revolutionary Iran are those expressing solidarity, and they tend to be used reciprocally (Keshavarz, 1988).

The creation and use of forms of address serve important functions. They enable speakers to express their distance and formality or intimacy and give clues to participants and observers of the social interactions about where each participant stands in the social structure. It has been argued that terms of address along with T/V pronominal systems constitute sociolinguistic universals.[18] The parameters determining choices, as well as the inventory, will vary cross-culturally. Any attempt to translate such terms literally will be doomed to failure, except for the most basic ones. What sort of feelings these alternative possibilities arouse cannot be rendered by any translation.

Consideration, therefore, of such cross-cultural perspectives is the *sine qua non* for one to understand clearly what constitutes politeness in a given society. But what is equally important is to appreciate the ways in which politeness may be perceived.

[18] See for instance, Brown and Ford (1964); Levinson (1978).

4
Perceptions of Politeness

'We speak with our vocal organs, but we converse with our entire bodies' (Hudson, 1980: 134, quoting Abercrombie). Thus, politeness cannot be limited to form and is not restricted to the linguistic medium. There are linguistic/verbal as well as non-linguistic/non-verbal norms of politeness. Informative communication is mainly verbal, whereas rapport communication involves much non-verbal behaviour as well. Emotive communication, as Arndt and Janney (1985: 282) call it, 'involves complexly interrelated verbal, vocal and kinesic activities'. These non-vocal manifestations complement the verbal manifestations in order to satisfy emotional needs which appear to be basic in communication. Politeness, in a broad sense, is what is behind this concern for our emotional needs and those of the other person.

Although the overwhelming majority of non-linguistic norms seem to vary from culture to culture, it has also been argued that at least some of them fall into the probably innate class (Goody, 1978a: 7; Morain, 1986: 74). They usually involve facial expressions, body contact, and gesture. The face, especially the eyes, can indeed be as rich a source of emotional information as language itself.

For Darwin, facial expressions were biologically determined and related to animal behaviour, and thus subject to less cultural variation than any other form of non-verbal behaviour. But as Graddol, Cheshire, and Swann (1987: 144) point out, 'more than a century of research in the area [of facial expression] has yielded very few insights beyond the obvious fact that our faces are capable of betraying our feelings, but that nobody quite knows how it is done'.

The significant relationship between facial expression and politeness has been emphasized by Arndt and Janney (1985: 290).

They maintain that the relationship between verbal and facial expression is complex and also that '*smiles* and *frowns* have a number of emotive communicative functions'. They may signal positive or negative feelings in neutral verbal contexts; may intensify positive or negative verbal cues; and may modify or contradict emotionally loaded verbal cues. This latter function of facial expressions is very important to politeness, because it enables speakers to indicate positive or negative feelings independently of whatever they may be conveying verbally. Similarly, Bates (1976: 316) observes that 'smile has been related to the set of innate signals that regulate aggression'.

Body contact, such as kissing, embracing, patting on the shoulder, hand-shaking, and body posture, even the distance between interactants are closely related to politeness and are utilized differently in different cultures. On this issue, Graddol *et al.* (1987: 138) maintain that 'the amount of touching that can be seen going on in public varies greatly from culture to culture'. They report Jourard's observation that 'around 110 touches per hour [were counted] in Paris, as opposed to none at all in London, and around 2 per hour in the United States'. It would, therefore, appear that the physical distance considered appropriate when people interact is culturally variable. Generally speaking, people from high-contact cultures, such as Arabs, Latin Americans, and Greeks, feel more comfortable at shorter distances when interacting than people from low-contact cultures, such as Americans and North Europeans (Morain, 1986: 72). The reasons why such differences between cultures exist are far from clear. The explanation offered by Hall (1966) is that they are related to differences in the conceptualization of the notion of 'privacy' and its boundaries. As Barnlund (1975: 431) points out, 'since all physical contacts are self-revealing. . . . Reducing the number of channels through which information is carried reduces the likelihood of self-exposure.'

The differential significance attached to body contact in different societies has also been related to the dimensions of power and solidarity. 'Touch may be regarded as a non-verbal equivalent of calling another by first name, that is, used reciprocally it indicates solidarity: when non-reciprocal, it indicates status' (Henley, 1973: 93). Likewise, Hudson (1980: 135) maintains that 'one very obvious aspect of non-verbal behaviour which helps to reflect power—solidarity is the distance one person stands from the other,' and adds that 'what varies from culture to culture is the distance which is thought appropriate for a particular degree of solidarity'. As Scheflen (1975: 161), drawing upon Hall, observes: 'traditional constraints about public touching and gazing in British culture are accompanied by a rather larger proxemic . . . or interpersonal spacing pattern. In fact, the British and the British-Americans not only tend to stand farther apart, but they also place seats at greater distance than do Mediterranean people.'

The English tend to impose restrictions on all these aspects of non-verbal behaviour (except for sexual partners, doctors, children, and pets), whereas for the Greeks non-verbal behaviour is not only tolerated but also highly desirable (Dendrinos, 1986: 47). In England, hand-shaking, for instance, is saved for more specific formal situations, such as congratulating somebody, rather than used more freely at both meeting and parting, even among friends, as is the case with Greeks and many other peoples, where the handshake is interpreted as a sign of access and solidarity (Schiffrin, 1981: 240). Even in ancient Greece, Schiffrin observes, hand-shaking 'was a welcoming sign of trust and friendliness'. Hand-shaking may be accompanied by kissing, embracing, or patting on the shoulder depending on the relationship of the interactants. 'In Britain, hand-shaking seems to be used to show that a relation is being given a fresh start, rather than as a sign of intimacy' (Hudson, 1980: 136). Although this interpretation does not seem to explain all cases of hand-shaking, such as congratulations, it does point to their relative infrequency in England.

Hand-shaking, however, is not the only restriction imposed on body contact by the English. Even looking directly into each other's eyes is restricted. 'In British and British-American culture men and women can look at each other's faces and shoulders but not into each other's eyes unless they are in courting relationship' (Scheflen, 1975: 161). More specifically, when we compare Greek and English eye-gazing practices, there is evidence that in both formal and informal interactions Greek speakers tend to employ far more eye contact than English speakers. Greeks tend to look fixedly at their interlocutor's eyes or lips, maintain a greater degree of proximity, and involve themselves in more tactile behaviour (Dendrinos, 1986: 43). Avoiding direct eye contact with one's interlocutor in Greece may be considered a sign of distrust and lead to inferences of dishonesty. The relationship between physical and social distance is assumed to be 'proportional . . . in all cultures' (Hudson, 1980: 135), even across cultures, I might add. This restriction of body contact is reflected in the English language as well. For instance, it could be argued that the absence of the singular *you* and the great reliance on indirect structures, mainly for requests and suggestions, represent related distancing devices, even if they are on a relatively subconscious level.

'The same observable behavior may or may not constitute a communicative act in different speech communities.' For example, a burp at the end of a meal does not constitute a communicative act if it is a sign of indigestion, but it does in societies where one burps to express thanks and appreciation for the meal (Saville-Troike, 1982: 30). Similarly, in Korea, loud smacking and sucking of the food are interpreted as compliments to the host or hostess, and also whereas it is impolite to blow one's nose, it is acceptable to sniffle throughout the meal at a Korean table (Morain, 1986: 72).

Non-verbal signals of politeness can be employed simultaneously with verbal expressions or without them.[1] De Silva (1976: 361) contends that societies which rely heavily on elaborate systems of kinesic and paralinguistic expression of politeness have, by and large, very few or no relevant politeness expressions (such as 'thank you', 'please', and 'sorry'), the one system thus replacing the other. An interesting consequence of such a difference is reported by Singh, Lele, and Martohardjono (1988: 51), who say that although Hindi speakers do not verbalize their gratitude as frequently as the English do, they express it habitually through non-verbal means. This difference, along with the lack of awareness that it exists, has contributed to the development of unfavourable stereotypes on both sides. On the one hand, native English speakers consider Hindi speakers impolite, since they interpret the infrequency of verbal gratitude as impoliteness; on the other, Hindi speakers consider the English impolite, since they interpret 'the profusion of verbal gratitude' to be lacking in any real feelings, and thus, to be hypocritical or insincere.

All societies share a certain amount of non-verbal behaviour, in spite of their differences, and in certain cases this can be linked to animal behaviour (Ferguson, 1981). It represents perhaps a fulfilment of the same needs in many animate beings: to belong to

---

[1] Markel (1975) uses the term 'coverbal' instead of 'non-verbal' to emphasize the complementarity of verbal and non-verbal behaviour.

groups with others, to help and be helped, and to avoid friction. These needs are also evident in children who are taught an extensive range of non-verbal means of communication, especially means relating to politeness, at a very early age.

4.2   ACQUISITION OF POLITE EXPRESSION

Any study of language use should include some account of children's acquisition (Ferguson, 1981: 33). Although most research has focused on the acquisition of lexical, morphological, and syntactic features of language, there has been increasing concern recently for the acquisition of speech acts and politeness.

Performing in a polite way is a complex ability which requires acquisition of a combination of linguistic, non-linguistic, and social skills. Children are reported to learn the structure of their language and its social functions simultaneously and at a very early age (Tannen, 1984a: 10; Hudson, 1980: 17). In her very interesting research on the acquisition of polite forms, Bates (1976: 295) observes that Italian children of about 2½ years of age are capable of using mitigating devices, such as diminutives and quantifiers, to soften the force of unsuccessful first requests. This tendency to mitigate requests, coupled with evidence that this is also the age when children start using the equivalent form of 'please', a fixed, overt marker of politeness, confirms the assumption that such performance is evidence of some concept of politeness. This development in understanding and using polite forms is related to the development of the 'more general ability to adopt the perspective of others' (Nippold, Leonard, and Anastopoulos, 1982: 193). Ervin-Tripp, Guo, and Lampert (1990) argue that politeness first manifests itself as 'social indexing', during a period in which addressees are differentiated by means of formal features, and then it develops as 'social tactics' or 'strategic politeness'.

The system of politeness is both taught and learnt directly, and acquired indirectly through the observation of the other members of one's society. Children, however, have to induce from their interactions with adults many more rules than those they are taught explicitly (Snow, Perlmann, Gleason, and Hooshyar, 1990). However, some form of politeness is taught to children at a very early stage. They are prompted to use gestures to indicate 'good-bye' and 'thank you' before they are able to vocalize the same concepts and later they are constantly reminded of these responses in similar circumstances. Bates, Camaioni, and Volterra (1976) argue that performative structures such as declaratives and imperatives are evidenced in children in the period prior to speech itself, in gesture, eye contact, and pre-linguistic vocalizations. In fact, 'the social uses of language, in the form of routines like *Bye bye*, appear as early as, if not earlier than, the referential use of language' (Gleason and Weintraub, 1976: 135).

Despite speculations by anthropologists of a possible instinctive basis of politeness formulas, the frequency of children's spontaneous production has been observed (Greif and Gleason, 1980) to be very low; parents have also been reported to put quite a lot of effort into teaching them. This insistence may have to do with the crucial significance of formulas in everyday interactions.

Politeness routines are fixed expressions with limited internal structure and variability and their significance derives from their use at appropriate moments. Thus, parents cannot really provide expansions of such formulas as is the case with most of the rest of the language. This difference leads to another difference, according to Gleason and Weintraub (1976). Parents are primarily concerned with their children's appropriate performance of such routines, rather than with their understanding of what the words mean.

Research on the acquisition of politeness can provide insights on social values. Hollos and Beeman (1978) investigated the acquisition of directives in Hungarian and Norwegian and concluded that children's issuance of directives exhibits the 'cultural communicative style' of their society. Thus, Hungarian children express their desires directly, whereas Norwegian children express them with indirectness, which increases as the degree of intimacy decreases. Snow *et al.* (1990) found that requests to children in American families tend to be relatively direct and unmitigated while not exceeding the limits of minimal civilized behaviour. Blum-Kulka (1990) observes cultural differences between American and Israeli parents issuing directives to their children and notes that the style is direct and richly, though differentially mitigated. Israeli parents resort to emotive language and nicknaming, thus minimizing the distance between family members, whereas American parents ensure their children's independence by resorting to conventionally indirect language and first names. Thus, in American families relations between parents and children are based on symmetrical solidarity, whereas in Israeli families the power difference is present.

4.3   FORMALITY AND POLITENESS

It is clear from what we have just seen in respect of children that politeness should not be equated with a certain style of speech, as has so often been the case. Style may certainly be described in terms of formality, but formality and politeness, although related, are not equivalent. Formality represents a divergence from the everyday norm, when the addressee is considered to be socially superior or the situation demands it, whereas politeness usually is the norm.[2] Furthermore, formality requires effort and is subject to more conscious monitoring, whereas politeness is to a greater extent habitual. The more attention a speaker pays to speech, the more formal the outcome will be (Labov, 1972*a*: 209). Moreover, ' "formality" is not, in fact, something which it is easy to define with any degree of precision, largely because it subsumes very many factors including familiarity, kinship-relationship, politeness, seriousness, and so on' (Trudgill, 1974: 107). Thus formality is related to politeness (see also Ervin-Tripp, 1972*a*: 235), but does not always indicate politeness and should not be equated with it. As Brown and Fraser (1979: 45) note, 'it is possible to be formally rude or casually polite'. It is simply not true that 'increased structuring of discourse necessarily brings about increased politeness' (Irvine, 1979: 775). Rather it brings about increased formality. The language used in courts, for instance, is highly structured and formal, but not necessarily polite. This social-norm view of politeness, reflects older conceptualizations, which link politeness with speech style and, thus, higher formality with greater politeness (Fraser, 1990: 220). Formality can be associated with most manifestations of negative politeness, but not necessarily with manifestations of positive politeness.

[2] See Atkinson (1982) for a discussion of formal interaction from a sociological point of view, and Irvine (1979) for an interesting discussion of aspects of formality from a sociolinguistic point of view.

4.4 URBANITY AND POLITENESS

If we accept the view that even animals exhibit some kind of politeness, then clearly politeness is not a matter of style, nor simply a characteristic of urban life. This association between politeness and urban life is clearly reflected in Goffman's (1956: 499) concluding remarks that 'these concepts [deference and demeanour] help us to grasp some aspects of urban secular living'. That this is not the case only for urban living is clearly illustrated by a kind of politeness code concerning apologies found in many rural areas of Greece. Here, before or after any mention of animals (particularly donkeys), vegetables like courgettes and cucumbers, or other words suggestive of excreta or genitals, villagers tend to use expressions like: *me siχoris* (sing.)/*me siχorite* (pl.) meaning 'excuse me'; or *me to simbaθio* meaning 'with your sympathy/my apologies'. Though interesting, the reasons behind this special code (Herzfeld, 1983: 159–62) are not germane to my argument that certain groups of people, irrespective of their rural or urban background, and for whatever reasons, develop and use their own means of appropriate polite behaviour. Some Greeks filling in a questionnaire for this study (see Appendix II/1) also pointed out that people living in the countryside are more polite than Athenians. Thus, it is difficult to justify the claim that politeness in general is of one form or that it is restricted to urban areas; it greatly depends on how we define the concept itself.

Views which equate formality and politeness and consider it characteristic of urban life seem to have sprung from some original conception evidenced in the etymologies of words for politeness (e.g. court → courtesy, city → civil, etc.) and their perpetuation through etiquette books. Etymologically, *polite* is derived from the Latin *politus*, past participle of *polire* meaning 'to smooth'. Thus, *polite* originally meant 'smoothed', 'polished', and subsequently 'refined', 'cultivated', 'well bred', and so on, when referring to people, and 'courteous', 'urbane', etc. when referring to manners. It appears that there is a clear connection between the Latin root and the Greek *poli* meaning 'city' and *politizmos* meaning 'civilization'. In any case, the connection between *politeness* and *city* is clearer in that *city, civil,* and *civilization* all come from the same root. All these clearly point to the association between urban life and polite, civilized manners, whereas rude, which does not only mean 'impolite', but also 'rough' and 'wild and untaught' is clearly associated with rural life. Thus, as Donaldson (1984: 208) observes, 'polished, mannerly, cultured, civilized life has come to be associated with the city, rough, rude, boorish life with the country'.

The Greek word for 'politeness', *evγenia*, reflects similar connotations. It is derived from *ef* meaning 'good' and *γenos* meaning 'descent', or 'origin'; thus politeness originated as an attribute characteristic of aristocrats. Of course, such etymological origins may be irrelevant for ordinary modern speakers, who just learn and use certain forms, but they can influence views and reactions of some people. An explanation for these associations might be Elias's views, reported by Donaldson (1984: 208), that the closer people have come to live together, the more each person has had to exert greater self-control. This view is reflected in most definitions of politeness.

4.5   AN ATTEMPT AT A DEFINITION OF POLITENESS

Lakoff (1975: 64) suggests that 'politeness is developed by societies in order to reduce friction in personal interaction'. Similarly, Leech (1980: 19) defines 'tact' as 'strategic conflict avoidance', adding that it 'can be measured in terms of the degree of effort put into the avoidance of a conflict situation'. Brown and Levinson (1978) view politeness essentially as a complex system for softening face-threatening acts. Thus, 'communication is seen as a fundamentally dangerous and antagonistic endeavor' (Kasper, 1990: 194). What seems to have been underplayed in such conceptualizations is that politeness is not just a means of restraining feelings and emotions in order to avoid conflict, but also a means of expressing them. To this end, Arndt and Janney (1985: 282) propose the idea of 'inter-personal supportiveness', a more positive and intuitively appealing notion.

However, people are not always on the verge of a war which they try to avoid by being polite. A more positive definition of politeness is offered by Hill *et al.* (1986: 349): 'Politeness is one of the constraints on human interaction, whose purpose is to consider others' feelings, establish levels of mutual comfort, and promote rapport.' This definition, although it acknowledges that politeness can be seen as a constraint on human behaviour, indicates that the constraint is not there just to reduce friction but also to enhance rapport and harmony. More recently Ide (1989: 225) defines politeness as 'language usage associated with smooth communication' achieved through the speaker's use of intentional strategies and of expressions conforming to prescribed norms.

At its most basic level, politeness is seen as consideration for the other person, according to expected norms. Does this mean that we are imprisoned in a world where we constantly have to consider other people's needs and feelings in order to be polite? What about our own, which may sometimes be in conflict with those of others? People in general do not feel forced to be polite. 'Politeness is a property associated with a voluntary action' (Fraser and Nolen, 1981: 96), and a combination of discernment and volition (Hill *et al.*, 1986).

People tend to be considerate because this repays them with a pleasant feeling of satisfaction; furthermore, they receive consideration in return and at the same time satisfy the needs of others. It is a multiple reward. This obviously does not mean that they behave in the way that they do because they have any ulterior motives (although this may be true in a few cases), or that they expect any tangible reward. It simply means that they have internalized the fact that in order to live in a harmonious society you give and take and thus participate in maintaining the necessary equilibrium of relationships. By treating others with consideration or more generally in the way you want to be treated by them, you feel satisfied as a person, contributing simultaneously to the satisfaction of others and thus to a more satisfied, comfortable life for everybody. As Hudson (1980: 115) contends, 'most people want to present to the world an image of considerateness, because this is most likely to make them popular' and adds that 'we usually try to avoid exposing other people's weaknesses, or raising heated controversy, unless we are sure that it will not affect the attitude of others towards us or we are indifferent to their opinion'.

What form this consideration will take and to whom it will be addressed largely depends on the cultural background of the participants, that is, their shared and thus expected norms of behaviour. For instance, in one culture, consideration may be expressed by holding the door open for the person coming behind, whereas in another it may be exhibited by taking off your shoes on entering somebody else's house. On the verbal level, consideration may be conveyed in one culture by sounding tentative and less sure, thus leaving the freedom of choice to your addressee, and in another by sounding decisive and assured, thus appearing to decide for them, though not by imposing but by assuming that you know what is best for your addressee. There is nothing inherently polite or impolite in any of these manifestations of consideration. The reasons which led to their establishment as such are intricate and depend on specific practical needs, which may no longer be evident, and on the general socio-cultural structure of each society. Each society agrees that certain forms of behaviour are acceptable and appropriate and for this reason such patterns of politeness are successful in those societies which support them. Thus, people have formulated expectations on the basis of which they judge anybody who differs. 'Rules of conduct impinge upon the individual in two general ways: directly, as *obligations*, establishing how he is morally constrained to conduct himself; indirectly, as *expectations*, establishing how others are morally bound to act in regard to him' (Goffman, 1956: 473–4). Consequently, one 'aspect of politeness is that whether or not an utterance is heard as being polite is totally in the hands (or ears) of the hearer' (Fraser and Nolen, 1981: 96).

Goffman (1956: 476) distinguishes between 'substantive' and 'ceremonial' rules of behaviour. These rules differ in that the former operate in respect of matters that have significance in their own right, whereas the latter operate in matters which are of secondary or even no significance in their own right, but merely as an accepted means of the individual's conveying a personal response to the situation. In other words, substantive rules reflect the law, the morality, and ethics of a society, whereas ceremonial rules reflect the etiquette. Ceremonial activity is seen as containing two basic components which overlap and which he calls 'deference' and 'demeanor'. Goffman (ibid. 489) defines deference as 'the appreciation an individual shows of another to that other, whether through avoidance rituals or presentational rituals' (see section 2.5). Demeanour is 'that element of the individual's ceremonial behavior typically conveyed through deportment, dress, and bearing, which serves to express to those in his immediate presence that he is a person of certain desirable or undesirable qualities'. Thus, deference requires communication of politeness to a particular individual, while demeanour presupposes the existence of no such recipient, but simply serves to show that the actor knows what etiquette is (Neustupný, 1978: 193).

Hymes (1986: 82) interprets deference as related to 'the negative face of the other' and demeanour as related to 'the negative face in respect to oneself' and maintains that they 'both have to do with a dimension that might be called "autonomy"'. Such an interpretation, however, leaves out a dimension which might be called 'involvement' which is clearly related to ceremonial activity according to Goffman's definition. Elsewhere, Goffman (1956: 486) discusses the common forms that presentational rituals can take, and states clearly that 'through all of these the recipient is told that he is not an island unto himself and that others are, or seek to be, involved with him and with his personal private concerns'.

Goffman (1956) does not use the term 'politeness', but for him it seems to be a broad concept covering both (deference and demeanour) aspects of ceremonial behaviour in actual encounters and is, moreover, irrelevant to substantive behaviour, because '"politeness" . . . refers to matters necessarily of no substantive import' (Goffman, 1981: 17).

A number of other studies (Fraser and Nolen, 1981: 98; Zimin, 1981: 41; Rintell, 1981: 32–3) view deference as the level of appropriateness inherent in utterances, irrespective of context, and politeness as that which depends on the particular context. On similar lines and on the basis of Korean sociolinguistics, Hwang (1990) argues that 'politeness' and 'deference' should be considered different, though interrelated, concepts. Deference is seen as a social fact a priori established by the positions individuals occupy in the social structure. As such it is encoded in the highly developed system of Korean honorifics. On the other hand, politeness is more dependent on the psychology of the individual, who is free, for instance, to choose among different levels of indirectness. This distinction seems to be closely related to that between 'discernment' and 'volition' (Hill *et al.*, 1986), respectively.

However, since politeness in a general sense covers both deference and demeanour, it seems to have become associated with formality in many Western societies. It is frequently seen as a feature associated with utterances, as well as with more general characteristics of human behaviour. In fact, as Goffman (1972: 325) points out, 'in our society terms such as politeness or tact fail to distinguish between the inclination to exercise such capacities and the capacities themselves'. I use the term 'politeness' in a more general sense, and see it as *the set of social values which instructs interactants to consider each other by satisfying shared expectations.* These shared expectations are assumed to constitute part of the socio-cultural knowledge of the particular interactants and include both intentional strategies and more fixed social indices. Such knowledge and its deployment guarantee and promote harmonious interpersonal relations, with the exception, of course, of the cases in which impoliteness is the speaker's intention. Since politeness derives from particular social values and satisfies shared expectations it will differ cross-culturally. Goffman (1956: 493–4) states that 'a frequent occasion for ceremonial difficulty occurs at moments of intergroup contact, since different societies and subcultures have different ways of conveying deference and demeanor, different ceremonial meanings for the same act, and different amounts of concern over such things as poise and privacy'.

A starting point which can guarantee validity of claims concerning politeness phenomena in different cultures should be the examination of what the concept means in the specific cultures under study.

4.5.1 *Native speakers' concepts of politeness*

In the questionnaire (see section 1.2.3 and Appendix II/1) concerning the concept of politeness, many of my informants reported that they found the first question extremely difficult to answer. This reflects the fact that although people recognize the existence of an important social value which they call 'politeness', 'tact', 'courtesy', and a variety of other related names, and although they can quite readily identify the behaviour, usually of others, by reference to these terms, the exact content of the concept 'politeness' seems to be far from clear and even puzzling. I believe that the problem is twofold. 'Politeness' is an abstract concept like, say, 'morality' or 'altruism', and indeed 'a very tricky' one (Bach and Harnish, 1982: 291). Furthermore, it manifests itself not only in verbal, but also in non-verbal behaviour.

The major overall difference found in the definitions of the concept of 'politeness' was that the English gave much clearer and more straightforward answers. By contrast, the Greeks were much more elaborate and gave very broad definitions.[3] An initial reaction to this finding could be that it is simply evidence that Greece has an oral culture to a greater extent than England.[4] In other words, 'Greeks talk a lot, and effusiveness is a highly valued and sometimes obligatory component of behaviour between people' (Mackridge, 1985: 338). Although such an interpretation appears to explain a certain degree of verbosity in the Greek definitions, it does not account for their expansion of the concept to include attributes such as self-abnegation, altruism, and sincerity. Consequently, the reasons for this finding must lie beyond any features which distinguish oral from literate societies.

I believe that Brown and Levinson's (1978: 134) views on the differences between positive and negative politeness offer a more plausible explanation: 'where positive politeness is free-ranging, negative politeness is specific and focused; it performs the function of minimizing the particular imposition that the FTA unavoidably effects'. Elsewhere, they emphasize that:

Unlike negative politeness, positive politeness is not necessarily redressive of the particular face want infringed by the FTA; that is, whereas in negative politeness the sphere of relevant redress is restricted to the imposition itself, in positive politeness the sphere of redress is widened to the appreciation of alter's wants in general or to the expression of similarity between ego's and alter's wants. (1978: 106)

In other words, negative politeness is narrower in that it addresses a specific act, whereas positive politeness is broader and considers the overall relationship between interactants. Thus, it appears that by definition negative politeness is more restricted than positive politeness in that the former reflects consideration for one of the addressee's basic needs—to be independent—whereas the latter reflects consideration for the addressee's perennial needs to be liked, approved of, admired, and so on. This negative politeness narrowness versus positive politeness broadness of orientation is exactly what is reflected in the differences observed in the

[3] The mean length in words of the definitions of politeness is 14.85 for the English and 33.77 for the Greeks.

[4] See Tannen (1980) for a discussion of the linguistic manifestations of the 'oral'/'literate' continuum. The use of the terms 'orality' and 'literacy' has been considered inadequate and perhaps misleading. For Tannen (1985) the issue should not be discussed in terms of 'orality' and 'literacy', but in terms of relative focus on interpersonal involvement.

definitions of the concept of politeness. This, I believe, partially justifies my hypothesis (see section 2.5) that Greece is a more positive politeness society than England. (Further justification, in terms of linguistic manifestations of politeness strategies, is presented in Chapters 6 and 7.)

The English defined politeness in clearer and more straight-forward terms. For them, it appeared to be the consideration of other people's feelings by conforming to social norms and expectations. These norms include the use of standard forms such as *please* and *sorry* in appropriate situations, requests rather than demands for people to do things for you and the display of 'good manners'. The issue of whether politeness is an innate attribute or not was for the most part not considered. Very few (2 out of 27) of my informants claimed that politeness is behaviour which should be taught at home and only one mentioned that it is acquired through the observation of appropriate behaviour.

The English were also clearer in their judgements concerning the degree of politeness of their compatriots (see Appendix II/1, Q. 4). The majority (23 out of 27) considered the English 'fairly polite', although some (9 out of 23) pointed out that this is relative and depends on whom they are being compared with, an observation reflecting common stereotypes that some societies are more polite than others. One informant judged them to be 'very polite' and one to be 'not polite'. One declined to answer this question on the grounds that he was not prepared to contribute to any stereotypical line of thinking, while another one judged them as 'boringly polite'. This is illustrated in Table 4.1.

In contrast, the Greeks defined politeness in very broad terms. They, too, included consideration towards others, but expanded their definitions to include attributes which might be better described in English in terms of altruism, generosity, morality, and self-abnegation. Another interesting difference between the Greeks and English is that several (15 out of 27) of my Greek informants considered politeness to be an innate attribute which has nothing to do with social or educational background, probably reflecting a certain distrust on overt markers to express real politeness.[5] Some of them (7 out of 15) distinguished between innate polite disposition and acquired 'good manners'. For some, 'good manners'

---

[5] Ferguson (1981: 22–3) argues for the possibility of innate predispositions to the use of politeness formulas.

are necessary indices of politeness, whereas for others they are conventions which conceal its essence. Two informants maintained that politeness is acquired through observation and parental teaching, and the rest had nothing to say on the subject. The Greeks' views concerning the degree of politeness of their compatriots were more diverse than those of the English. Fifteen rated them 'fairly polite' and seven 'not polite', while pointing out the relativity of the question. Two assessed them to be 'very polite' and three declined to answer (see Appendix II/1, Q. 4). This is illustrated in Table 4.1.

TABLE 4.1 *Responses to question 4, Appendix II/1 expressed as frequency and percentage of a sample of 27 informants of each nationality*

Degree of politeness	English		Greeks	
	No.	%	No.	%
very polite	1	3.7	2	7.4
fairly polite	23	85.1	15	55.5
not polite	1	3.7	7	25.9
other	1	3.7	0	0.0
no response	1	3.7	3	11.1

Some Greeks also described their compatriots as possessing *filotimo*. This is a uniquely Greek concept which is difficult to translate and define, as Triandis and Vassiliou point out:

A person who has this characteristic is polite, virtuous, reliable, proud, has 'a good soul,' behaves correctly, meets his obligations, does his duty, is truthful, generous, self-sacrificing, tactful, respectful and grateful. . . . The best way to summarize what is meant by this concept is to say that a person who is *philotimous* behaves toward members of his ingroup the way they expect him to behave. (1972: 308–9)

It seems to me that while it is essential to be 'polite' in English, it is more essential to be *filotimos* in Greek. The concept of *filotimo* is still very strong in smaller places, such as villages, but its repercussions are evident throughout Greek society. Clearly, this idea overlaps that of politeness because it is *filotimo* which is demonstrated 'by a foreign visitor who later sends a postcard to thank for a villager's hospitality' (Herzfeld, 1980: 343), but it is not restricted to such situations. *Filotimo* is revealed in all socially appropriate behaviour (ibid.) and is associated more with deeds than with words.

Although the number of my informants was somewhat limited, I believe that their answers clearly illustrate that the conception of politeness differs in the two cultures and also that the folk notion of tact is not as highly valued in Greek as it is in English society (Brown and Levinson, 1987. 14). Furthermore, the examples cited by my informants indicating polite and impolite behaviour (see Appendix II/1, Qs 2 and 3) confirmed these differences. Where socio-cultural experiences differed, responses from the two groups varied, but the most significant variations were those reflecting the differential conception of politeness in the two cultures. Greek informants, for instance, mentioned cases of body-part donation as examples of polite behaviour. They also attributed politeness to poor people who helped others in need, to children who collected money for charities, and to those who offered gifts. No English informant mentioned such examples as indicative of polite behaviour.

The major similarity between the two groups was in their view of politeness as a form of consideration towards others, including giving up a seat to someone more in need of it, helping an old or blind person to cross the street, carrying something heavy for someone, and so on. Other similarities related to impoliteness, which included swearing, insulting, talking loudly, and offensive behaviour both verbal and non-verbal.

The English (15 out of 27) much more than the Greeks (4 out of 27) emphasized the necessity of expressing apologies and especially gratitude verbally, even in minor situations, and appeared to value immediate verbal reciprocity in polite behaviour more highly. All those English informants who included linguistic observations in their answers emphasized the significance of polite expressions such as *please* and *thank you*, and the importance of sending letters and notes to express gratitude. They also pointed out the necessity of a certain amount of formality in language and the fact that declarative and imperative constructions should be avoided in favour of the more polite conditionals and interrogatives. Only one suggested that saying *sorry* is not always an indication of a polite person, while another mentioned that the omission of polite expressions might be indicative of shyness and lack of confidence rather than impoliteness.

By contrast, the Greeks did not appear to appreciate such overt markers of politeness to the same extent. Of only four who did deem these expressions necessary two considered their compatriots 'not polite', obviously because they do not use them frequently enough. Another pointed out that such expressions should be accompanied by a friendly smile and a pleasant disposition. Moreover, another five subjects emphasized that, although some people think of politeness in terms of such overt expressions, these markers are habitual and conceal real, innate politeness since they are frequently used as distancing devices. This is, of course, true. 'Politeness can express warmth, certainly, but it can also, and simultaneously, express the threat of rejection' (Herzfeld, 1983: 152). Likewise, Lakoff (1973: 295) points out that the use of *please* is not always an indication of kindness, since it can equally well signal a break in the relationship.

Another difference which should be noted is that the Greeks (7 out of 27) more than the English (2 out of 27) pointed out that a warm look, a friendly smile, and in general a good-humoured disposition and pleasant facial expression are integral parts of polite behaviour. The significance of facial expression to politeness has already been pointed out (section 4.1). These observations, it may be argued, do not reflect exactly what happens in actual situations, because as Graddol, Cheshire, and Swann (1987: 140), drawing upon Stier and Hall, state, 'people's beliefs and perceptions may run contrary to observed facts'. They do, however, signal at least different expectations.

Though both Greeks and English emphasized the importance of acknowledging the arrival of somebody else on the scene by greeting them, I believe that there is a difference here. Although greeting somebody you know in the street is imperative in both cultures, the Greeks, much more than the English, expect an exchange of greetings when they join a group. Lack of such behaviour is interpreted as indifference, perhaps signalling a problem in the relationship. 'Indifference is a real insult' for the Greeks 'and is somewhat related to the notion . . . that most Greek social relations are characterized by greater intimacy' (Triandis and Vassiliou, 1972: 315). 'To be indifferent is not neutral; it is essentially hostile' (ibid. 316). The English, on the other hand, seem to prefer to join in more quietly, and greetings in this context are perceived more as an interruption of the ongoing conversation. 'The rules [for interaction] may already be codified in the form of aphorisms, proverbs, or even laws' (Saville-Troike, 1982: 147); witness the English 'politeness costs nothing', versus the Greek 'saying "good morning" costs nothing'.

Consideration for the other person is seen as an integral part of politeness in both cultures, but it seems that what is construed as consideration differs. For instance, one aspect of Greek behaviour which strikes foreigners as uncalled for, even improper and impolite, is what they call 'intensive curiosity' about people's income, marital status, and so on. Generally speaking, however, this is clearly not conceived as curiosity by the Greeks themselves, but rather as an expression of concern and interest, a friendly way to approach people. If not just having children, but having many children is (or rather was) considered by Greeks to constitute wealth, as Herzfeld (1980: 347) points out, then asking or advising to that end is an expression of care and consideration rather than interference in somebody else's affairs.

Dendrinos (1986: 43), drawing upon Laver, distinguishes between 'committed' and 'uncommitted' statements in interaction, and points out that Greek verbal and non-verbal behaviour seems to belong more to the 'committed' category, whereas English behaviour seems to be much more of the 'uncommitted' type. Consequently, Greek behaviour is often misjudged by the English as 'too intimate' and perhaps 'intrusive', whereas the Greeks are likely to condemn English behaviour as 'distant' and 'insincere'. Greek behaviour may also be related to the significance of the in-group–out-group distinction (see section 2.5.1), in that it is an attempt to place the addressee into one or the other of these groups as soon as possible. The definition of a polite person given by one of my English informants as 'being considerate, though not over-interested, but fairly distant and cool' cannot stand as a definition of a polite person in a Greek context, but rather as that of a cold, even inhuman individual. Thus, consideration clearly is measured on a different scale.

Another aspect of Greek behaviour which strikes many Greeks and foreigners alike as irritating and impolite is reckless driving, queue jumping, and, perhaps above all, the unhelpfulness of some civil servants and shop assistants. There are, however, various reasons which may explain this kind of behaviour. It may be due to lack of training or due to the fact that some people feel that providing a service is demeaning. However, the major source of such behaviour is the in-group–out-group distinction. Clearly, people you do not know, such as the other drivers in the street or customers in a shop, belong to the out-group. Thus drivers' competitiveness and/or assistants' unwillingness to be helpful, wherever it may occur, is understandable. Is it justifiable though? Possibly to a certain extent. This in-group–out-group distinction is so deeply ingrained in the society that it actually determines individual behaviour. This process, however, is *unconscious*. Thus, it would appear to be the *conscious* attempts by individuals to offend, degrade, or hurt others which may truly be construed as impolite. Politeness lies not just in showing consideration for others, but in conveying what the specific addressee will perceive as considerateness in a specific context.

4.6   CONCLUDING REMARKS

From our discussion so far it has become clear that the concept of politeness seems to be universal in some form or other, presumably because it satisfies universal needs. What differs cross-culturally and subculturally is the weight these needs bear, which consequently leads to differential choices from the repository of possible realizations on both the verbal and the non-verbal levels. True, there is a danger of becoming anecdotal in attempting cross-cultural comparisons of this sort, especially so far as non-verbal behaviour is concerned, but this is unavoidable to a certain extent because 'so far, our knowledge of intercultural differences in this sphere [the typological study of cultures and languages in relation to interpersonal rhetoric] is somewhat anecdotal' (Leech, 1983: 150). More specifically, 'Greek conversational behavior has not been the subject of investigation up to this point, and there is serious lack of information concerning communicative interaction among Greek speakers' (Dendrinos, 1986: 38).

Nevertheless, the responses of informants to questionnaires and face-to-face queries do appear to substantiate certain generalizations. First, the major difference between Greek and English politeness is not a matter of degree, but arises from the differential conception of what constitutes politeness. This is in line with both Brown and Levinson's positive versus negative politeness dimensions and with the observation presented by Leech that whereas the English tend to give prominence to tact, in Mediterranean cultures the emphasis is placed on generosity. In other words, different cultures give precedence to different values, which are, moreover, interpreted differently. Secondly, there seems to be more tacit consensus among the English subjects as to what constitutes politeness than among the Greeks, who define politeness in broader terms covering more areas of behaviour. This perhaps explains the diversity of their judgements concerning the degree of politeness of their compatriots. In other words, the Greeks appear to expect more diverse attributes to be characteristic of a polite person, and they are, therefore, less unanimous in judging the politeness of others. Thirdly, Greeks appear to attach more importance to non-verbal aspects of politeness, which seems to counterbalance the relatively secondary significance they assign to overt polite expressions. This may be related to their emphasis on the innateness of politeness in contrast with acquired polite forms.

It should be noted that there is no intention to evaluate the kind of politeness preferred by each group under study; this would be unjustified. The main concern is to point out that there are basic differences in the conception of what politeness means, and, consequently, in its manifestations, and that these two factors give evidence to my hypothesis that the Greek and English systems of politeness are different, the former being predominantly positive and the latter predominantly negative.

5
Speech Act Theory and Politeness: Requests

5.1 INTRODUCTION

Speech act theory has also touched on the question of politeness, particularly as it has been advanced by Austin and Searle. Both of these philosophers consider linguistic communication to be not just a means of conveying information, but a tool people use to achieve a variety of goals. When people use language, they do things or have others do things for them: they apologize, promise, request, thank, and so on. The things people can do linguistically have been grouped into a few categories, each with its own subcategories. Regrouping Austin's extensive list, Searle (1979) proposed a system of five different categories of speech acts. These are: *assertives*, whose function is to describe states or events in the world, such as asserting, boasting, and claiming; *directives*, whose function is to direct the addressee to perform or not to perform an act, such as ordering and requesting; *commissives*, whose function is to commit the speaker to a future course of action, such as promising and threatening; *expressives*, whose function is to express the speaker's attitudes and feelings about something, such as thanking, pardoning, and congratulating; and *declarations*, whose function is to change the status of the person or object referred to by performing the act successfully, such as christening and sentencing.

Leech (1983: 107) contends that 'as far as Searle's categories go, negative politeness belongs pre-eminently to the DIRECTIVE class, while positive politeness is found pre-eminently in the COMMISSIVE and EXPRESSIVE classes,' adding that assertives are usually neutral as regards politeness, and that declarations, being institutional rather than personal actions, can hardly involve politeness. However, the specific situation and the participants by whom these speech acts are employed and received determine the kind and degree of politeness, which is also relative to socio-cultural values.

There are a number of social factors, such as the age, sex, familiarity, and social status of participants, the spatio-temporal setting, the weight of the particular imposition, and so on, which determine the kind of politeness strategies that will be employed in performing these speech acts. The importance of each one of these factors is not invariant, but dependent on all the others, and together they constitute part of the social knowledge each member of any society has. The fact that societies vary in respect to the importance they assign to these factors explains why different politeness strategies are predominantly used in different societies. Brown and Levinson (1978: 256) suggest that 'in societies where high D [distance] relations dominate in public encounters . . . one would expect symmetrical use of high-numbered strategies to be most evident'.

For Brown and Levinson, England is a society in which relatively high value is placed on social distance, and consequently negative and off-record strategies will prevail in social encounters. There may also be a preference for not performing the act at all, if the degree of loss of face is great. They also suggest that 'in societies where low D is the emphasis and P is minimized . . . symmetrical use of bald on record and positive politeness would be expected'. However, Greece appears to be a society where relatively low emphasis is placed on social distance or, to put it differently, where intimacy and solidarity are valued more than distance, especially in in-group encounters, so that positive and bald-on-record politeness strategies will prevail in daily encounters. There are, of course, cases of asymmetrical power in both societies, that is, cases in which the interactants will have different statuses. In such cases, we would normally expect the 'lower-status' interlocutor to use high-numbered strategies, the 'higher-status' interactant to use low-numbered ones.

Brown and Levinson (1978) give a detailed account of the linguistic means that underlie the realization of each one of their four strategies or 'super-strategies', as they call them: (1) baldly on record, (2) positive politeness, (3) negative politeness, and (4) off record. One of their basic claims is that their model is of universal applicability. The above superstrategies are assumed to be in order of increasing politeness, although cross-cultural variation has been acknowledged between the two most basic strategies, that is (2) and

(3), or in other words, between preferences for more positive or more negative politeness orientation.[1]

Bearing in mind that positive and negative politeness interact in intricate ways, it is important to consider mainly these two superstrategies and to examine whether and to what extent their linguistic manifestations present themselves in the data collected from both languages. If indeed it is the case that, on the one hand, linguistic realizations of positive politeness strategies appear to prevail in the Greek data, and on the other, linguistic realizations of negative politeness strategies appear to prevail in the English data, then this may constitute a partial justification of the hypothesis that Greece is a positive politeness society when compared to England. Moreover, this will confirm the broader hypothesis that Greeks are not less polite than the English, but polite in a different way due to a different conception of what polite verbal and non-verbal behaviour is, a conception which largely derives from different cultural norms and values. Here, I have restricted myself to examining the area of requests, although occasionally I resort to examples from other areas, such as compliments, offers, greetings, and thanks. Requests have been extensively studied, particularly in English, though not to the same extent in Greek.[2] Nevertheless, it may be argued that they are worthy of attention because they are frequent in a variety of everyday encounters, permit a variety of strategies, and are mainly responsible for judgements on the extent to which societies are classified as polite. Furthermore, the conventionalized realizations of requests, as well as their frequency, are perhaps the clearest indicators of whether one society is orientated to positive or negative politeness. Moreover, the fact that requests have been studied extensively also provides a framework for this work and safeguards the validity of interpretations and conclusions concerning a culture and language which are not my own.

---

[1] However, Baxter (1984) argues that, in some respects, positive politeness is considered more polite than negative politeness and Blum-Kulka (1987), among others, argues against the highest degree of politeness attributed to off-record strategies.

[2] See Green (1975); Davison (1975); Gordon and Lakoff (1975); Ervin-Tripp (1976); Blum-Kulka and Olshtain (1984); Tannen (1982), to mention but a few.

5.2   THE SPEECH ACT OF REQUESTING

According to Searle, directives

are attempts (of varying degrees, and hence, more precisely, they are determinates of the determinable which includes attempting) by the speaker to get the hearer to do something. They may be very modest 'attempts' as when I invite you to do it or suggest that you do it, or they may be very fierce attempts as when I insist that you do it. (1979: 13)

For Bach and Harnish (1982: 47), who have borrowed the term 'directive' from Searle, 'directives express the speaker's attitude toward some prospective action by the hearer,' but 'they also express the speaker's intention (desire, wish) that his utterance or the attitude it expresses be taken as (a) reason for the hearer to act'.

Requests fall into this group of directives. Although a number of subcategories of requests can be distinguished, such as requests for action, requests for information (Bach and Harnish, 1982: 47), requests for attention, and requests for sympathy, 'all requests are basically requests for an action of some kind from the other person' (Labov and Fanshel, 1977: 63). Thus, the speech act may succeed, yet the addressee may fail to fulfil the request for reasons which may have nothing to do with the discourse.

For both Austin and Searle the success of a performative act depends on certain preconditions—'felicity conditions'—that must be fulfilled. Searle (1979: 44) says that 'each type of illocutionary act has a set of conditions that are necessary for the successful and felicitous performance of the act'. For Labov and Fanshel (1977) these are preconditions for an utterance to count as a request which are not stated directly but which underlie the rules of request. These are similar to the rules of syntax in that they are obligatory and below the level of consciousness; consequently, people can make jokes because they can violate such rules.

Although both Green (1975: 125) and Leech (1983: 106) prefer the term 'impositive' to 'directive' in respect of requests, it seems that the latter is more appropriate than the former because although requests always 'direct' the addressees to perform the action, they do not always 'impose' it on them. If the latter were the case, we would expect fewer requests, a lot more non-compliance with them, and a lot more and frequent elaboration in performing them. Speakers, however, in performing requests assume compliance or at least good will on the part of the addressee. That this is the case is evinced by the fact that non-compliant responses tend to be more elaborate than their compliant counterparts, which can be omitted altogether.

Requests are usually considered to be a very good example of speech acts which imply intrusion on the addressee's territory and limit freedom of action. In other words, they are intrinsically face-threatening activities, threatening the addressee's negative face (Brown and Levinson, 1978: 70), and therefore comprise a category of inherently impolite acts in which negative politeness is essential (Leech, 1983: 106). How far, however, is it a valid assumption that requests always threaten the addressee's negative face and, therefore, to what extent is negative politeness important? It could be argued that this will be the case only when negative face is more important and valued more than positive face. Requests can also imply closeness and intimacy, in the sense that one must feel close enough to ask somebody else to do something, and consequently positive politeness is important, too. Furthermore, there are requests, such as those addressed to shop assistants, which are not face-threatening, imposing acts.

It is true that every language affords its speakers a variety of grammatical possibilities they can choose from to avoid or mitigate the impact of a possible face threat. But it is also true that the choice among these and other alternatives may indicate intimacy. For instance, by using an embedded imperative one might indicate concern for the addressee's negative face by mitigating the imposition through indirectness, whereas using a bald imperative in a construction including a diminutive may indicate concern for the addressee's positive face through the emphasis of affection.

Requests are made up of two parts: the core request and the various peripheral elements. The core request is the main utterance which fulfils the function of requesting, irrespective of its form, and can stand by itself; that is, it can be used successfully without any peripheral elements. However, in most cases this is preceded and/or followed by expressions which mitigate or aggravate its force, but which do not change its propositional content. These peripheral elements include address terms, various introductory utterances, explanations and justifications for the request, hedges, *please*, and so on. These are modifications of the request, when explicitly stated, and some of them, such as address terms, explanations, and so on, can stand as requests themselves in the absence of a core request. In addition to this external modification of requests, we can also have internal modification,[3] that is, devices which affect the core request, such as number, tense, and diminutives. Requests in both Greek and English can be realized linguistically with imperatives, interrogatives, negative-interrogatives, and even declaratives. Sometimes even elliptical forms are found.

Very briefly, imperatives can function as requests: *pass me the butter, please* or *δose mu to molivi su se parakalo* 'give me your pencil please'. Interrogative constructions appear to be the most prolific group of request means in English. In Greek, they are common, too, though not as common as in English largely because imperative constructions are socially more acceptable.

Interrogative constructions range from simple questions such as *what time is it?* or *ti ora ine?*, to embedded imperatives, such as *could you tell me the time?*, or *θa borusate na mu pite ti ora ine?*, and are commonly introduced with a modal. In Greek, unlike English, a great number of everyday requests are realized with present indicative constructions, for example, *mu δinete ti fotja sas?* 'do you give (pl.) me your fire (lighter)?' Requests in question form can be both yes–no questions and wh-questions and can also take the form of highly elaborate interrogative constructions, such as, *would you be kind enough to sign this for me please?*, *mipos θa iχate tin kalosini na mu ipoγrapsete eδo parakalo?* 'would you happen to have the kindness to sign for me here please?'.

Negative constructions can also be found as requests, though less frequently than interrogatives, especially in Greek:

I wouldn't mind another piece of cake.				[NB]

δe θa	'leγa	oχi s'ena	γlik*aki*.	[NB]
I wouldn't	say	no to a	sweet-*dim*.	

Combinations of interrogative-negative constructions are more frequently encountered in Greek than plain negative ones:

δe θa	fas tipota esi?		[NB]
aren't you going to	eat anything?		
can't I stay with him?			[OR 4: 243]

---

[3] This distinction between external and internal modification is borrowed from Faerch & Kasper (1984: 224).

Finally, statements can also function as requests. They fall into two main groups. The first group includes examples of what Ervin-Tripp (1976) and others have called 'need statements', such as *I want you to check this possibility*, *χriazome/θelo ena pistopiitiko jeniseos* 'I need/want a birth certificate', which occur in specific environments. These also include more widely applicable, elaborate, and conventionalized constructions implying or stating needs, usually introduced with *I'd like*, in English and *θa (i)θela* 'I would want' in Greek. For example:

I'd like to see you for a minute [NB]

| θa 'θela | na su po | kati | [NB] |
| I would want | to tell you | something | |

The second group consists of cases which have been called 'hints',[4] such as *there's not enough light here* or *to fos δen ine arketo eδo*, intended by the speaker as a request for the addressee to do something such as turn on a light, move if obstructing it, and so on. Abbreviated request statements such as *coffee, please*, or *ena kafe parakalo* 'one coffee please' can also be found in both languages.

It appears then from this brief account that both languages afford their speakers similar, though not identical, linguistic means to perform requests. This is not surprising because, as Bolinger (1981: 91) contends, 'grammatical functions probably started as social functions thousands of years ago'; and he adds that 'as societies grew more complex, the simpler social functions became diversified and the old forms had to be adapted to new purposes'. Societies, however, developed differently, and the needs and values which sprang from their development were also different. The basic structural patterns may be similar, but there will be differences in detail, some of which will be considered later. Furthermore, the choice of structures open to speakers in making requests is not entirely free since it conveys different attitudes, different social norms and values, as well as personal differences. For instance, the choice of a negatively constructed request implies a strong negative attitude as far as the outcome of the request is concerned—linguistic pessimism. Question forms and modals, especially in their past tense form, indicate mild or strong hesitation and tentativeness. Imperative and declarative constructions, on the other hand,

---

[4] Hints can also be expressed in interrogative form.

indicate optimism that the outcome of the request will be successful. Finally, more talkative and effusive people may tend to employ more elaborate constructions (not more formal, but rather more verbose), whereas more taciturn individuals may choose simpler forms. However, what is perhaps of major significance is the question of which of these structures, whether similar or different in the two languages, are conventionalized for different situations, a question which we shall consider in more detail later.

5.2.1 Prominence devices

Requests, as has been pointed out (section 3.3) clearly indicate the kind of social relationship which holds between the interactants. The choice of the kinds of constructions we have been talking about is, of course, of the utmost importance. This choice includes, among other things, a decision regarding the entity that will be placed in the prominent position. Requests in both languages include explicit or implicit references to the speaker, the addressee, and the action requested. (This, of course, is not true of non-conventionally indirect requests—see section 5.2.2.) Speakers have at their disposal a number of alternatives so that they can place any of these entities in the prominent position. Which one they choose is partly determined by cultural norms and partly by personal idiosyncratic characteristics. Four possibilities can be distinguished:

- (a) The speaker made prominent, as in 'can *I* open the window?'
- (b) The addressee made prominent, as in 'could *you* open the window?'
- (c) Both the speaker and the addressee made prominent, as in 'could *we* open the window?'
- (d) The action made prominent, which is achieved mainly through impersonalization or passivization.

In the first case, where the speaker is made prominent, we can have two varieties: 'permission requests' and 'permission directives' (Ervin-Tripp, 1976: 37). For instance, 'Can *I* have your pencil for a second?' versus 'Can *I* have my pencil back?' The former variety is far more common than the latter, because the speaker asks permission to perform an act, whereas in the latter it is the addressee who will have to perform the act and the request may also imply criticism. The difference between these forms is that the latter, unlike the former, involves another action that has already taken place. Both varieties may be introduced with either *may* or *can* in English, whereas in Greek, since there is no verb rendering the meaning 'may', the only possibility with auxiliaries is the verb *boro* 'can'.

The second possibility, in which the addressee is made prominent, includes most cases of what Ervin-Tripp (1976) calls 'question directives', e.g. 'could *you* open the window please?' *Can* but not *may* can introduce requests of this type. Imperative requests fall into this category, although the subject *you* is hardly ever made explicit. Sometimes, even 'innocent' *you*-questions can be used instead of *I*-questions as indirect requests, e.g. 'are *you* making tea?' instead of 'could I have some tea?'

Although the above appear to be the most frequent means of performing common, everyday requests, there are also interesting ways with which both the speaker and the addressee can occupy the prominent position, e.g. 'can *we* clear up the mess?' Besides the cases in which such constructions are used to request the addressee's help, they may also be employed to indicate either 'you' or 'me'. Brown and Levinson (1978: 132) have pointed out that this phenomenon is found in both Tamil and Tzeltal, as well as in English, where *let's* can also function in this way. Their examples 129 and 130 are:

> let's have a cookie, then (i.e. me)
> let's get on with dinner, eh? (i.e. you)

Ervin-Tripp (1976: 48 and 1981: 198) contends that this inclusive 'we' implies a pseudo-participation and is appropriate only downwards in rank. However, in Greek there is no such restriction concerning rank. The first person plural form of the verb (the subject pronoun is not usually needed), apart from the normal 'both' can also be used to mean 'you' or 'me'. Among equals, for instance, *δe θa pjume tipota?* 'aren't we going to drink anything?' may be a request for a drink if the speaker is in the addressee's house. Such an utterance could also be perceived as an offer on the part of the speaker when acting as a host.

Since in many cases it is difficult to assign one clear interpretation without having a fair amount of background knowledge of who the speaker is, such utterances can lead to misunderstandings (Ervin-Tripp, 1976 and 1981). For instance, *na aniksume to paraθiro?* '[can] we open the window?' might mean that it would be a good idea if the addressee opened the window, although it might also mean that the speaker will do it.

Such forms are also frequently used towards children. For instance, a mother may say *ine ora na kimiθume* 'it is time we went to bed', but what she really means is that this applies to the child, not to herself. Moreover, children seem to recognize this implication, because although they may nag and invent reasons to postpone going to bed, they rarely demand that the mother should go to bed. This is basically a positive politeness strategy in that the speaker presumes that he or she knows what is beneficial for the addressee and involves both people in the action, even though only conventionally.

I would like now to consider another use of Greek plural, called the 'royal plural', which single speakers usually use of themselves. I will exclude those cases in which the president or head of an organization, etc., speaks on behalf of its members, and also the 'plural of majesty' that is, the kind of language used by monarchs. The plural forms in the 'royal plural'—or 'plural of splendour' as it is called in Greek—are not confined to verb forms, as is the case with the polite second person plural forms, but can extend to any kind of predicate structure, whether nominal, adjectival, or verbal. These can also be used along with second person plural forms to a single addressee, although this is not always the case. These first person plural forms are rather a characteristic of lower groups' colloquial use to indicate distancing from an addressee who belongs to the same group. Thus, they tend to indicate tension in the relationship rather than politeness, and since they are mainly used by uneducated people, there is a considerable inconsistency in the use of the singular and plural. For example:

| eγo (sing.) | omos, | na to kseris (sing.) | [E 1: 28] |
| I, | however, | you should know | |

| δen epireazomaste emis (pl.) | ap' afta . . . |
| we are not influenced | by these . . . |

A common use of the plural, where one would normally expect singular, is found in certain fixed colloquial expressions used among close friends. In such cases the pronominal object or the pronominal object and the verb can be in the plural. Again this use indicates tension or teasing rather than closeness alone. Something similar is encountered in English with imperative constructions and a first person plural pronominal object:

give us a fiver, mate

ase (sing.) mas (pl.)	re	katerina	[AN 1: 21]
leave us [alone]	(re)	Katerina	

jati δe mas (pl.) lete (pl.)	ke mas (pl.)	[NB]
why don't you tell	and us	

First person plural forms, especially of fixed polite formulas, are sometimes employed by single speakers usually belonging to lower classes to express extra formality and politeness. For example:

mas siχorite (pl.)	ja tin enoχlisi	[NB]
excuse us	for the disturbance (for disturbing you)	

efχaristume (pl.)	poli	[NB]
we thank you	a lot	

Such cases appear to involve a special code of politeness which associates politeness with any manifestation of plurality. The speaker appears to act not as an individual but as a member of a group, thus increasing the amount of gratitude or apologies offered.

What is perhaps more interesting is the availability in many languages of impersonalizing pronominal devices which work in the opposite direction of 'inclusive we', or first person plural constructions. Thus, in English we have *one* followed by third person verbal constructions, as for instance, *one wouldn't want to correct essays during the holidays*, uttered by a lecturer in class to justify his refusal to accept essays just before the Easter holidays.[5]

---

[5] What the lecturer really meant was *I wouldn't want to . . .*, but that would have sounded too abrupt a refusal. He could also have said *you wouldn't want to . . .*, thus inviting his students to be more understanding and co-operative by approaching the issue on a more personal and friendly basis. However, by choosing *one*, he presented his refusal as something more general, having almost nothing to do with either his students or himself, thus distancing himself from the abating refusal by implying that it was not a personal choice, but a more general rule applicable in such situations. Such use reflects the negative politeness strategy 'state the FTA as a general rule'. By stating the face-threatening activity as a case of some general social rule or obligation, the speaker attempts to dissociate both himself and the addressee from it (Brown and Levinson, 1978: 211).

The fact that such constructions with *one* cannot be rendered in Greek does not

The use of *one* in such constructions has an important distancing effect, but will not be discussed here since it is not directly related to requests. This usage with *one* cannot be rendered in Greek.⁶ What is possible, however, in both languages is use of relative and indefinite pronouns, such as *kanis* (m.) or *kamja* (fem.) 'anybody' and *anybody* in English, followed by a third person verbal construction;⁷ these, however, are different from the English *one* constructions. For example:

eχi	kamja sas	kali	ora?	[KA 2: 103]
does	anybody have	the right	time?	

who'll give me a glass of whisky?   [PN 2: 105]

turn off the light somebody   [PL 1: 10]

This device is not used to avoid mentioning the addressee but rather to suggest either that the speaker does not know or that it does not matter who the appropriate addressee is, as long as the request is executed.

Distancing can also be achieved in Greek by manipulating the use of lexical items. For example, general terms of address can be used in the nominative instead of the vocative. Such cases are related to *one* constructions in that they take third person verbal inflections. This practice is more common with children, and less frequent with strangers; among friends it implies jocular behaviour. Generally speaking, this use is rather limited. For example:

mean that Greek lecturers are friendlier and closer to their students than the English; the contrary would sound a more plausible assumption since such status differences seem to be observed in Greece more than in England. The difference stems from the fact that each language affords its speakers and conventionalizes those patterns which reflect general cultural values, and social distance is a positive cultural value in England. For an interesting account of the multifunctionality of *one*-constructions in English and their relationship to *you*- and *they*-constructions (as impersonalizing devices) and the passive, see Antonopoulou (1991).

⁶ Modern Greek lacks even the device for utter impersonalization—the infinitive. As Mackridge (1985: 282) points out on this issue, 'the lack of an infinitive . . . makes it impossible for a verb to be used without at least an implied subject,' and adds that 'the complete impersonality of reference found in an infinitive cannot be achieved in MG [Modern Greek]'. The example he cites is Hamlet's famous line 'to be or not to be' which could be rendered as *na zi kanis i na mi zi* translated literally as 'should one live or (should one) not live'.

⁷ Such uses of indefinite and relative pronouns are discussed in detail by Clark and Carlson (1982).

θα iθele o kirios (nom.)   mia fotoγrafia?   [NB]
would the gentleman want   a photograph [taken]?

ti θeli to moro mu?   [NB]
what does my baby want?

The use of the demonstrative *ekinos/i/o* 'that' instead of *aftos/i* 'this' can also be indicative of distancing in English, though less so in Greek. For example:

will you put that magazine down a moment, please? [A 2: 120]

That magazine is the magazine the addressee is reading, which from a Greek speaker's point of view is not all that far away. Note also:

— . . . what about that tea?   [OS 1: 14]
— (still behind the [news]paper) what tea?
— put that kettle on
— don't say that   [PN 3: 166]

That is also frequently used with 'stop'. For example:

please! will you stop that?   [OS 1: 91]

This kind of distancing in English with the use of *that* cannot be rendered in Greek. Instead, the definite article can be used in similar constructions, or perhaps the demonstrative *aftos* 'this' rather than 'that'. In actual fact, *aftos* can often be used in cases in which 'that' would be used in English:

pjos ine aftos o anθropos eki pera?
who   is   this   man   over there?

In other words, in Greek *aftos* 'this' can be used for a much wider range of distances than it is in English, where it is employed to indicate immediate proximity both in space and time. The demonstrative *ekinos/i/o* 'that' sounds more formal and cannot be used for people or items which are relatively near the speaker. From the above English examples, the only one which could be rendered with *ekino* 'that' in Greek is *what about that tea?*, but even this would sound more appropriate with a follow-up like *ti ejine me ekino to tsai pu leγame?* 'what happened with that tea we were talking about?', which is implied even if not stated. This follow-up indicates actual time lag and implies some kind of prior agreement or perhaps anger for the delay. This kind of interpretation could, of course, hold true for the English utterance, too.

All the differences discussed above are not unrelated.[8] They all clearly point to a more positive politeness orientation of Greek society as compared to English. 'Just as the use of proximal demonstratives etc. [preferred in Greek] can convey empathy and involvement . . . so the use of distal markers [preferred in English] can convey social distance, anger, or avoidance' (Brown and Levinson, 1978: 210). Such variations from unmarked usage are called 'point-of-view operations', which are discussed in some detail (ibid. 123).

Impersonal verbs also seem to offer very good examples of distancing devices. Thus, instead of requesting with *do you have . . .?* or *could I have . . .?*, languages provide ways of avoiding the *I* and *you* pronouns with expressions like *is there anything . . .?*, or *iparxi kaθolu . . .?* in Greek. However, the most common and pervasive means of impersonalization shared by many unrelated languages is offered by the passive. The literature on the subject is vast and I will not go into detail. The purported synonymy of active and passive constructions was challenged, and a variety of solutions have been proposed both within and outside the transformational model.[9] Do we really need passive constructions, whether explained in terms of the order of constituents and morphological changes or in terms of grammatical relationships or even in terms of subject demotion, since they are so closely linked to their active counterparts? It seems that we do, since they are evinced in so many different and unrelated languages, and for reasons outside the strict grammatical domain. 'Both grammar and pragmatics conspire to provide an explanation of the passive: one explains how the passive is formed, the other explains the conditions under which it is likely to be preferred to the corresponding active' (Leech, 1983: 22).

---

[8] It should be noted here that there are similar differences in the use of verbs of movement, such as *come* versus *go*. Although 'English seems to encode a basic positive-politeness "taking the role of the other" point of view in the usage of *come*' (Brown and Levinson, 1978: 126), Greek seems to go even further. For instance in cases like (ibid.) '{come/go} and meet me at my favourite restaurant . .' 'do you want to {come/go} with me to the movies?' where both options are possible in English, in Greek only *erχome* 'come' is acceptable. For some Greek speakers, even the use of *here* and *there* can be similarly affected. For them, *here* is only where they are.

[9] See, for example, Perlmutter and Postal (1977) and Comrie (1977), for contrasting views.

Shibatani (1985), in a very interesting article on passives, discusses their relationship to other constructions, besides the well-known reflexives and reciprocals, such as honorifics and plurals to single addressees. He argues that passives and their correlation to such other constructions can be better understood if pragmatic factors are taken into account. His position is that 'their fundamental function has to do with the defocusing of agents' (ibid. 831). Thus, what passives share with the impersonalizing constructions mentioned above is that they fulfil the speaker's need to express distance and formality, features which have very often been associated with politeness. 'Passives and impersonal expressions . . . tend to create a sense of distance between speaker and utterance, or speaker and addressee. Hence sentences containing these forms tend to be interpreted as polite' (Lakoff, 1973: 299). Likewise, Brown and Levinson (1978: 279) suggest that 'impersonalization serves basic politeness ends . . . and the passive exists (at least partially) to serve these ends'. They also argue that the basic motive involved in English passives is to demote and possibly delete the subject. In this way the responsibility is shifted off the subject, which reflects politeness and formality conventions.[10] The restriction on passing information explains the need for and existence of the circumstantial voice in Malagasy and most Polynesian languages and also the strong preference for passive and circumstantial instead of active forms; this facilitates the expression of impersonalization and indirectness (Keenan, 1976).

There is evidence which supports the assumption that passive constructions are not so frequently used in Greek as they are in English in daily encounters.[11] Moreover, passive constructions of the sort *it would be appreciated if . . .* can introduce formal requests in English but cannot in Greek. The source for this variable preference is closely associated with the general tendency for more directness and informality in Greek.

Impersonalizing devices whose main function is to avoid overt reference to either the speaker or the addressee are related to the interesting phenomenon of indirectness which is encountered in

[10] As is well known, passives characterize the written scientific medium as a means of formality and distance since the author is the authority, but formality rather than politeness would more appropriately describe such discourse.

[11] See, for instance, Warburton (1975); Wasow (1977); Lascaratou (1984); Lascaratou and Philippaki-Warburton (1981 and 1983–4); Marmaridou (1987).

many diverse languages and which is discussed in some detail in the following section.

5.2.2 *The politeness of indirect requests*

Most work regarding indirectness relates mainly to requests, since they exhibit a rich variety of features of the phenomenon. This may suggest a greater intrinsic face-threatening element being involved in requests than in other speech acts, as a result of which politeness has been regarded as the most basic motivation of indirectness.

Given a specific situation, speakers can select from among a variety of forms of request ranging from the direct and straightforward to the mildly or strongly indirect. For instance, one can request somebody else to open a window by saying *Open the window, please, Would it be possible to open the window, please?*, or *It's hot in here.* The first utterance is the direct way of performing the act, whereas the second and the third alternatives have been regarded as indirect ways (though not unquestionably—see Davison, 1975). The basic formal difference between these two main types of indirect acts is that although the parts of both are explicit, the force of the former is a clear directive whereas the force of the latter has to be inferred. It has been suggested that direct requests are either neutral or impolite, whereas indirect requests have a strong relationship to politeness.

In addition to inhering in single acts, indirectness can permeate the whole exchange. It is this kind of indirectness which is cherished by the Japanese (Loveday, 1983) and the Chinese (Young, 1982). A similar phenomenon 'with a cumulative summing of associative hints' is reported by Brown and Levinson (1978: 221) for Malagasy speakers. Thus, indirectness is a broad term which can have a variety of facets and can underlie phenomena such as irony, metaphor, and understatement. 'In a sense, all interpretation in context is indirect' (Tannen, 1982: 225); consequently, 'a full understanding of conversational organization will have to await an adequate account of indirect communication' (Brown and Levinson, 1978: 217).

'If speakers always said what they meant, then there would be few problems for speech act theory or for discourse analysis' (Stubbs, 1983: 147), and obviously fewer misunderstandings. There are, however, various reasons which lead interactants to express themselves indirectly, in some cultures perhaps more than in others.

Indirect speech acts have been analysed and grouped together in various ways. The details of the arguments extend beyond the scope of this discussion; thus, only the issues which are directly relevant will be considered. The major concern expressed has been the importance of the literal meaning of the indirect speech act. For Searle (1975) there is a difference between 'literal sentence meaning' and 'speaker utterance meaning', and addressees follow a procedure from sentence meaning towards utterance meaning in order to interpret what they have heard. Morgan (1978), expanding Searle's analysis, distinguishes between 'conventions of language' which refer to the literal meanings of utterances and 'conventions of usage' which govern the use of utterances, and argues that they are both necessary for a full understanding of what the speaker intends to convey. A similar procedural approach is suggested by psycholinguists, notably Clark and Lucy (1975) and Clark and Schunk (1980), who argue that literal meaning is essential to the correct interpretation of indirect speech acts.

For Gordon and Lakoff (1975: 87) 'the conversationally implied meaning (the request) can be conveyed only if the literal meaning (the question) is not intended to be conveyed and if the hearer assumes that it is not'. Green (1975: 132) strongly objects to this and argues that there are 'whimperatives that would be ungrammatical as questions' and, even worse, 'whimperatives whose "literal, question meaning" is nonsensical,' such as constructions with *would* as in *Would you get me a glass of water*. It has also been suggested that the presence of a strong linguistic and situational context is more essential than the literal meaning for an understanding of the conveyed meaning of a request (Gibbs, 1979; Raskin, 1979).

For Davison (1975: 144), an indirect speech act may contain a verb of saying and may be accompanied by various other elements in addition to the 'core' of the speech act. These additional elements do not contribute to the meaning of the sentence; that is, they do not make it more informative, though they provide additional features not shared by the corresponding direct act. The question of indirect acts, their identification, classification, and potential has been discussed in some detail not only by Davison, but also by Gordon and Lakoff (1975), Haverkate (1988), and Bach and

Harnish (1982). However, the value of their findings in relation to politeness is perhaps best observed in the work of Clark and Schunk (1980).

Clark and Schunk conducted experiments which confirmed their assumption that it is the literal meaning of a speech act which is crucial in conveying politeness with both requests and their responses. They suggest that since all options available to interlocutors to perform indirect requests carry the same non-literal meaning, their degree of politeness is, consequently, determined directly from their literal meanings. They (ibid. 111) claim that 'the more the literal meaning of a request implies personal benefits for the listener, within reason, the more polite is the request,' and also that 'the more attentive the responder is to all of the requester's meaning, the more polite is the response'. They suggest, for instance, that *May I ask you what time it is?* is more polite than *Won't you tell me what time it is?*, because the literal meaning of the former demands very little of the addressee and offers the option of giving permission, whereas the literal meaning of the latter demands a great deal of the addressee. Similarly, a response *Sure/Yes, it's six* is more polite than simply *It's six*, because the former takes both the literal and the non-literal meaning of the utterance into account. Clearly, there is a wide range of phenomena included under the rubric of indirectness, and linguists are not unanimous as to (*a*) how to group them, (*b*) what the role and importance of the literal meaning is, and (*c*) the extent of their relationship to politeness.

Tannen (1982: 218), drawing upon Lakoff (1973), says that 'sociocultural goals, broadly called *politeness*, lead people to express opinions and preferences in widely varying linguistic forms'. The association between indirectness and politeness has been espoused by many scholars.[12] Searle claims that as far as directives are concerned, politeness is the main motivation for indirectness. Likewise, Leech (1983: 108) states that 'indirect illocutions tend to be more polite (a) because they increase the degree of optionality, and (b) because the more indirect an illocution is, the more diminished and tentative its force tends to be'. In contrast, experiments conducted by Holtgraves (1986) failed to confirm expectations that indirect questions would be perceived as more polite than

[12] Heringer (1972); Lakoff (1973 and 1977); Clark and Schunk (1980); and Brown and Levinson (1978 and 1987) are among them.

direct questions. The explanation offered is that this may be true only for requests for information, which were examined, due to the fact that they do not encode as high a degree of imposition as requests for action. Overall, however, most scholars have argued that to a great extent the degree of indirectness determines the degree of politeness.

The main reason for linking politeness and indirectness must be the fact that analyses of speech acts are mainly based on English, where on-record indirect structures constitute the majority of conventionalized means for polite requesting, usually in the form of questions. If one looks at other languages, for example Greek, Polish, and Hebrew, people can be and are polite without relying so heavily on such indirect constructions. The ethnocentricity of the association between indirectness and politeness is revealed by Irvine's experience in a Wolof-speaking community in Senegal reported by Hymes (1986: 79). 'She learned that a direct request or demand was actually more polite than an expression that was hedged or qualified by mention of the wishes or situation of the speaker.'

Furthermore, even within English one can find a variety of reasons for which people decide to be indirect: teasing and joking, irony, lack of confidence, or even sarcasm and rudeness. Stubbs (1983: 163) says that Lerman's analysis of Nixon's language in the Watergate transcripts has provided 'fascinating data on the depth of indirection which may be involved in giving directives'. Obviously all these observations have nothing to do with politeness. 'Indirect speech acts are invoked in too many different contexts to be accounted for by one [i.e. politeness], or one main, motive force' (Fotion, 1981: 118).

Structures, whether direct or indirect, are not inherently polite or impolite—they acquire such characteristics from the speakers' intentions, the addressees' expectations, and various other social factors present in the situation. Davison (1975: 149) also contends that individuals who possess politeness attributes 'do not use indirect speech acts exclusively and in all situations. Utterances can be said politely without being overtly (syntactically) marked for politeness.' Politeness is related to both pleasant and unpleasant things, as Davison points out, whereas 'indirect speech acts seem to be associated most of the time with bad news, unfavourable opinions, and intrusive questions'. Indirect speech acts enable one to distance oneself from the unfavourable message and mitigate the intrusion or imposition (Davison, 1975: 153). Since distance and politeness are closely related in some cultures, it is not surprising that many scholars have explained indirectness in terms of politeness needs.

As is evident from this discussion and the relevant literature, there is only limited consensus among scholars about what constitutes indirectness or otherwise. However, for me, the two generally accepted forms of indirectness exemplified by *Would you mind opening the window please* and *Its hot in here* are of fundamental importance in considering politeness. I have chosen to regard both as indirect acts and I will call the first type 'structural' indirectness and the second one 'pragmatic' indirectness. This distinction reflects Brown and Levinson's 'on-record' negatively polite or 'conventional' indirectness and 'off-record' or 'non-conventional' indirectness respectively. Although the terms 'conventional' versus 'non-conventional' have been widely used (Blum-Kulka and Olshtain, 1984; Blum-Kulka, 1987) to describe the two types of indirectness, they conceal the important fact that pragmatic indirectness can also be a conventionalized means for requesting.

Structural or conventional indirectness includes what Ervin-Tripp (1976) has called 'imbedded imperatives', 'permission directives', and 'question directives' and relies heavily on structural elaboration, mainly in the form of hedged interrogative constructions. Pragmatic or non-conventional indirectness comprises mainly 'hints' which are structurally simple statements or interrogative constructions. These are usually produced when Grice's maxims of efficient communication are violated and, thus, conversational implicatures are invited in order to arrive at the intended message.

As far as politeness is concerned, off-record utterances have been attributed higher degrees of politeness on the grounds that they minimize impositions more successfully. Blum-Kulka (1987), among others, has challenged Brown and Levinson's ranking of politeness strategies suggesting that, at least for requests, politeness is associated with conventional indirectness, but not necessarily with non-conventional indirectness, leaving room for cross-cultural variation. Her basic argument is that a certain interactional balance between clarity and non-coerciveness is necessary for any utterance to count as polite. This balance is achieved in the case of structural indirectness, constructions which are rated in her experiments as the most polite. In the case of direct constructions, clarity overrides non-coerciveness and in the case of pragmatic indirectness non-coerciveness overrides clarity; thus, they can both be perceived as less polite than structurally indirect constructions since the necessary balance is destroyed. Brown and Levinson (1987: 19) admit that there may be an 'efficiency' factor involved in assessing politeness, but argue that Blum-Kulka's experimental design and results do not offer genuine counter-cases to their ranking of off-record strategies as generally more polite than negative politeness strategies.

Blum-Kulka (1987) examined perceptions of directness and politeness in Hebrew and English. However, what she called 'English informants' are all native speakers of American English. This choice of informants seems to have an important consequence, because although it is a truism that, to a great extent, the Americans and the English share the same linguistic code, it cannot be denied that they do not share socio-cultural values and attitudes to the same extent, witness Brown and Levinson's observation of the different politeness orientations of the two societies. It is, therefore, not unreasonable to assume that results may have been different had the informants been native speakers of British English, bearing in mind Gumperz's (1982a: 135) assumption that the English are a lot more indirect than the Americans. In other words, American speakers ranked what have been called 'query preparatory' strategies of the form *could you . . .?* and *would you mind . . .?* as the most polite ways of performing requests followed by off-record 'hints'; therefore, English speakers, being more indirect, may have ranked the same 'hints' as the most polite constructions for the realization of requests. Such evidence could partially justify Brown and Levinson's insistence on a greater degree of politeness in off-record strategies, at least in English culture which, however, cannot be cross-culturally valid. However, the above observations do not suggest that this is the case; they only point to the need for further cross-cultural investigation of the subject, as Brown and Levinson (1987: 21) accept.

Thus, before making or accepting claims concerning the degree of politeness encoded in indirectness universally, the cultural specificity of the phenomenon should be considered. It is indeed hard to see in what sense it could be objectively verified that an English husband who may request coffee with *Would you mind making me a cup of coffee?* is more or less polite than a Greek husband who may say *ftiakse mu ena kafeδaki* 'make me a little cup of coffee' or *δen ine akoma eksi* 'isn't it six o'clock yet?', implying that he would like his coffee. The difference between these constructions lies in the type of (in)directness involved and the extent of conventionalization rather than in the degree of politeness. The consequences of such requests offer ample evidence for this claim. All other factors being equal, the husbands above will receive their coffees and the wives will not feel that they have been treated impolitely. Thus, it seems that in addition to being asked to rate utterances according to their degree of politeness, informants should also be asked to consider and evaluate the speaker's intentions and the addressee's reactions in response to such utterances. If the speaker did not intend to be impolite and the addressee did not feel imposed upon in conforming with the request, then such considerations provide ample evidence that the constructions used were appropriately polite. Such differences give rise to puns or misunderstandings, especially when interlocutors belong to different sexes or do not share the same cultural and subcultural background (Gumperz, 1982*a*: 135; Tannen, 1982: 217).

Greeks tend to prefer more structurally direct requests than the English, who tend to prefer more structurally indirect constructions. For example, imperative constructions constitute appropriate requesting forms in many more contexts in Greek than in English. However, existing research concerning Greeks (Tannen, 1982) finds that they are very indirect. Do we have a contradiction here? No, because the apparent impasse stems from the fact that we are dealing with the two different types of indirectness, discussed earlier.

Although Tannen compares Greeks and Americans, Gumperz (1982*a*: 139) also assumes that the English are more indirect than the Americans. A very first tentative conclusion which can be drawn from the above observations is that both the Greeks and the English are more pragmatically indirect when compared with Americans. In an attempt to investigate such first assumptions and determine whether and to what extent the Greeks and the English differ in terms of pragmatic indirectness preferred in daily exchanges, I constructed a questionnaire (see section 1.2.3 and Appendix II/3). All the situations depicted involve the off-record strategy, 'give association clues', which, according to Brown and Levinson (1987: 214) violates the relevance maxim. The first interesting finding is that both the Greeks (65.7 per cent) and the English (63.5 per cent) found the indirect interpretation more plausible and that they both move on a very close level of pragmatic indirectness (see Table 5.1).

TABLE 5.1 *Frequency and percentage of occurrence of direct (D) and indirect (I) interpretations for utterances from 4 situations of a sample of 35 English and 35 Greek informants.*

Situation	English		Greek	
	No.	%	No.	%
Friend asking for information (D) or	7	20.0	8	22.8
requesting a lift (I)	28	80.0	27	77.1
Wife asking for husband's wish (D)	24	68.5	18	51.4
or expressing her wish (I)	11	31.4	17	48.5
Mother asking for information (D) or	1	2.8	1	2.8
requesting action (I)	34	97.1	34	97.1
Husband asking for information (D)	19	54.2	21	60.0
or requesting the newspaper (I)	16	45.7	14	40.0
TOTAL (D)	51	36.4	48	34.2
TOTAL (I)	89	63.5	92	65.7

The results, although preliminary, suggest that there is a slight difference regarding preferences for pragmatic indirectness between the two societies. Moreover, independent evidence also indicates that the Greeks tend to prefer more off-record strategies than the English. There are a number of classic off-record strategies which include rhetorical questions, ellipsis, and the use of proverbs (Brown and Levinson, 1978: 217). Greeks use rhetorical questions very frequently either as responses to other questions or in order to emphasize a certain issue and achieve greater vividness (see section 8.3). Some of these rhetorical questions have acquired a formulaic nature. This characteristic of the language cannot be unrelated to the abundance of situational formulas encountered in Greek when compared to English (Tannen and Oztek, 1981) and to the highly idiomatic nature of the language (Mackridge, 1985: 343). Actually Mackridge assumes that these features of the language may be related to indirectness. Ellipsis also exhibits greater flexibility in Greek than in English (see section 6.5).

If we accept Brown and Levinson's hierarchy of politeness strategies, then Greeks appear to be slightly more polite than the English. However, such an assumption cannot be justified because, first, it would be making unrealistic claims of higher degrees of politeness in some societies, and secondly, and more specifically, because it contradicts earlier claims of differences in the politeness orientations of the two societies.

Structural indirectness may indicate the speaker's concern for the addressee's freedom and, consequently, the politeness encoded may be motivated by a wish to reduce the imposition involved. However, as far as pragmatic indirectness is concerned a number of issues deserving our attention seem to be involved, extending beyond the notions of pragmatic clarity, avoidance of coerciveness, and efficiency. First, much depends on what has been conventionalized to function as more polite or more formal in the specific context. If questions concerning the ability or willingness of the addressee to perform the act are conventionally understood as negatively polite requests, it may be argued that utterances stating reasons (Haverkate, 1988) and questions concerning location can be understood as conventional requests in many contexts. It has been suggested that utterances expressed as hints require a lot more mental endeavour on the part of the addressee than embedded imperatives, which in turn require more effort than straightforward imperatives. The speaker obviously does not choose to employ indirect expressions in order to place interpretive demands on the addressee. Conventionalization diminishes the length of the inferential process necessary for the interpretation of both structurally and pragmatically indirect constructions and contributes decisively to the balance between clarity and non-coerciveness and, thus, to the assumed degree of politeness. The difference in terms of conventionalization between structural and pragmatic indirectness is mainly that the former, unlike the latter, has been studied extensively; thus, its manifestations are overt, to a great extent typical, and readily recognizable as such. Off-record utterances, therefore, cannot be seen as more or less polite irrespective of their degree of conventionalization in the particular society under study.

Members who use indirect utterances of this type must share certain knowledge with the other members of their group which guarantees correct interpretation and success. If that is the case, the process of interpretation is not lengthier and there are actually no more options really open to the addressee(s) but to conform to the request, than there would have been had the speaker used a different construction. Nonconformity without reason or a request for more specific information might have had unpleasant consequences, such as annoyance or anger. People can be ambiguous and indirect but in so doing they subconsciously follow cultural and subcultural rules and expectations, and to question them can have dramatic results.

Secondly, another important related issue is the notion of imposition which such devices are supposed to mitigate. One of Brown and Levinson's (1987: 18) basic arguments for the correctness of their hierarchy is that off-record politeness has not been found to be used for smaller FTAs or to lower-status addressees whereas negative and positive politeness have.

However, their conviction does not seem to account for the great variety of off-record utterances used in familiar and familial contexts, at least in Greek. One wonders in what sense the mother who says to her little son, for instance, *Where are your boots?*, and implies 'put them on', is performing a serious face-threatening act and would want to be extremely polite. Or, similarly, in what sense the husband who requests to be given his newspaper by *Where is the newspaper?* is superior in status to his wife or is committing a serious imposition requiring the highest degree of politeness? Simple considerations such as these cast doubts on the ranking of politeness strategies and its universal validity. Brown and Levinson (1987: 12) offer an explanation when they note that in cases in which off-record utterances have only one defensible interpretation, they 'may occur with lesser requests or to less distant or elevated addressees', but add that it is very difficult to verify empirically the idea of ' "having in context only one defensible interpretation" '. Conventionalization and specific socio-cultural norms seem to restrict the success of alternative interpretations, to a certain extent.

However, it could be argued that the main source of the disagreement regarding off-record requests is the assumption that they derive their politeness from minimizing impositions. Although this may be one motivation, it cannot be the only one, nor even the most basic one, holding for all situations and cultures. Another equally important yet less considered motivation is that the addressee is provided with the opportunity to volunteer. This double function of off-record utterances explains why both the Greeks and the English can perform on very similar levels of pragmatic indirectness, despite their different politeness orientations. Off-record strategies do not form an independent category, but mix with both positive and negative politeness strategies and can be interpreted in different ways (Brown and Gilman, 1989). Thus, for instance, someone who requests a lift from a friend with a hint like *Are you going to the University tomorrow?* may be either leaving the options open to the addressee because they do not want to impose or because they do not want to deprive the addressee of the pleasure of offering and indicating consideration for the speaker's needs. In other words, in societies where the principles of distance and non-imposition prevail it will be essential to take all linguistic measures to ensure minimization of coerciveness. By contrast, in societies where greater importance is attached to solidary relations and dependence, the weight of impositions is assessed differently and is considered of secondary importance. The main concern is to satisfy the need for involvement rather than that of independence, a concern which derives from social norms which constitute part of the shared knowledge of the interactants. Consequently, in such cases, pragmatic indirectness will not be chosen by speakers eager to soften impositions, but by those willing to provide the addressee with the opportunity to offer without being requested. This prevents the face-threatening, 'inherently impolite' request from ocurring and at the same time paves the way for an 'inherently polite' act, the offer.[13] In this context, offers do not necessarily involve tangible goods but cover acts which indicate that inter-actants are on the same wavelength and are eager to be of service out of their own free will. This is but a reflection of the greater importance attached to in-group relations in Greece.

[13] It is worth noting that Brown and Levinson (1987: 72) consider both requests and offers face-threatening acts, while Leech (1983: 83) views offers as inherently polite in contrast to requests and orders. Ethnomethodologists (Schegloff, 1979: 49) argue that offers are structurally preferred to requests. For a detailed discussion of the functions of off-record requests, their relationship to offers, and the concept of imposition, see Sifianou, 1993.

In short, interlocutors in negative politeness societies will probably prefer structural indirectness to indicate their distance and through this their consideration for the other person; in positive politeness societies, however, interlocutors will prefer more structurally direct configurations to indicate their closeness and through this their consideration for others. Positive politeness and negative politeness techniques 'operate, respectively, as a kind of social accelerator and social brake for decreasing or increasing social distance in relationships' (Brown and Levinson, 1978: 98).

Pragmatic indirectness, on the other hand, can characterize both types of societies. This is possible because, as Brown and Levinson (1987: 213) suggest, many off-record strategies when used in context acquire on-record explicitness, and consequently their manifestations can be either positively or negatively polite. Furthermore, socio-cultural norms inform the context and determine the functions to be performed by particular constructions. The needs of 'rapport' and 'defensiveness' served by indirectness (Tannen, 1984a: 14) have different values in different societies.

From what has been said so far, it is not unreasonable to assume that the English use pragmatic indirectness as a strategy which enables speakers to give options to addressees to interpret the utterance in the way they wish, and yet reserve the right to deny the addressee's interpretation if that endangers their own face. In other words, it protects both the speaker's and the addressee's negative face. By contrast, the Greeks use pragmatic indirectness as a strategy by which the speaker expresses rapport with the addressee, a rapport which recognizes each other's needs and the desire to satisfy them. In other words, it enhances both the speaker's and the addressee's positive face.

5.3 THE NOTION OF REQUEST

Before proceeding to a detailed examination of the realization of requests in the two languages, some more general points are worth considering; in fact, they are fundamental in explaining the differing conceptions and realizations of requests in the two cultures.

Requests, as has already been mentioned, can be grouped into two broad categories; namely, requests for information and requests for action. These latter requests can be subcategorized into requests for goods, requests for help, and so on. Their main common characteristic in English is that all types of requests can be reported with *ask* rather than *tell*. The verb *ask* in English means, among other things, both 'request' and 'enquire' (cf. Green, 1975: 140). Doesn't this then point to an implicit assumption in the language that *to request* means *to ask* and that, consequently, there should be a tendency and preference for question forms to express requests?

In Greek, on the other hand, requests for information are reported with the verb *roto*, which means 'ask', 'enquire', but not 'request'. Requests for action are reported with *zito*, which means 'ask for', and possibly with *leo*, meaning both 'say' and 'tell', but not with *roto* 'ask'. As mentioned in section 5.2.2, there seems to be a difference between these two types of requests, in that the latter involve a higher degree of imposition. This distinction covers requests which are seen as part of the normal everyday tasks, which people who live or work together perform for each other, such as opening and closing doors or asking the time, as well as tasks related to socially determined roles, such as cooking, which is seen as a woman's duty. Such requests tend to be structurally simple and unembellished. If, however, the request for action or information is seen as something more serious, extraneous to simple or socially determined duties, then the request itself is more elaborate and it is reported with the verb *parakalo*, which means something between 'request' and 'plead'.

Furthermore, it is interesting to note here that there is no single word in Greek which can render the meaning of the English verb *request*. For those rather formal cases in which the verb *request* is explicitly stated in English, the verb *parakalo* would be the most appropriate in Greek. For instance, *I requested her to let me in, if she wouldn't mind coming down to the door*, (example from Davison, 1979: 424), would be translated as *tin parakalesa na* . . . This, however, does not mean that all occurrences of the verb *request* could be successfully rendered with the verb *parakalo*. The derivative noun *paraklisi* again sounds too formal to render appropriately all occurrences of the noun *request*.

Are these differences significant, or are they simply idiosyncratic peculiarities of the languages? Obviously the former because as Coulmas suggests, the intertranslatability of names, or rather, descriptions of speech acts in different languages should be investigated. Names of speech acts may serve as a valuable heuristic device for the investigation of functions of language, but they should not enter unquestionedly into the metalanguage of the description of speech situations and linguistic routines. Limitations in intertranslatability hint at differences between the structuring of speech situations and habitual speech activity in different communities, which should then be analyzed in detail. (1979: 243–4)

These differences in the description of speech acts clearly indicate different conceptions that native speakers have of the social meanings and functions of their linguistic actions (cf. Verschueren, 1981), because the descriptions of speech acts available carry socio-cultural information. According to Hudson (1980: 111), 'concepts used in classifying speech-acts will be typical of cultural concepts,' and consequently 'we might expect them to vary from one society to another, and that is . . . what we find'. The above observations justify the concern shared by various scholars, namely that speech act categorizations are largely based on English, and as such cannot be applied universally. They are, however, useful in that they provide insights; consequently, we can agree with Coulmas (1981*b*: 70) when he says that we can 'start out with kinds of speech acts as defined in a given socio-cultural and linguistic system, and then proceed to look for similar or equivalent linguistic acts in another culture'. He illustrates this with the investigation of thanks and apologies in Japanese and English and points out that although both speech acts may exist 'as generic types of activities across cultures, it is obvious that the pragmatic considerations of their implementation are culturally defined' (ibid. 89). Though related to thanks and apologies, his observations appear to be valid for requests as well, and indeed for any speech act category.

The importance of looking through native language terminologies has also been emphasized by various other scholars. For instance, Hymes (1968*b*: 110) maintains that 'one good ethnographic technique for getting at speech events . . . is through words which name them'. On this issue Wierzbicka (1986: 365) asserts quite strongly that 'the set of speech act verbs which a language has is usually a valuable source of insight into the culture associated with that language'. To support her views, Wierzbicka (1985*b*: 496), drawing upon Hudson, cites a very interesting example from Walmatjari (a language spoken in Western Australia). Walmatjari has a special word which could be rendered as 'kinship-based requests', and a characteristic of such requests is that they cannot be refused. 'But in calling this speech act a "request", one is, of course, committing an error: An act which, in the speaker's view, cannot be refused is not really a "request".'

Examples of such cross-cultural variations in speech acts are extensive, but are beyond the immediate scope of this work. What is important and, hopefully, clear is that the concept of 'request' is embodied differently in Greek and English. More specifically, it appears that the English cover term 'request' embraces many more utterances than it does in Greek. For a Greek, a *paraklisi* 'request' would include only one part of the English requesting constructions, namely, the more formal realizations. The other segment of English requests simply includes questions or expressions of a desire of the speaker. These expressions of desire lack a label in Greek, perhaps because they are an integral part of common everyday acceptable behaviour, and so are not recognized as a special category. It may be the case, as Verschueren (1981) argues, that such acts are performed so automatically that their cognitive salience is diminished and they have, consequently, escaped lexicalization.

In spite of these differences, in this study, all utterances that would be considered to be requests in English have been included, because otherwise it would be extremely difficult to draw a clear distinction and would exclude large areas which the definition of requests includes.

6
Requests: Form and Function

6.1 IMPERATIVES

As we have already observed, requests can be performed with a variety of constructions. In the previous chapter we focused upon prominence devices and indirectness in relation to requests and politeness. In dealing with the form and function of requests, we shall move on from these considerations to more straightforward request constructions such as imperatives and interrogatives, and later with their possible modification.

Imperative constructions usually include a verb and an object, if the verb is transitive, and if intransitive, some other complement. They do not include a subject unless special reasons such as emphasis require an overt subject.[1] In addition to these, they may or may not contain some kind of modification to mitigate or aggravate their force.

In English, direct imperatives are usually defined as constructions appropriate for commands and instructions (Lyons, 1968: 307); consequently, they are thought of as less appropriate or even unacceptable for making requests. This inappropriateness has led to great restriction on the use of imperatives as requesting devices, and their use is condemned by laymen and scholars (Clark and Schunk, 1980: 111; Wardhaugh, 1985: 162) alike as downright impolite: for Searle (1975: 64) 'ordinary conversational requirements of politeness normally make it awkward to issue flat imperative sentences (e.g., *Leave the room*) or explicit performatives (e.g., *I order you to leave the room*), and we therefore seek to find indirect means to our illocutionary ends (e.g., *I wonder if you would mind leaving the room*).'

For both Lakoff (1977: 101) and Leech (1983: 119) imperatives are the least polite constructions when compared to declaratives

---

[1] In the relevant literature there are many arguments as to the existence of an underlying 'you' subject, which does not surface because of a deletion rule. See, for instance, Postal (1964); Katz and Postal (1964); McCawley (1968); Bolinger (1967); and Downes (1977), among others.

and interrogatives. Leech's explanation of this is that 'an imperative impositive is tactless in that it risks disobedience, which is a fairly grave type of conflict situation'.

These views are of course valid to a certain extent, as far as the English norms of politeness or rather formality are concerned, but they are not and cannot be universal principles of polite linguistic realizations. According to Thomas (1983: 102), 'polite usage in Russian permits many more direct imperatives than does English' and adds that 'transferred into English, such direct imperatives seem brusque and discourteous'. In Greek, imperatives can express command, but also desire and wish (Triandafillides, 1978: 308), suggesting that their force will be different. Their frequency is such that they are remarkable even to observers who do not speak the language well, and if those observers happen to be English, they may easily become offended and annoyed by the degree of Greek 'impoliteness' and 'authoritarianism'. This important definitional difference seems to stem from the fact that the Greek morphological system for marking the imperative is more elaborate than the English. In English, the imperative is an uninflected form and is marked for neither aspect nor number. In Greek, on the other hand, there is a distinct morphological system marking imperatives for singular and plural, active and passive voice as well as for the present, past, and occasionally the present perfect tenses. It should be noted that with imperatives the present/past distinction does not specify any time, which is determined by the context, but simply indicates aspect. More specifically, the present imperative is used for progressive or habitual actions (e.g.: *pleke* 'knit'), whereas the past imperative is used for momentary actions (e.g.: *plekse* 'knit'). The terms 'imperfective' and 'perfective' have been used to express these differences, respectively (Mackridge, 1985: 102).

In English, the understood subject of an imperative is in most cases a second person addressee, whereas in Greek there is also a periphrastic form for a third person addressee, formed with *as* 'let' and the third person verb form borrowed from the subjunctive, as for instance, *as pijeni* meaning roughly 'let him/her go'. In some rare cases we can also have a first person plural imperative, usually formed periphrastically with *as* 'let', and a few verbs have their own monolectic forms for the first person plural, like *pame* 'let's go', etc. (Triandafillides, 1978: 315). Commands are usually issued directly, that is, they require a second person addressee. This flexibility explains why imperatives in Greek are not exclusively related to commands but can equally well express the wish or desire of the speaker.

The second person singular present or past imperative forms when negated, borrow the equivalent forms from the subjunctive, using the subjunctive negative particle *mi(n)* rather than the indicative *δen*. Furthermore, in cases in which the verb is irregular and does not exhibit a full paradigm of all imperative forms, the missing forms are supplied by the equivalent subjunctives. In many cases, subjunctive equivalents can also be used along with the imperative forms, the two moods being semantically interrelated: *γrapse* 'write' (past imperative) or *na γrapsis* '(you should) write', (past subjunctive).

Thus, it appears that there is some kind of affinity between these two moods in Greek, and they can both be utilized to perform requests as well as the indicative. The availability of such alternatives in the language partly explains why the demand for embedded imperatives and elaborate constructions is not so heavy in Greek as it is in English.

However, what is noteworthy here is that the majority of requests performed with imperative constructions utilize the past rather than the present imperative. Mackridge (1985: 123) contends that 'since the imperfective imperative is often used to order the immediate inception or cessation of an action, it is often felt to be less polite than the perfective'. Furthermore, the present tense expresses a progressive or repetitive action, notions which are quite incompatible with requests so that the past tense, which emphasizes the action rather than its duration, has been established as a more appropriate requesting form. These aspectual distinctions obviously reinforce the predilection for the past over the present imperative forms as requests. A Greek speaker who gets very angry or who intentionally issues a command will more often resort to the present imperative:

stamata (present tense) pja   [E 3: 114]
stop it

rather than *stamatise* (past tense) *pja*, although the overt meaning would be the same.

[among friends]
vale (past tense)   sava li*y*o   kras*aki*   na to tsugrisume
pour   Sava a little wine-*dim.*   to toast   [E 1: 28]

This is rather similar to what Wierzbicka (1985*a*: 154) reports for Polish, where when someone gets really angry, they will avoid the imperative and resort to the impersonal, bare infinitive. In other words, languages provide their users with a different construction to express stronger, offensive feelings.

It should be pointed out here that the above distinction in Greek is a tendency rather than a clear-cut rule, because one can find various exceptions. Moreover, present imperatives of some commonly used verbs have acquired pejorative connotations, such as *δine tu* which literally means 'give him', but in actual use means 'clear off' (Mackridge, 1985: 123). However, since the imperative is not the only mood utilized in Greek to perform requests, the present/past distinction is not the only one marking the difference between polite and impolite discourse.

Brown and Levinson (1978: 100) contend that 'direct imperatives stand out as clear examples of bald-on-record usage' and distinguish two categories. The first includes those cases in which there is no minimization of the face threat because other needs override face concerns, for instance, in cases of real or metaphorical urgency, of sympathetic advice, of warnings, wishes, and so on. The second category includes those cases in which the minimization of face threat is conveyed by implication. The speaker performs the face-threatening activity in an attempt to alleviate the addressee's anxiety not to impose on the speaker, for instance, in cases of welcomings, farewells, and offers. It is noteworthy that most such uses indicate concern for the addressee and a kind of intimacy. However, since few of these cases are requests they will be dealt with very briefly.

In both languages unembellished imperatives are found in cases of urgency, in which quick reaction is obviously more important than the loss of face and 'redress would actually decrease the communicated urgency' (Brown and Levinson, 1978: 101). For example:

*y*ri*y*ora tote.   siko,   trekse,   disu.   [MR 4: 88]
quickly then.   get up,   run,   get dressed.

Come on, hurry up, my flight number's been called. [PL 2: 70]

In such cases of urgency, nouns are also used in Greek. So 'help!' will be rendered as *voiθia*, which is the noun of the verb *voiθo* 'help', rather than any singular or plural imperative form. The preference for nouns is perhaps determined by the fact that the noun is a shorter form, and brevity is very important in such contexts. Furthermore, the verb has to be followed by an object in order to be complete. Even in English it is unclear whether the *help* cry is a noun or a verb, since as a transitive verb *help* should be followed by an object.

In Greek the imperative of *voiθo* 'help' is saved instead for cases of task-orientated activities as well as for cases of begging, used either by beggars or other people who are emotionally desperate. For example:

voiθa (imperfective)	na katevaso	ti valitsa	[KA 2: 173]
help [me]	to bring	the suitcase down	
(he kisses her hands)	voiθise (perfective)	me . . .!	
	help	me . . . !	
			[KA 3: 267]

The use of *voiθa* in the first example rather than *voiθise* implies criticism or anger and reflects the distinction discussed earlier between perfective and imperfective aspects of imperatives in Greek. *Help* is a general purpose urgent cry but with more specific ones indicative constructions can also be used. For example:

keγome
I am on fire

Related to the above kind of real urgency are cases of metaphorical urgency, in which the speaker speaks '*as if* maximum efficiency were very important' (Brown and Levinson, 1978: 101). Good examples of this are the so-called 'attention-getters' (see section 7.2.3.4).

Brown and Levinson (1978: 101) say that 'this metaphorical urgency perhaps explains why orders and entreaties (or begging), which have inverted assumptions about the relative status of S [speaker] and H [hearer], both seem to occur in many languages with the same superficial syntax—namely, imperatives'. Beggars tend to make direct demands in Greek:

eleiste (perfective—pl.)	to ftoxo
give charity	to the poor (man)

δoste (perfective—pl.)   kati
give   something

However, although beggars in Greece use imperatives and sound direct, they use the perfective plural form, and tend to accompany their requests with wishes of well-being. They frequently use the word *ftoχos* 'poor man' to describe their situation, which is one way of debasing themselves. All these devices suggest that they follow certain rules of politeness to mitigate the impact of the directness of the imperative, and yet retain its urgency. It seems that entreaties of this sort do not 'have inverted assumptions about the relative status of S and H', but rather imply that the fear of loss of face is minimal or non-existent. This also explains why prayers to God also include unembellished imperatives, and in Greek can also be expressed in the present imperative. For example:

voiθa (imperfective)   me   θe mu
help   me   my God

It would be presumptuous to suggest that this is an example of impoliteness. On the contrary, it is an example of intimacy or perhaps of total subordination, as Friedrich (1972: 285) points out.[2] Furthermore, 'one needs to know about the place of beggars in social structure, the rights and duties associated with them in relation to others, and the evaluation that others would give to their forms of utterance' (Hymes, 1986: 80).

Unmodified imperatives are also found with metaphorical and formulaic entreaties, according to Brown and Levinson (1978: 102). For example:

excuse me

don't forget us!

Formulaic entreaties, which in English are usually made with imperatives, are usually conveyed in Greek with nouns or present tense indicative constructions. Thus *pardon me*, *excuse me*, and so on are rendered with *siγnomi* which is a noun meaning 'pardon' or *me siχorite*, which means 'you excuse me', rather than the

---

[2] Wadman (1983) examines the kinds of politeness strategies used by George Herbert in his poems directed to God. She argues that the choice defines the kind of relationship between the speaker and God and any changes reveal changes in the relationship, too.

imperative forms, such as *siχoreste me*, which sounds more like pleading for forgiveness after some serious infraction.

Metaphorical entreaties, which favour imperatives in English, are more often expressed with subjunctives in Greek. For example, *send us a letter* will be rendered *na mas γrafis* rather than *γrafe mas*, and *don't forget us* as *mi mas kseχnas*. These constructions indicate concern and interest in the addressee's welfare, a kind of optimism that s/he will conform to the request.

In both languages unmodified imperatives were found in activity-orientated situations, that is, in cases in which the focus of the interaction was the task to be performed, possibly for the benefit of both the speaker and the addressee. In such situations face redress is rather irrelevant (Brown and Levinson, 1978: 102). For example:

> fer'   to karotsi   [P 1: 32]
> bring the wheelbarrow
>
> fetch me 'ammer   [B 2: 132]

It appears that where the focus of the interaction is the task to be performed, maximum efficiency is again important. Furthermore, a lack of distance is presupposed in order to engage in such activities, so imperative configurations, as well as contracted and elliptical forms, are frequently used with such requests. Thus, instead of *fetch the hammer*, just *the hammer* would be sufficient in appropriate situations. Ervin-Tripp (1976: 35) says that she has also found in her data many imperatives in interactions between parents and children involved in activity-orientated tasks.

Although recipes and instructions are not requests, Brown and Levinson (1978: 102) explain the predilection for imperatives with recipes and instructions as a further case of task-orientation. In Greek, recipes favour the present tense first person plural, rather than the imperative, thus including both the addressee and the instructor in the activity.

Imperatives were also found in both languages in cases of extreme tension, that is, in cases which were loaded with either negative or positive emotions, where they had an impact of either an order or begging:

> go away . . . shut up! I'm sick a' the lot of yer! leave my room
> at once   [B 2: 54]
>
> give us a kiss   [OR 2: 91]

skase,   skeftome . . .   [MR 4:95]
shut up,   I am thinking . . .

sfikse me   [P 2: 47]
embrace me tightly

In such cases face considerations might be irrelevant or less
important. The temper of the speaker clearly influences what is said
and how it is said. Although repetition of truncated forms is quite
frequent here, elaboration is not common. Since Greek society is
more tolerant of the open expression of both positive and negative
feelings, we can anticipate a more frequent use of such blunt
imperatives.

Imperatives are also found in cases of physical distance and in
many cases of power difference, in the former case because
efficiency is more important and in the latter because face redress is
not necessary. Brown and Levinson (1978) add more cases in which
imperatives are tolerated in English, such as sympathetic and
comforting advice, offers, warnings, welcomings, and farewells. In
Greek, such cases are realized with either imperatives or nouns, or
configurations involving indicative and subjunctive forms. (I have
excluded such cases from this study since I concentrate on the
realization of requests, rather than on the various uses of the
imperative.)

Larkin and O'Malley (1973: 318) list a few more cases in which
imperative configurations are appropriate in English, such as
advertisements, prescriptions, and giving directions, and add that
'with such a variety it is curious that linguists still talk primarily
about imperatives being commands and orders'. Blum-Kulka
(1983: 46), reporting Higa's remarks, points out that in a Japanese
social context such a free use of direct imperatives in advertisements is
unthinkable. Thus, it is clear that specific culture-bound social
norms affect the illocutionary force of imperatives.

From this brief account two findings emerge. First, since the
Greek imperative system is more elaborate than the English, and it
can also express the desire or wish of the speaker, it is not
surprising that imperatives are more frequently used as requests in
Greek than in English. Second, a wider variety of constructions are
appropriate in Greek for bald-on-record usage. What really matters
in cases of real or even metaphorical urgency, is quick reaction on
the part of the addressee; consequently, the shortest linguistic form,

whether that is a noun or an imperative, etc., will be the best candidate for conventionalization.

Having discussed the morphological and semantic differences between the two systems of imperatives and cases in which imperatives are acceptable in both languages, we will now proceed with one striking difference which also accounts for the fact that more imperatives were found in my Greek data. In cases in which the requested item was coffee, drinks, food, etc., and the participants were couples, close friends, or relatives, especially in household environments, there was a strong predilection for imperative constructions in Greek, whereas more elaborate constructions were more common in English. Furthermore, such requests were less frequent in my English data, as a whole, which perhaps implies that the risk of loss of face is perceived as great and for this reason the English choose not to perform the face-threatening activity at all (Brown and Levinson's strategy 5). For example:

ftjaks'	ena kafe				[S 8: 89]
make	a coffee				

fere	to konjak				[E 3: 123]
bring	the cognac				

ande	vale na fame . . . anikse	ke	mja	bira	
come on	set the table . . . open	and	a	beer	
					[MR 3: 69]

How can we account for this finding? Should we accept that in such cases we have status or power differences? May we suggest that Greeks very often act as bullies, assuming power differences which do not exist and issuing commands? Or should we assume that they are simply inconsiderate and impolite? Any such claims would be preposterous and would sidestep deeper issues.

Even a cursory observation of the household behaviour of many, especially older, couples in Greek society reveals that there are still strong built-in preconceptions about the different tasks allocated to each member of the household. In spite of the socio-political changes, for many people, especially men, roles and duties are still clearly defined as men's and women's. Thus, setting the table, making coffee, and all sorts of domestic tasks are still (unfortunately) seen as the woman's responsibility. Here, therefore, imperatives cannot be seen as orders, since both participants tacitly accept this kind of social order. Downes (1977: 89) argues that 'the command potential varies with content and speaker's and hearer's belief of its truth from specific situation to specific situation,' and Leech (1983: 219) maintains that the difference between a command and a request is that, whereas in issuing the former the speaker assumes that the addressee will comply, in issuing the latter the speaker assumes or 'purports to assume' that the outcome will be successful only if the addressee agrees to conform. Thus, imperatives used in Greek in such situations are more like reminders of a duty, expressing the desire of the speaker, which can often be seen as a desire of the addressee, since compliance means conforming to one's duties. Should we then conclude that what we really have here is a sex-based power difference? Such a claim cannot be justified for two reasons. First, when the host is a man, imperatives are also used. For example:

> [among male friends]
> ... konjak.   fere   konjak   [KE 3: 105]
> ... cognac.   bring some   cognac

These imperatives then appear to express role-dependent duties rather than sex-dependent ones, although the fact that it is mainly women who act as 'hosts' makes them appear to be receiving most of this kind of imperative. Secondly, imperatives are reciprocally used, whereas in situations where there are power differences we would not expect this kind of reciprocity. Power-based imperatives are employed downwards but not upwards, and clearly this is not the case here. For example:

> Male: fere   to konjak   [E 3: 123]
>   bring   the cognac
> Female: δoz' mu ki emena
>   give me too

Ervin-Tripp (1981: 195) makes a similar point, namely that 'explicit imperatives occurred more often than modal questions like "could you . . ." to familiar peers doing expected tasks, close at hand,' and adds that 'the form taken to realize the act, then, captures some of the social properties of the interaction too'. Stubbs (1983: 161) also points out that there is an important relationship between the verbal act performed and the social role of the speaker, and concludes that 'the correct interpretation of the illocutionary force, therefore, depends both on the linguistic form of the utterance, and also on an understanding of the social network'. His point concerns mainly the authority status of speakers, but, I believe, it is valid here, too.

The verbal behaviour delineated above is clearly related to Goffman's (1967) notion of 'free goods'. By this, he means those material goods which can be used by another person without special permission. This notion can be extended to cover goods which can be seen as not exclusively belonging to the addressee; in other words, goods which can be easily shared where asking for them does not constitute a great imposition on the addressee. In Greek, such goods can be obtained without even asking. 'Generally speaking, what an individual regards as "free goods" varies according to relationships and situation. . . . Cross-culturally, too, perceptions of what constitutes "free" or "nearly free" goods differ' (Thomas, 1983: 105). Thus, the forms more frequently used among Greek friends in such situations tend to be past imperatives. Consequently, it is understandable that requests like,

ftjakse	enan kafe!	[S 4: 41]
make	a coffee!	

δose mu	ta tsiɣara!	[S 4: 42]
give me	the cigarettes!	

will be frequent in Greek, but rather inappropriate in English. We have already seen that this kind of directness does not imply impoliteness, and we could test this by employing very elaborate indirect forms in cases in which something simpler and more direct is expected. Our prize for being 'more polite' will be strange looks, teasing comments about our linguistic innovations, frustrated questions of the sort *what's wrong?*; or we might even cause a breach in the relationship. Over-politeness can also be insulting (Brown and Levinson, 1978: 234).

I am not suggesting that imperatives are the only appropriate requesting configurations in such contexts, but rather that more direct, less elaborate forms are preferred in Greek versus English. To share 'small' goods in Greece is seen as a kind of social obligation, and everybody willingly and subconsciously conforms to this and expects everybody else to do the same. This attitude appears to be similar to the Wolof logic of etiquette reported by Hymes (1986: 79). 'For a large number of possible everyday requests, the Wolof view is that participants in situations are entitled to make them in relation to what is evident in the surrounding context. . . . If there is coffee, you are entitled to some; ask for it directly.'

As has been discussed in section 2.5.1, Greek in-group relationships tend to be closer than those in England. 'Both food-sharing and T-exchange are intimate behaviours' (Levinson, 1978: 23; Brown and Levinson, 1987: 45). Thus, entirely different choices of politeness strategies seem to be involved in the two cultures, because what constitutes 'small' things and the extent to which these can be shared differ in the two cultures—they are more face-threatening acts in England, less or even not face-threatening in Greece. Consequently, the English appear to decide between not committing the face-threatening activity at all and using elaborate negative politeness or off-record constructions, whereas the Greeks appear to prefer more direct positive politeness or off-record constructions.

We could then justifiably claim that the frequency with which imperative request constructions are employed in English and Greek in such contexts reflects the different conceptions of what politeness is; this in turn depends on differing social norms which determine social roles, rights, and duties as well as a different conception of the accessibility to goods belonging to others. What is in question is not politeness as such, but an understanding of what is considered to be socially appropriate in the culture (Wierzbicka, 1985a: 154). To be able to make correct judgements and reach valid conclusions 'one has to know the social structure in which the forms of utterance occur and the cultural values which inform that structure' (Hymes, 1986: 80).

Brown and Levinson (1978) draw a distinction between 'optimistic' and 'pessimistic' ways of performing face-threatening activities and point out that this is perhaps the most important difference between positive and negative politeness ways of performing face-threatening acts. They elaborate on this by saying that 'such optimistic expressions of FTAs seem to work by minimizing the size of the face threat . . . implying that it's nothing to ask (or offer, etc.) or that the cooperation between S and H means that such small things can be taken for granted' (ibid.: 131).

Thus, imperatives can be seen as devices indicating optimism that the addressee is willing to carry out the act requested by the speaker. This kind of presumed willingness and co-operation springs from the social rule which prescribes it as the duty or even obligation of every individual to help others, thus creating the opportunity for everybody to live in a harmonious in-group. The preference for imperative requesting constructions is, I believe, partial justification for the claim made earlier that Greeks tend to resort to positive politeness devices while the English tend to resort to more negative politeness devices.

However, in discussing the degree of politeness encoded in particular constructions, one should not forget the importance of the modification these constructions accept. Although theoretically the two can be separated, in actual encounters they usually occur and function together. Modification is discussed extensively in Chapter 7, thus, suffice it to say that in both Greek and English imperative requests are mitigated, but with different softening devices, which clearly reflect different values, and, more specifically, different kinds of politeness.

6.2 INTERROGATIVES

As has been pointed out in section 5.3, requests are not associated with interrogative forms in Greek to the extent that they are in English. An instance of this is a set of common, rather formal requests, which are declarative in Greek but would be better rendered as interrogatives in English. These contain *parakalo* 'please', 'request', or 'plead' used performatively:

> θa sas parakalusa, ean δen to χriazosaste,
> would you please, if you do not need it,
> na mu to δanisete.   [Q 10: S.2]
> to lend it to me?

In both languages, interrogative requests can range from simple to elaborate interrogative constructions. The main formal difference between Greek and English common, everyday interrogative requests is that in English there is a stronger preference for more elaborate constructions with modals, whereas in Greek they are

very frequently formulated with present indicative or past subjunctive
constructions:

mu pjanis   ti feta   ap' eki?   [P 2: 31]
do you catch (give) me   the feta (cheese)   from there?

na anikso   to paraθiro?   [NB]
may I open   the window?

would you mind posting this for me please?   [NB]

The main question which arises is what is it that allows the present
indicative to be used so frequently with direct requests in Greek,
but not in English. In English we have the continuous present tense,
which usually describes what is happening at the time of speaking,
and the simple present, which indicates habitual action. In Greek,
there is only one present tense, whose range of meanings
encompasses those covered by the two English present tenses. It
may be the clear difference in meaning between the two English
present tenses which makes them unacceptable for use as requests,
because while one may request people to do things more or less
immediately, one would hardly request an action which is already
in progress or occurs habitually, in the same way that we would not
knowingly request an action that has already been done.

A more plausible interpretation of this difference may be a
contrast in the speakers' need to distance themselves from acts
which can be viewed as encoding peremptory behaviour. The
indicative expresses a certainty and/or a reality, whereas the
subjunctive expresses the unreal. Similarly, both past and future
tenses express non-actuality and thus mark situations distant from
the speaker's deictic centre (Fleischman, 1989: 9). The English
speaker then seems to be enabled to soften the directness and
assertiveness of face-threatening acts by shifting the focus away
from present reality. By contrast, Greek speakers do not need this
kind of distancing to the same extent so that present indicative
constructions are appropriate requesting means. In other words, it
seems that we have a differential preference for involvement versus
detachment.

Anijis to paraθiro? could be translated literally in English as 'are
you opening the window?' or 'do you open the window?' and *mu
δinis ena tsiɣaro?* as 'are you giving me a cigarette?' or 'do you give
me a cigarette?' These are perfectly acceptable and indeed very

frequent requesting constructions in Greek, but not in English, and literal translations cannot render this force. In English, if such constructions are used, they will sound like questions for information about a habitual action, or about one in progress, and as such it is extremely difficult, if at all possible, to think of an appropriate context where they could be used as requests. We will have to resort to modals to render the above constructions in English. Thus, *anijis to paraθiro?* can be *can/could you open the window?* This is a conventionalized structure and, at least theoretically, leaves more choice to the addressee than an unmodified direct question.

Tentativeness and lack of commitment are English cultural values, and obviously explicit, simple present tense questions apparently do not sound tentative or pessimistic enough to be regarded as appropriate requesting means, whereas modals offer this possibility. It is the notion of tentativeness conveyed through conditionals, which renders them more polite than corresponding indicatives lacking this feature. Present indicative constructions may be used as requests in English only when they are negatively phrased and are followed by a question tag, or when they are indirect, that is, when their requesting force is implicit. For example:

you don't have a pen, do you?	[NB]
are you making coffee?	[NB]

Thus, the necessary tentativeness, which leaves more options open to the addressee, is offered through other means.

Question directives, as Ervin-Tripp (1976) calls the simple yes/no questions with possible directive force, are very often ambiguous, suggesting either a question for information or a directive; moreover, in most cases 'there is a substantial possibility that the listener cannot comply' (ibid. 40). On the other hand, imbedded imperatives, although also potentially ambiguous, are more often than not understood as requests since the acts requested are more clearly within the choice of the addressee.

Here, we need to distinguish two types of simple yes/no questions with possible requesting force: explicit or direct and implicit or indirect. For example:

mu δinis	ena molivi?	[NB]
do you give me	a pencil?	

exis	ena molivi?	[NB]
do you have	a pencil?	

In the first example, the desired act is explicit and the speaker appears optimistic that the addressee has got a pencil and will be willing to lend it, so there is no ambiguity involved. It is clearly and directly a question directive. In the second example, the speaker sounds more tentative and rather pessimistic as to the outcome of the request. This second example may be interpreted ambiguously either as a question for information or as a question directive. The addressee who may not wish to comply is thus offered a clearer escape route to respond negatively to an assumed information question. English social norms of politeness do not allow the first type of construction at all—the force of the imposition would be too great to be acceptable. By contrast, in Greek, this is one of the conventionalized, most frequent means of request. The second construction can function as a request in Greek, but there is a more literal ring to it.

Are the English then more considerate towards the addressee and, thus, more polite since they minimize impositions by leaving more options when they ask others to do things for them? Such a suggestion cannot be justified. Although whimperatives sound more tentative and less of an imposition, they are conventionalized, which means that although they appear to leave more choice to the addressee, in actual fact, unless a substantial, real, or contrived reason is presented, one cannot refuse to comply any more easily than the Greek who receives a more direct question directive. Here again, the differential preference between Greek and English interrogative requests seems to stem from the concept of imposition. In Greek, 'small' everyday tasks are seen as less or not at all imposing and can be requested with more direct constructions, especially between familiars and equals. Whimperatives and present tense indirect questions are utilized in situations of real uncertainty or in cases where there is distance between the interlocutors. By contrast, in similar contexts in English, whimperatives are the conventionalized means for requesting, and indirect present tense questions are saved for cases of greater uncertainty.

Thus, the conventionalized interrogative request forms in Greek point to a positive politeness society, whereas those in English point to a negative politeness society, where social norms restrict the appropriateness of directness.

Why-interrogatives in both languages are questions asking for reasons:

> to paraθiro . . .   to paraθiro   jati to klisate?   [KA 3: 259]
> the window . . .   the window   why did you shut it?

In certain contexts this might be understood as an indirect request to open the window again, but it would more often than not be understood as a literal question, with a hint of criticism, or a suggestion. Criticism is more obvious with *why*-negative-interrogative constructions. For example:

> jati δe me proseχis   pu   su milao?   [P 1: 34]
> why don't you listen to me   since I am talking to you?

Why-constructions can also imply sympathy in appropriate contexts:

> ela tora,   maritsa, jati kles?   [MN 1: 55]
> come on now,   Maritsa, why are you crying?

Green (1975: 128–9) distinguishes 'intentional hints', such as *why aren't you quiet?*; 'unintentional clues', such as *why aren't you cooking dinner? It's 8.30*; and true orders or requests, such as *why don't you cook dinner? It's 8.30*. Literal equivalents for these in Greek could be questions or suggestions, sometimes with critical intention. It appears that, in Greek, *why*-questions could be used as requests on very rare occasions. Perhaps the fact that there are more structural possibilities for expressing requests has excluded *why*-questions from the requesting function. *Why*-questions cannot function as requests in Polish (Wierzbicka, 1985a). Thus, it would appear that Fraser, Rintell, and Walters (1980: 79) are wrong in claiming that the requesting strategy illustrated in English by the question *why don't you do that now?* is a requesting strategy which is shared by all other languages.

Thus far, we have observed that apart from these present indicative requests, imperative forms offer a wider range of possibilities in Greek than in English. However, there are also periphrastic forms considered to be remnants of the optative (these are outside my immediate area of study), and the past subjunctive[3]

---

[3] Arguments have been advanced against the existence of a distinct subjunctive mood in modern Greek (Lightfoot, 1979). Even if we accept that there are no inflectional differences between the indicative and the subjunctive in Modern Greek,

to which forms of request I shall now address myself. Consider the following examples:

> na kano   ena tilefonima?   [NB]
> can I make   a phone call?

> na peraso   liγo?   [NB]
> can I go through   a little?

The Greek subjunctive is 'marked' for mood (Lyons, 1968: 307)[4] and can be seen as equivalent to constructions with modals in English. By using the subjunctive the speaker expresses a desire or need and asks whether the addressee agrees or not. These are permission requests, which in English require the modals *can* or *may*. In Greek *boro* 'can' could be used here to indicate formality. For example,

> boro   na kano   ena tilefonima?
> can   I make   a phone call?

or more elaborately and formally,

> θa borusa   na kano   ena tilefonima?
> could   I make   a phone call?

In even more formal contexts the verb *epitrepo* 'permit' could also be used. For example:

> mu epitrepete   na kano ena tilefonima?
> do you permit me   to make a phone call?

It should be noted here that, as is the case with imperatives, the present/past tense distinction specifies aspect rather than time. Thus, the past subjunctive does not indicate any distancing in the past, but rather views the act as a completed whole.

Subjunctives can have a variety of functions and meanings (Pavlidou, 1986). They can function as commands, as in *na pas* 'go', which can be a suggestion or a command rather than a request. Imperative requests can also be reported or repeated in the subjunctive, especially when preceded by the reporting verb: for

---

the particles *na* and *as* and the negative particle *mi(n)* are distinct markers of the subjunctive which carry semantic differences (Veloudis and Philippaki-Warburton, 1983; Philippaki-Warburton and Veloudis, 1984).

[4] Although Lyons does not refer specifically to the Greek subjunctive, his comments apply.

instance *anikse to paraθiro* 'open the window' becomes *ipa na aniksis to paraθiro* 'I said that you open the window'; however, the force has also changed from a request to a command. As we have noted earlier, there is an affinity between the imperative and the subjunctive in Greek in that they can both express a command, wish, or desire. There is, however, an element of doubt and uncertainty sometimes implicit in subjunctives which is absent from imperatives. This explains why 'token tags' such as *ti les* and *e*, meaning roughly 'do you agree?' or 'did you hear?', may be more easily used with subjunctives than with imperatives. For example:

> na mas γrafis, e?
> [will] that you write to us, OK?

Another interesting difference between subjunctive and imperative constructions is that whereas imperatives imply a certain immediacy, subjunctive constructions imply lack of any such immediacy (Veloudis, 1987). This explains, among other things, why certain formulaic expressions utilize imperative constructions and not subjunctives and accords with Fleischman's (1989) observations that subjunctives mark a shift to an unreal, hypothetical, and more distant world. It is true and compatible with the above observations that requests utilizing subjunctive constructions sound a little more formal than those with imperatives, but appear less formal than other constructions (Pavlidou, 1986). Nevertheless, this is difficult to judge with any precision because imperatives involve the addressee in the action, whereas subjunctives usually involve the speaker.

Thus, it appears that Greek and English differ significantly in the classes of conventionalized interrogative requests. In English, there is no way one can use present indicative to say politely *do you open the window?* or *are you opening the window?* as a request; one could only imagine it to be a threatening, impolite request of the reverse activity.[5] Nor is there the possibility of employing the subjunctive to express requests, which must, therefore, be conveyed by the use of modals.

---

[5] Similar to Greek, Italian also employs a more flexible system for interrogative requests (Bates, 1976).

6.2.1 Modals

'*Mood*, like tense, is frequently realized by inflecting the verb or by modifying it by means of "auxiliaries"' (Lyons, 1968: 307). The English mood system is not inflectionally elaborate enough to accommodate the variety of attitudes a speaker needs to express; consequently, an elaborate system of modals has been developed to make up for this 'deficiency'. By contrast, in Greek the modal system is not developed to the same extent (*may* and *can* are both rendered as *boro* and *will* is a particle rather than a modal), since the inflectionally marked mood system is richer.

However, modals are mainly used to introduce interrogative requests in both languages. Most common are those concerning the addressee's ability to perform the action, that is, *can* in English and *boro* in Greek. An alternative corresponding to *are you able to* does not exist in Greek. The past tense *borusa* 'could' cannot be used to introduce requests, because it can only refer to the ability to perform an action in the past and that is incompatible with the requesting function. What is used to mark the request as more polite or formal is the conditional form *θa borusa*, roughly meaning 'I would be able to'. Thus, it seems that distancing in the direction of the past is unacceptable, unless it is through a conditional. For example:

> boro/*borusa/θa borusa   na anikso to paraθiro?
> can/could/would I be able to open the window?

In Greek, the present tense *boro* is conventionally used to introduce requests, especially when there is lack of familiarity, when the requested action is seen as beyond the socially acceptable duties of the addressee, or when a special ability for the performance of the request is involved. The conditional *θa borusa* sounds more formal and, as such, is saved for cases in which there are status differences or where the imposition is considered to be more than the minimal. In most situations in English either *can* or *could* can be used, although *could* is considered to be more polite since past tense modals indicate a hypothetical action (Leech, 1983: 121). Their equivalent forms *will/would be able* to have not been conventional-ized and, as such, they are less appropriate to introduce requests. Sadock (1974) actually argues that such forms cannot be requests at all.

Leech (1983: 70) points out that *can/could* requests appear to be more polite than the *will/would* ones because the addressee can more easily decline by alleging inability rather than unwillingness. The same is true in Greek, where *boro* 'can' requests have been conventionalized as requesting realizations, which is not true of the future tense of most other verbs. In English, ability questions have been so conventionalized as polite requests that native speakers are more likely to interpret them as requests than as questions of ability. Although this has been assumed to be a universal feature of ability questions (Fraser, Rintell, and Walters, 1980), this is not completely true for French and Russian (Thomas, 1983: 101).

In Greek, as we have seen, *may* does not exist as a separate form while in English, in contrast to *can*, it cannot be employed for requests with *you* (Green, 1975: 134). On the other hand, in affirmative constructions *might* can be employed, as in *you might pay this bill for me*, but only in very friendly exchanges; otherwise, it would sound rude and reproachful.

Will and *shall* have only one realization in Greek, the particle *θa*, which does not show the same flexibility as its equivalents in English. The simple future tense can occasionally be used with requests in Greek, but usually has overtones of prior unwillingness to conform. When the future is used, it is mainly in the indicative simple question form, but not in the continuous or in the conditional. For example:

θa aniksis   to para*θ*iro?
will you open   the window?

*θa anijes/*θa anijis   to para*θ*iro?
would you open   the window?

However, in English, *would you . . .?* questions are conventionalized for polite requests.[6]

The modal *prepi* 'must' cannot be used with requests either in Greek or in English (Green, 1975: 135). It expresses necessity or obligation so it is quite incompatible with requests; nevertheless, it is more appropriate than *may* or *should* for offers, as Lakoff (1972) argues. Moreover, she emphasizes the importance modals play in

---

[6] In Polish (Wierzbicka, 1985a) *would you . . .* questions sound odd and amusing as requests, and in ·Russian (Thomas, 1983) they would most probably be interpreted as genuine questions about the addressee's preferences rather than requests.

the expression of English politeness by noting that the use of modals in English is governed by the same assumptions of politeness which govern the use of honorifics in the languages which exhibit such systems.

6.3 NEGATIVES

Negative constructions in general have a more restricted distribution than their positive counterparts and constitute different speech acts (Givon, 1978). In requests, negatives are not very common, and are less so in Greek than in English. They are usually used when what is intended is that the addressee should avoid or stop the performance of an action, situations in which the positive requests would perhaps sound more abrupt. Negatives express a corrective intention on the part of the speaker rather than a new desire; for example:

> min   anavis   to fos   [AN 1: 73]
> don't   turn on the light
>
> please don't do that. Don't switch the lights on,
> please   [PL 1: 11]

They are more frequently employed in tense situations and can be easily interpreted as commands or threats.

> kleopatra, mi me eksoθis   os t'akra   [MR 2: 38]
> Kleopatra, don't push me   too far
>
> don't keep on about it   [B 2: 58]

Tension may be either positive or negative; thus, negatives may also be used appropriately to express sympathetic advice and even begging; for example:

> Oh, don't get upset. There's no point   [PN 3: 183]
> ... min kles,   staθi mu ...   peδi mu ...   min kles
> ... don't cry, my Stathis ... my child ... don't cry
>   [MN 1: 24]

In English, unlike Greek, we can find negative constructions as indirect requests:

I suppose you wouldn't lend me your new shirt . . .   [Q 1: S 5]

I wouldn't mind another drink.   [SR 2: 65]

In Greek, the former cannot be a request and the latter could only be an answer to an offer, as for instance *δe θa leγa oχi* 'I wouldn't say no' as a response to *θa 'θeles liγo akomi?* 'would you like a bit more?'

What is found more frequently in Greek, as well as in English, are interrogative-negative constructions:

jani, δen pas   na feris tin turta?   [E 1: 43]
Jani, don't you go to bring the cake?

In English, this might be better rendered as a *why not* or *won't you* request. What is negatively phrased here is not the actual request, but its opener. Green's (1975: 137) claim that *won't you close the window, please* is a more polite request than *will you close the window, please* does not hold for Greek. The former can be used without *please* as a reprimand for the addressee's failure to perform the action, because he or she had been told before or should have known better. In Greek, negative-interrogative constructions in the present tense such as *δen klinis to paraθiro* 'don't you close the window' can be used as suggestions or reprimands rather than requests.

English interrogative-negative constructions are almost always followed by a question tag:

you wouldn't seriously think of leaving us, would you?

                                                      [OS 1: 28]

I don't suppose you've got anything you could give me, have you?   [Q 35: S 1]

you won't ring this girl, will you?   [OR 2: 98]

Ervin-Tripp (1976: 39) contends that 'we know very little about the social distribution of the negative forms, but would expect that they might occur, like statements, under conditions when leaving the maximum choice to the listener to refuse may be important'. Stubbs (1983: 113) associates this provision of choice with politeness and asserts that negative constructions are often used to mark politeness in discourse, as in a shop assistant's request for change, *You wouldn't have anything smaller I don't suppose?* Such a request form strongly predicts that the answer will be *no*, makes a rejection of the request easier and, therefore, does not put the customer on the spot. Such examples, common in English, cannot be rendered in Greek. The nearest equivalents would be an interrogative *(mipos) exete psila?* 'do you perhaps have change' or an interrogative-negative construction, *δen exete kaθolu psila?* 'don't you have any change at all?'

In other cases, however, where similar constructions are used, the assumption is conventional rather than real:

> you couldn't rustle something up for me. I am starving.
>
> [Q 50: S 1]

The fact that this negative form is followed by a colloquial expression seems to provide further evidence for the conventionality of the assumption, since it implies familiarity. Furthermore, such a request can hardly be expected in situations where there is no familiarity. All this points to only a marginal possibility of the addressee's refusal. In the shop assistant example, a customer who does not have any smaller change cannot really be held responsible for inability to comply with the request; but in the last example, an addressee who cannot or does not want to offer the speaker some food that he or she presumably has will appear to be uncooperative. In this case, the addressee would have to produce strong reasons for non-compliance, whereas in the first case *sorry* in English and a *no* response in Greek would be sufficient.

In what sense then are these negative constructions more polite? One might argue that they are less polite because the speakers make negative assumptions about the addressees and simultaneously place them under even greater obligation to comply. Thus, the point here seems to be the extent to which the speaker is allowed by social conventions to make assumptions about the inability of the addressee to conform. 'Negative questions are sometimes polite whimperatives and, in other cases, rather impolite' (Green, 1975: 137). They are polite only in the sense that they are pessimistic, reflecting Brown and Levinson's (1978: 179) contention that 'encodings of polite pessimism in English are found in negative usages'. This kind of pessimism is a polite device used in negative politeness societies. For instance, in Korean and Japanese 'a question is more polite when phrased negatively' (Applegate, 1975: 275).

In both Greek and English there is a set of negative questions, those which presume a *yes* answer, which can function as a positive politeness device in that these indicate that the speaker knows the addressee's tastes, wants, and so on. These, however, are offers, expressions of opinion, etc., rather than requests, as Brown and Levinson (1978: 127) point out. For example:

> wouldn't you like something to drink?
>
> isn't it a gorgeous day?

6.4 DECLARATIVES

The declarative is another formal variant which can function as a request in both languages. Declaratives fall into two main groups: 'hints' and 'need statements'. 'Hints' perform the requesting function indirectly; that is, their surface structure does not easily reveal their force, as discussed in section 5.2.2. Sometimes great effort is required by the addressee to understand the speaker's actual intention, and an outsider may not even realize that a request has been made. This can obviously lead to misunderstandings, as well as to teasing and joking. On the whole, however, such requests are considered polite in that they leave options open to the addressees to interpret them in the way they wish, so that they do not feel compelled to conform to something they do not want to do.

Some of these hints—for instance, *it's cold in here*—are so conventionalized that they require no extra effort to be understood as requests than do their more direct equivalents; nevertheless, even here the addressees might have to think a bit about what exactly they are expected to do. As Ervin-Tripp (1976: 48) suggests: 'there is a variation in the extent to which questions and hints have become routinized by experience in the particular social group'.

On the other hand, 'need statements' are very direct; the speaker's intention or desire is explicitly stated:

> I'd like some more wine. [PN 3: 250]
>
> θα 'θελα   ena potiri nero [Z 4: 66]
> I would want [I'd like]   a glass of water
>
> Come on, Alexei . . . you can spare a moment. I need some
>   help. [PL 2: 69]

. . . mana,   θelo   na su miliso!   [MN 1: 50]
. . . mother,   I want   to talk to you!

In English, *I'd like* is a conventionalized way of stating a desire, the *would* enhancing the unreal and hypothetical. The verbs *need* and *want* are not conventionalized and are usually avoided since they sound too direct to be polite. In Greek, the verb θelo 'want' is a frequent way of introducing requests of this sort. The same is true of Hebrew, where 'want statements' are usually phrased as *I want you to do (x)* (Blum-Kulka, 1987: 138). In Greek, the verb θelo is often used in the conditional future, or even in the past, that is, *(θa) (i)θela*, literally 'I (will) wanted', which is equivalent to the conventionalized *I'd like* in English. The full conditional form is more formal than the past.

The most explicit, that is, the less elaborate of these are frequently used by children (Ervin-Tripp, 1976). Such simple requesting declaratives also tend to be used within families in Greek since a lot of shared knowledge and solicitude among members is taken for granted. For example:

θa iθela   na mu ton feris   [Q 17: S 4]
I would want you   to bring it for me

θa iθela   na tsibiso kati   [Q 35: S 1]
I would want [I'd like]   to nibble something

A requesting declarative among close friends and relatives may also assume other forms besides constructions with θelo 'want'. Since subjunctive, and more frequently indicative constructions can have requesting force in Greek, they are sometimes used in the declarative rather than in the interrogative form. As Mackridge (1985: 126) points out, 'the imperfective non-past is very commonly used to express a polite request, normally (but not always) enunciated as a question'. For example:

na sas akuo   ki eγo   parakalo   [Z 1: 121]
[I'd like] to hear you too   please

θa foreso   to pukamiso su   [Q 31: S 5]
I will wear your shirt

perno   ena tsiγaro,   pjanu ine?   [NB]
I am having a cigarette,   whose are they?

The fact that *parakalo* 'please' in Greek is literally a verb enables it to introduce declarative requests used either in the present tense or in the conditional. For example:

. . . parakalo . . .	parakalo	na kanete pjo
. . . please (come on)	please (come on)	(to) fix more
eksotiko	to makijiaz tu aleku	[MN 2: 35]
exotically	the make-up of Alekos	

θa sas parakalusa	na erχeste	stin ora sas	[NB]
would you please	that you come	on time	

Such constructions, however, which involve the verb *parakalo* 'please' are used in more formal contexts.

Second person affirmative subjunctive forms are also used as requests to express the wish or desire of the speaker, cases in which imperatives are usually used in English. For example:

na mas	γrafis
that you	write to us

Related to this is the usage of subjunctives as formulaic wishes in Greek, whereas in English imperatives are employed. For example:

na zisete (wish to newly weds)
[may] that you live a long life

na sas zisi (wish to parents of a newborn baby)
[may] that it live to you

na perasete kala
[may] that you have a nice time
have a nice time

Declarative requests are also found in office settings. Here, they are used among colleagues since specific personal responsibilities are usually beyond question. In English, they are frequently used by superiors to subordinates (Ervin-Tripp, 1976). Although this is true in Greek, they are also used by customers and clients in shops and offices, where it is not always clear who is superior. Here, it is the setting which facilitates the occurrence of such statements. The logic behind such use is that the customers are there to be helped and, thus, have to state their need directly. For example:

I'd like your autograph   [PG 1: 33]

θa iθela   ena pistopiitiko jeniseos
I would like   a birth certificate

They may also be used by clerks and/or doctors in giving instructions about what the customer/patient has to do. For example:

na mu ferete   ena pistopiitiko
[you should] that to me you bring   a certificate
ja to ɣnisio   tis ipoɣrafis   [P 2: 57]
to authenticate   the signature

I want a urine sample in that jar   [PG 1: 38]

Such declarative requests can be viewed as answers to a real or hypothetical question such as *what would you like?*.

6.5   ELLIPTICAL CONSTRUCTIONS

Besides the full grammatical constructions discussed so far, we can also have elliptical ones, that is, cases in which a part of the request is not explicitly stated but is understood either from the linguistic or the extra-linguistic context of the ongoing encounter, or from the knowledge participants share. Ervin-Tripp (1976: 30) says that 'in situations where the necessary action is obvious, it is common to produce elliptical forms specifying only the new information—the direct or indirect object'. She gives the example of a customer asking the waiter for *Coffee, black*. However, these types of utterances may also be interpreted as answers to explicit or implicit requests for service, such as *what would you like?* As such, they have been conventionalized as requests, in the absence of the initial question, and answers are usually elliptical to avoid unnecessary repetition. As Hymes (1986: 66) suggests, service encounters present a direct linguistic interest, 'because a logically expected part may so often be omitted and implied'.

Ellipsis appears to fall into three broad categories related to the structure of the utterance, not just one as Ervin-Tripp (1976) seems to assume. The first concerns utterances in which the verb is missing; the remaining part can be a noun, an adjective, or adverb, depending on the verb omitted, and can be modulated in the same way as full requests:

[husband to wife at home]
maria,   ena maksilar*aki*   [E 1: 12]
Maria, [bring]   a cushion-*dim.*

[at a restaurant]
garson   δjo kila arni   se parakalo   [P 2: 34]
waiter [bring]   two kilos of lamb   please

[husband to wife at home]
quiet! give the lad a chance   [OR 1: 46]

[at a restaurant]
... waiter! another bottle of Corvo Bianco ...   [PN 3: 250]

In the above examples, a verb is missing. It is usually a verb like *bring, be, wait, speak* or *give*. This kind of ellipsis appears to occur mainly in service encounters, such as in restaurants and garages, and also in in-group encounters such as those at home among close friends and relatives where it indicates shared knowledge. Thus, the verb appears to be redundant since the new information is sufficient in itself. This explains why verb ellipsis is also used in cases of emergency:

[in the street after an accident]
ena asθenoforo!   t' asθenoforo.   [AN 1: 80]
[call] an ambulance!   the ambulance.

A second category of ellipsis involves utterances with the noun object missing; for example:

[wife to husband]
... δoz' mu ena   [S 2: 14]
... give me one [cigarette]

[between friends]
put them in water [the flowers]   [B 1: 51]

Noun ellipsis with requests seems to be more common in Greek than in English. In the above examples, the noun missing is recoverable from either the linguistic or extra-linguistic context. Brown and Yule (1983: 175) discuss this phenomenon in recipes in English. They say that the writers select a ' "topic entity" for a sequence of events within a sentence', and then they do not repeat that entity again in the same sentence. Recipes, of course, do not deal with single sentences, but with a group of utterances which constitute a speech act in Hymes's (1972c) terms. The closest phenomenon to noun ellipsis in English requests is that of co-reference, which is also found in Greek. In other words, nouns can be omitted, leaving a lexical item behind, usually a pronoun which acquires specific meaning by referring to something which has already been mentioned. It seems that in English it is more difficult to omit the object of a transitive verb. For example:

> [between sisters]
> krata   [AN 1: 26]
> hold [the glass]

The third sort of ellipsis concerns cases in which the performative verb *parakalo* roughly 'plead', or the politeness marker *please*, or even an address term are used alone or in combination. To be understood, such elliptical requests rely on what has been said before or on the shared knowledge of the participants. For example:

> [husband to wife's sister on an ongoing unpleasant
> conversation]
> alexandra!   [MR 1: 56]
> Alexandra!

These are usually used in emotionally loaded situations, and have the force of a plea or a threat.

Another case which might also be considered ellipsis in a broad sense, is that of a statement, which could be interpreted as a request; for example:

> [between friends]
> A: δen efera   pali tsiɣara   [NB]
>   I haven't brought again cigarettes
> B: δen pirazi,   eχo eɣo
>   it doesn't matter, I've got (enough)

Ellipsis appears to be related to repetition. The more repetition there is, the more the context becomes shared knowledge, and thus the importance of constructing complete utterances for full understanding is diminished (see also Tannen, 1983). For example:

> F: —... klise to   paraθiro   [AN 1: 8]
>   ... shut the   window

S: — ma kale   baba θa skasume
     but good (please)   father we'll suffocate
F: — ipa   klise!
     I said   shut!

Ellipsis appears to be more frequently employed in Greek than in English, and with a wider variety of possibilities. English has a predilection for elaborate requests, as has been shown, and this may have led to the restriction of elliptical forms, which probably sound too abrupt to be considered acceptable and polite. On the other hand, by using ellipsis the speaker gives the addressee a task to perform—that is, to fill in the gaps—and this acknowledges shared knowledge making the addressee a more active participant and possibly encouraging questions or clarification. Mackridge (1985: 342) contends that 'verbless sentences are far more common in Greek than in English, and are perfectly acceptable in written styles'. He also gives examples of idioms which depend on this facility of the language.[7]

Tannen (1983) also reports ellipsis as a frequent device in Greek and adds that a possible explanation for this is the regular use of non-verbal expression. This may be a valid hypothesis, but does not invalidate the observation that in most cultures, the more intimate and informal the relationships, the less precise and articulate the participants tend to be.

For Brown and Levinson (1987: 111) ellipsis is a positive politeness strategy, since the comprehensibility of an elliptical utterance depends on mutually shared knowledge. Moreover, shared pragmatic and cultural knowledge plays a significant role in the decoding of elliptical utterances and in the understanding of the problems that such utterances pose to non-native speakers (Kato, 1986: 418).

Another type of ellipsis is that involving incompleteness; in other words, the utterance is left unfinished. This is an off-record device, according to Brown and Levinson (1987: 227), deriving its high degree of politeness from the fact that the addressee is not actually requested to do something, but is left to decide how to react.

---

[7] Mackridge (1985: 342) states that in Greek the possibilities for ellipsis are narrower, because tenses and verb forms do not depend on auxiliaries so that the verb has to be repeated, as in θa fao psaria an θa fas ki esi 'I'll eat fish if you *will* [eat] (too)', (his example). However, this is a different kind of ellipsis called 'strict ellipsis' (see Kato, 1986: 417).

However, as we have already noted (see section 5.2.2), most off-record strategies can receive various interpretations. They may be used to indicate either that one does not want to impose on the addressee, leaving the options open for the addressee to decide how to interpret the utterance (negative politeness); or they may imply that the speaker and addressee are so close and share so much knowledge that completion of the utterance would appear redundant (positive politeness); furthermore, the addressee is given the opportunity to volunteer. Thus, for instance, the incomplete utterance *my car* . . . may lead a close friend conversant with specific contextual factors to offer a lift immediately, whereas somebody more distant will have to decide whether to interpret the utterance as a request for a lift or as a statement with which they might simply agree, go on to suggest that there is a taxi-rank nearby, and so on. Nevertheless, bearing in mind the extent to which Western cultures cherish 'elaborate explicitness', we cannot expect such elliptical constructions to be common to the extent they are favoured in Japan (Loveday, 1983: 181).

In this chapter an attempt has been made to examine the possible and conventionalized request constructions in Greek and in English. Although it appears that the constructions employed to make requests are similar, there are substantial differences. The striking one is the conventionalization of present indicative constructions in Greek, forms which are impossible as direct requests in English. Further differences relate to subjunctive and imperative constructions. Subjunctives are freely used in Greek, constructions which may be seen as roughly equivalent to those with modals in English. The more elaborate Greek system of imperatives renders them more appropriate for requests in Greek than in English. The different patterns available contribute to more straightforward requests in Greek, whereas the necessary use of modals in English contributes to more elaborate utterances. Moreover, the formal second person plural used to single addressees further restricts the need for elaboration in Greek. ' "You" (plural) can be understood as motivated by exactly the same wants that . . . account for conventional indirectness' (Brown and Levinson, 1978: 204).

7
Requests: Modification

7.1 INTRODUCTION

Although, as we have just seen, the form and function of requests vary considerably in English and Greek, it is commonly accepted that the force of a request does not depend solely, nor even mainly perhaps, on the construction employed. The kind of modification chosen is also a determining factor contributing greatly to the force of the utterance. Therefore, having discussed the possible and preferred request constructions in English and Greek we will proceed with the types of modification available, whose function is to soften or to intensify the impact of the request. These, too, reveal interesting differences related to politeness between the two societies. In other words, the speaker has to make a number of choices on various levels which have a cumulative effect on the result, and clearly this is not just a matter of linguistic knowledge. The speaker must also be equipped with socio-cultural knowledge along with context knowledge, and so on.[1]

The fact that in English intensifying devices are rarely used with requests (House and Kasper, 1981: 177) has perhaps led to an extensive study of softeners with requests, but not of intensifiers, or 'upgraders' as House and Kasper call them. The process of softening or mitigation is defined by Fraser (1978: 22) as 'the intentional softening or easing of the force of the message—a modulation of the basic message intended by the speaker'. Besides mitigation, however, intensification is also used with requests in Greek. It appears that aggressive verbal behaviour is, generally speaking, socially more acceptable in Greece than in England; such behaviour is related to the looser restrictions on the expression of feelings in Greece, as has already been pointed out.

Turning now to the kinds of modification that are present in requests, we should distinguish between 'internal' and 'external' modification. Internal modification is achieved by means of

[1] For a discussion of these types of knowledge see Faerch and Kasper (1984) and Keesing (1979).

linguistic elements within the same speech act which can either mitigate or intensify its force, whereas external modification is achieved by mitigating or intensifying devices which occur in the immediate linguistic context rather than in the speech act itself (Faerch and Kasper, 1984).

Internal modification can affect directly either one specific element of the speech act, such as the verb or the noun, or the whole act. Examples of internal modification could be items such as *a little*, *a bit*, *possibly*, and *sort of*. Internal intensifiers were found mostly in Greek but rarely in English. Further examples of internal modification are choices among different grammatical structures (e.g.: imperatives versus interrogatives), or tenses (e.g.: present versus past), as well as the addition of other elements, which I call 'fillers'. Although not semantically void in other contexts, these fillers become semantically void but remain pragmatically meaningful (see section 7.2.3).

Examples of external modification are various reinforcing devices which can appear in the form of separate short clauses or lexical items, which often contribute nothing to the meaning of the utterance (see section 7.3).

Figure 7.1 illustrates the kind of classification I have outlined so far. It is based on similar classifications by Edmondson (1981), House and Kasper (1981), and Blum-Kulka and Olshtain (1984), although it does differ from these in a number of respects.

7.2   INTERNAL MODIFICATION

7.2.1 *Openers*

For me, these are the opening words and expressions which seek or assume the addressee's co-operation, which express the speaker's gratitude or indebtedness, and which modify the request as a whole. However, I exclude modals since they have already been discussed (section 6.2.1). Examples of openers are *would you mind . . .?*, *I don't suppose . . .*, and *I would be grateful* in English, and in Greek *θa sas piraze . . .?* 'would you mind' and *θa sas xrostusa evγnomosini* 'I would be grateful'. These Greek expressions, especially in the plural, are used in cases where extra formality is needed or where the speaker feels that the addressee would indeed

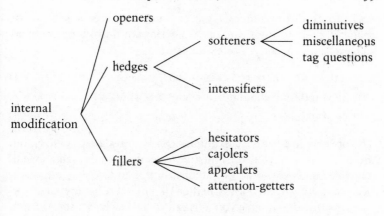

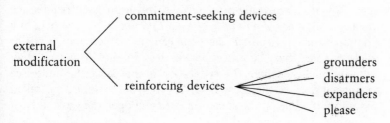

Fig. 7.1 Modification

mind performing what is requested. Such expressions usually initiate the request, although they can sometimes be tagged on to the end; for example:

> do you think you could open the window?
>
> could you open the window, do you think?

Some of them, when put at the end, take the form of if clauses, in which case, however, they become external modifiers:

> you wouldn't mind opening the window, would you?
>
> make me a cup of tea in the red mug, if you wouldn't mind, please   [NB]

From my data it is evident that these kinds of introductory items are much less frequently used in Greek than in English. This perhaps indicates that in English they represent a more conventionalized way of introducing requests, whereas in Greek they tend to retain their literal meaning, and as such do not introduce everyday requests so frequently. For example:

> is there any chance of a sandwich? [Q 6: S 1]
>
> do you think I could borrow your new shirt? [Q 18: S 5]
>
> do you think I could have a cigarette? [R 1: 14]

The openers in the above examples can be translated in Greek but are not conventionalized to introduce requests to the same extent. The first sentence would be rather insulting in Greek as a request, because asking somebody whether or not there is any chance— *iparχi periptosi*—to give you a 'small thing', such as a sandwich to eat, is a rather unacceptable way of requesting it. If, however, what is requested is something more serious, for instance, a friend's car, then *iparχi periptosi na mu δosis to aftokinito su . . .*' is there any chance of giving (lending) me your car . . .' is acceptable; but in such a case this initiating phrase has its literal rather than conventional meaning. The suggestion is that since the addressee may need the car, the speaker wishes to avoid making a mistaken assumption while, at the same time, leaving open the possibility of something being arranged.

As far as the second and third examples are concerned, the Greek verb for 'think' can be used only when there is cogitation involved. In other words, it is used to ask for the addressee's opinion, rather than to make the tentative request of its English counterpart. In Greek, the equivalent of the third example could only be used if the cigarettes did not belong to the addressee but to somebody else who was not present. What might be found in Greek, on occasions is the verb *leo* 'say', which in one idiomatic use means 'think of' rather than 'think', as in *leo na fiγo* 'I am thinking of leaving'. For example,

> ti les, na valo to pukamiso su?
>
> what do you say, [could] I wear your shirt?
>
> [Q 10: S 5]

although here again the speaker seems to be asking for the addressee's opinion.

Lakoff (1977: 83) says that in English such openers are pragmatically related to tags and 'do not describe an act of cogitation; rather they have a softening effect on the declarative illocutionary force of the sentence'. A similar point is made by Drazdauskiene (1981: 57), who states that such openers indicate a 'degree of personal involvement, diminished assurance and therefore courteous detachment and optional treatment of the subject matter'. This tendency to express things as tentatively as possible has led to an extensive use of negatively phrased openers, which are usually followed by a question tag. This tag, however, does not correspond structurally to the opener, but rather to the verb of the request which follows; for example:

> I don't suppose you could collect my books for me,   [NB] could you?

In both Greek and English, the negative *don't you think* sounds more like a reprimand. In Greek the only negatively phrased opener in my data was δe *mu les* . . .? 'don't you tell me . . .?', which asks for the addressee's opinion.

Although it is true that tentativeness helps the speaker sound less abrupt and consequently more considerate and courteous towards the addressee, this detachment from the subject matter and the lack of assurance, which reaches a peak with the use of negative constructions, cannot be positively valued in all societies. Furthermore, such openers imply social distance between interactants and the strong pessimism of the speaker about the outcome of the request, both of which features are again not universal. It is also noteworthy that openers can be used in situations in which people do not want to be courteous (Wierzbicka, 1985a: 161), or even in cases in which such expressions are absolutely redundant because extra-linguistic factors make them unnecessary.

The verbs which are found as introductory items in Greek, but not in English, are θ*imame* 'remember' or its negative counterpart *kseχno* 'forget' in appropriate contexts. For example:

> θimisu (imp.) / θa θimiθis (fut.)   na mu paris   ena
> remember   / will you remember   that you buy me   one
>
> min   kseχasis   na mu ton paris   [Q 57: S 3]
> don't   forget   that you buy it for me

The difference between the verb *remember* versus *think* or *mind* is that if the request is not executed, the requestee cannot be held entirely responsible for the outcome; that is, the addressee might have been willing but may simply have forgotten to carry out the request. It is interesting to note that this kind of opener was found in Greek with requests to mothers to buy a magazine (see Appendix II/2, S.4); that is, to older people, who may be more prone to forgetting, an implication which might be insulting for an English mother.

A few verbs, such as *exo* 'have' and *θelo* 'want', can be used in the conditional to introduce requests:

θa iχes	kati	na mu δosis?	[Q 52: S 1]
would you have	something	to give me? (to eat)	

These verbs are used with a variety of expressions concerning the addressee's kindness or willingness to perform the act. They are, however, saved for circumstances in which either there is some degree of social distance or the act is seen as falling beyond the addressee's normal duties:

θaχes[2]   tin kalosini na mu paris
would you have   the kindness that you buy me
tsiγara ...?   [Q 26: S 6]
cigarettes ...?

The verbs *χrosto* 'owe' and *ipoχreono* 'oblige' can also be used in the conditional as openers with requests in fixed expressions like *θa me ipoχreones* 'you would oblige me' and *θa su χrostusa evγnomosini* 'I would owe you gratefulness'. In the singular, these can be used among friends when the imposition is seen as great. In the plural they also express formality. Similar constructions can be found in English where they can be seen as negative politeness devices in that the speakers, attempting to minimize the imposition, explicitly state their indebtedness to the addressees (Brown and Levinson, 1978: 215). Is this then a negative politeness strategy used in a positive politeness society? It may be, although it can also be seen as an example of a 'hybrid strategy' which is the result of a combination of positive and negative politeness elements (ibid. 235).

The notion of obligation definitely deserves investigation, but intuitively it appears to be basic to the Greek politeness system. Many routines in daily life are called 'social obligations'. Very

---

[2] *θaχes* is a contracted form of *θa iχes* 'you would have'.

often, instead of or along with thanking expressions, Greeks use expressions which involve the concepts of debt and obligation, such as *sas ime ipoχreos* 'I am obliged to you', *meno ipoχreos* 'I remain obliged', or *epifilasome* 'I owe you'. The expression *ipoχreosi mu* 'my obligation' is an appropriate, though rare, response to thanks. This sense of obligation may be of a different type and not as strong as it is in Japan or India,[3] but it appears to play a significant role in everyday exchanges, where minimization of the imposition is achieved by a kind of implicit or explicit promise on the part of the speaker to conform to the socially determined duty to reciprocate the benefit. This may have led to the restriction of overt thanking and apologizing expressions in Greek compared to English because they seem to be interpreted as attempts to eschew the obligation to behave in the expected manner, and thus, as ways of distancing oneself from the in-group.

What is also used in Greek as an introductory item is *mipos*, a kind of *wh*-word, roughly meaning 'perhaps', 'by any chance', or 'I wonder'. In this sense, it is a dubitative marker, a tentativizer used with both questions and requests (in question form only), when the speaker is not sure whether the requested item or information is available, or whether the requestee is able to perform the action, and so on; that is, it suspends the preparatory conditions for the request rather than any other felicity conditions. It is used as a politeness marker when there is social distance between the interlocutors, but not usually between friends. For example:

[said to somebody superior]
mipos θa borusate   na mu δanisete   to vivlio?   [Q 3: S 2]
could you perhaps   lend me   the book?

Among friends it could only be used when there is real doubt about the possibility of the act being performed.

In English, however, 'when *perhaps* or *maybe* are appended to predictions about a future act of the hearer, the speaker claims less authoritative knowledge about the hearer and his acts and correspondingly the hearer is, or appears to be, less bound to do the act' (Downes, 1977: 90).

The conventionalized openers used in English contribute to the elaboration of the requests, a feature associated with formality

---

[3] See Brown and Levinson (1978) and Coulmas (1981*b*).

which is not necessary in Greek since formality is indicated by the change in number. Moreover, it appears that cultural values explain and determine in intricate ways the reasons why certain expressions can become conventionalized in one language but not in another. This is an important point which has to be borne in mind before levelling any criticisms against non-native speakers of English or Greek as being too abrupt or rude.

7.2.2 *Hedges*

According to Brown and Levinson (1978: 150), 'a "hedge" is a particle, word, or phrase that modifies the degree of membership of a predicate or noun phrase in a set; it says of that membership that it is *partial*, or true only in certain respects, or that it is *more* true and complete than perhaps might be expected'.

Brown and Levinson's use of the term 'hedge' is broader than that in other accounts and 'hedging can be achieved in indefinite numbers of surface forms' (ibid.: 151). In general, hedges are assumed to soften the force of the face threatening acts. Brown and Levinson (ibid. 152) distinguish between 'weakeners' (mainly acting as tentativizers) and 'strengtheners' (mainly acting as emphatic items). However, it is not at all clear that the basic function of hedges is to modify the propositional content or the illocutionary force in order to avoid or minimize interactional face threats. There must be other motivations for the wide variety of linguistic devices which can be used as hedges in addition to that of mitigating impositions. In a negative politeness society where almost all interaction is potentially face-threatening, hedges will normally serve negatively polite functions. What about positive politeness societies? Can we assume that hedges will be restricted to softening face-threatening acts or to safeguarding vagueness? It can be argued that lack of explicitness serves another equally important function, that of offering the addressee the opportunity to provide support, understanding, sharing, participation, etc.; in other words, to show that both speaker and addressee are on the same wavelength. Furthermore, the speaker, for various reasons, may not want to minimize the impact of the act, but on the contrary to reinforce it. Thus, hedges may be grouped into 'softeners' and 'intensifiers', with softeners mitigating the force of the request in at least the two ways stated above and intensifiers aggravating the impact of the request.

Softeners include diminutives, tag questions, and a variety of other devices while intensifiers include such items as *for God's sake* and *come on*.

7.2.2.1 Softeners

7.2.2.1.1 Diminutives Greek is morphologically a very rich language, both inflectionally and derivationally. One of the derivational processes used extensively is the production of diminutives. This is a feature of many other European languages but not English, or at least not to the same extent. Diminutives in Greek are usually formed by a wide variety of special types of suffixes.[4]

Morphologically, diminutives are produced from a variety of word classes, although the most productive class of all is that of nouns. They occur most frequently with neuter nouns, somewhat less frequently with feminine nouns, and seldom with masculine ones.[5] Sometimes the same stem can be given either one (e.g. *-aki*) or another (e.g. *-uli*) diminutive suffix; for instance, *moraki* and *moruli* 'little baby'. Most often the diminutive suffix occurs in a neuter form (both *-aki* and *-uli* are neuters), but occasionally the diminutive suffix may indicate sex; for instance, *γataki* 'small cat' either male or female, but *γatula* 'small cat' female only. It is worth noting that some diminutive forms are produced through the addition of more than one diminutive suffix, as in *γata* 'cat' → *γatula* → *γatulitsa*.

In English, on the other hand, diminutive suffixes are fewer and diminutives themselves are not so frequently used. Examples, such as *-ette* in *kitchenette*, and *-let* in *piglet* and *starlet* are becoming used with decreasing frequency (Quirk *et al.*, 1972: 994). Another group of suffixed diminutives common in English consists of words accepting the *-ie* suffix (sometimes *-y*) such as *doggie* and *mummy*. Although the flexibility of this suffix is greater than those mentioned above, it is still limited because although *doggie* and

---

[4] See Triandafillides (1978) for an extensive list. For an extensive discussion of the relationship between diminutives and politeness, and the notion of imposition, see Sifianou, 1992.

[5] This may be due to the fact that masculinity is associated with powerfulness and toughness; consequently, diminutive forms associated with endearment are rather inappropriate with masculine nouns.

birdie are common, there is nothing like *headie* or *cowie* (Wierzbicka, 1984: 126). This ending can also be observed in shortened forms, such as *hankie* for *handkerchief* and *hubby* for *husband*.

Another group of morphological derivatives in English akin to diminutives are contracted forms of longer words. Examples such as *daffs* for *daffodils* and *veg* for *vegetables* are common and new ones are continually being introduced. Abbreviations of this sort are common in the jargon of certain groups with shared interests, groups that tend to use the same stock of words very often. For instance, *info* for *information* and *memo* for *memorandum* are common.

The primary function of diminutives, as the term suggests, is to express the idea of 'little' or 'small'. However, they may also be employed to indicate affection, tenderness, and positive emotions or, conversely, negative feelings and contempt. Diminutives have 'a number of affective connotations which range from endearment to tenderness through mild belittlement or deprecation to outright derogation and insult' (Haas, 1978: 82).

Augmentatives (the opposite of diminutives), expressing large-ness, are found in Greek but not in modern English. They are related to diminutives in that, especially when used with children, they do not indicate largeness, but rather affection and tenderness. When used for adults they may indicate praise or on occasion, contempt. For instance, from *χeri* 'hand' we can have *χerukla* 'big hand'; referring to a child's hand this is endearing, but when referring to an adult's hand it is rather disparaging. The meaning might not always be that of large, e.g. *koritsaros* from *koritsi* 'girl' usually means 'beautiful, attractive girl'. Haas (1978) says that in general augmentatives are much less commonly found and that, although the presence of an augmentative implies the presence of a diminutive, the reverse is not true. Apart from being a restricted, less productive group of lexical items, augmentatives mainly characterize in-group spoken language and are not usually used outside this domain. However, their existence clearly indicates a richer system of diminutives in Greek.

In many cases diminutives are used when talking or referring to children. Nouns indicating children's parts of the body, their toys, food, and so on, and concrete nouns referring to their immediate environment and concern constitute the most prolific groups. Diminutive forms, however, are not restricted to interactions with children; perhaps they originated in such contexts and then developed to cover similar items of the immediate environment and concern of adults. Diminutives are not usually used when there are status differences. There is a conflict between intimacy and status, and diminutives expressing intimacy and familiarity would be incompatible in situations where participants were of different status.

Adults use diminutives to convey factual information, such as smallness, or to indicate social relationships, endearment or contempt, towards a particular item, feelings which extend towards the addressee-owner. For example:

poli orea   i   bluz*itsa*   su   [NB]
very nice the sweater-*dim.* your

When speakers use diminutives to refer to their own possessions, achievements, or characteristics, the connotations may be those of affection but may also be attempts to reduce the possibility of the utterance being interpreted as self-praise. For example:

aγorasame ke mis ena spit*aki*   [NB]
we bought, too,   a   house-*dim.*

Diminutives in Greek can also be used pejoratively, though less frequently, and only when used towards adults. There are certain older endings such as -*iδio* and -*iskos*, which tend to carry insulting connotations (Triandafillides, 1978: 124). For example:

[NB]

me   δjo   tria   arθriδ*ia*   θeli   proaγoγi
with two three articles-*dim.* she wants promotion

The same is true of the English diminutive ending -*ling*, especially when added to word-classes other than nouns; then it acquires a mildly contemptuous flavour, as in *underling* and *weakling* (Quirk et al., 1972: 994).

Perhaps the most interesting feature of diminutives in Greek is that, although they mainly concern morphological alternations on the word level, they affect the force of the whole utterance and/or piece of interaction. In other words, they serve a variety of positive politeness needs. Diminutives are restricted to everyday informal speech and mainly involve routine actions dealing with the exchange of 'free goods'. Requests are perhaps the best examples of the pragmatic force exhibited by the use of diminutives, which clearly serves politeness needs. For example:

[among friends]
δose   mu   liγo   ner*aki*   [NB]
give   me   a little   water-*dim*.

[at the supermarket]
ke   liγo   kaser*aki*   na mu kopsete   [NB]
and   a little   cheese-*dim*.   to cut for me

[not well-acquainted neighbours]
siγnomi,   mipos eχete kanena   rantz*aki*
excuse me,   do you happen to have any   camping-bed-*dim*.
mono ja apopse?   [NB]
only for tonight?

As is clear from the above examples, diminutives are not restricted to certain structural patterns; that is, they may be concurrent with imperative, subjunctive, and indicative constructions. The diminutivized object mitigates the impact of the imperative so that it does not sound like an order to the native ear but rather like a friendly request. This function, however, is not achieved through minimizing the imposition because it would be a strange, if not a rude way of softening the force by presenting the favour or item asked as something very small. What is then the function of diminutives here? In the first example, 'small things', such as 'water', can be obtained without even asking; consequently, requests for them are not face-threatening acts. Since there is no imposition to be minimized, the diminutive indicates in-group solidarity. In the second example, where actors perform specific roles, requests are not perceived as impositions, and diminutives show readiness for co-operation in a friendly atmosphere. In the third example, although there is imposition involved because of the social distance between interactants, this is acknowledged and mitigated through other means; that is, the apology and the elaborate construction realized in the polite plural. The redressive force of the diminutive derives from its association with in-group language. The speaker expresses her wish for the establishment of an in-group context where both interactants are co-operating members. Thus, the speaker, by presenting the item requested as a 'dear little thing' necessary for her, has made a vulnerable assumption of solidarity whose effectiveness will depend on the addressee's acceptance of this assumption.

Diminutives are by no means restricted to requests. Since diminutivization is one of the most prevalent suffixation processes in Greek (Joseph and Philippaki-Warburton, 1987: 217), diminutive forms are frequent in everyday exchanges. For example:

| θa pame | mja ekδrom*ula* | tin kirjaki | [NB] |
| we'll go on | an excursion-*dim.* | on Sunday | |

			[NB]
ma ela,	pare liγes	patat*ules*	akoma
but come one	take a few	potatoes-*dim.* (chips)	more

There is also some equivalence of affinity between slang words and diminutives, since they both expess familiarity. For example:

| I'll be back in a jiffy | [NB] |
| give us a tenner then (imp.+slang) | [B 2: 113] |

| δoz' mu ena | δekarik*aki* (imp.+dim.) |
| give me a | ten-drachma-*dim.* coin |

Diminutives, therefore, appear to be closely linked to children's needs and environments and imply affection through the emphasis of smallness. Their use and implication can extend to adults, implying the same kind of endearment and affection together with familiarity through the assertion or assumption of solidarity. It is among adults that they have also acquired pejorative connotations.

'Rich systems of diminutives seem to play a crucial role in cultures in which emotions in general and affection in particular is expected to be shown overtly' (Wierzbicka, 1985*a*: 168). Greeks tend to express both their negative and positive emotions overtly. Since they value spontaneity, 'they find no obvious advantage in being systematic and emotionally controlled' (Vassiliou *et al.*, 1972: 111). Thus, diminutives appear to be an extremely useful and frequent aid to facilitate the expression of feelings. By contrast, the 'Anglo-Saxon culture does not encourage unrestrained display of emotions' (Wierzbicka, op. cit.) and, therefore, it is not surprising that expressive derivation has not been developed to the same extent.

7.2.2.1.2 *Miscellaneous* Another way of expressing diminution in both Greek and English is by means of syntactic modification, namely, by using the words *liγo* 'little' and *mikro* 'small' plus a noun. In Greek, the collocation of such items with already diminutivized nouns is also common. Such constructions can be found in English as in *little doggie* from baby talk, but are rather restricted to such environments. These combinations further emphasize the smallness and thus the endearing aspect of what is mentioned. The English form *a little* can also modify nouns and is used in similar ways as other quantifiers such as *a few* or *some*. For example:

> I could do with some tea.   [SR 2: 82]
>
> I'd like a few words with you   [OR 3: 172]
>
> if you don't mind, I'll walk with you a little way . . .   [PL 2: 117]

Theoretically, in combinations with nouns, *liγo* can be ambiguous between a quantifier reading and a politeness marker, but in context the intentions and meanings are clear. Evidence for this is the fact that interactants do not usually act on the literal meaning of the utterance; that is, the quantity offered is not determined by the presence or absence of *liγo*. Furthermore, such constructions can be replaced by diminutives. For example:

> aleko fertu   liγo   nero.   [KE 3: 82]
> Aleko bring-him   a little   water.

> fere   liγo   konjak.   [E 3: 127]
> bring   a little   cognac.

> se pirazi?   θa se piraze   na kano   liji   δulja?
> do you mind?   would you mind   that I do a bit of work?
>   [P 1: 11]

A variety of other expressions in both languages can perform a similar politeness function. For example, *mja stiγmi* 'a moment', *ena lefto* 'a second', and *mja γulja* 'a sip' in Greek, and *a moment*, *a second*, and *a sip* in English. In English, they themselves can also be modified by *just* and in Greek by *mono* 'only'. In English, but not usually in Greek, they can be preceded by *for* as in *for a minute*, etc.

The modifier *liγo* 'a little' or 'a bit' in Greek; and *a (tiny) little* or *a bit* in English can also modify verbs, encoding extra politeness. The Greek *liγo*, however, seems to be more flexible than its English equivalent form. It can collocate with a variety of verbs and it is not restricted in terms of the grammatical construction with which it is employed. For example:

na peraso	liɣo?	[NB]
[could] that I go by	a little?	

patas	liɣo	to oχto	[NB]
do you press	a little	the eight	

mu lete	liɣo	to onoma?	[NB]
do you tell me	a little	the name (of the client)	

These collocations are not ambiguous. They cannot be interpreted as meaning that the requester wants the actions carried out partially or necessarily for a short time, and such examples cannot be rendered literally in English. Clearly then *liɣo* in the above example does not minimize the imposition by minimizing the action requested. It could be suggested that in such contexts, *liɣo* has lost its literal force and is an informal variant of *parakalo* 'please', which can be used instead of or along with it. Its positional flexibility is indicative of the fact that its function is related to that of *please*. For instance, instead of *anijis liɣo to paraθiro?* we can equally well say *anijis to paraθiro liɣo?*, although we can rarely say *liɣo anijis to paraθiro?* In initial position *liɣo* functions more as an attention-getter. But even *please* in initial position can be thought of more as an attention-getter or as an apology for the interruption (Ervin-Tripp, 1976: 48); that is, its function is slightly different from the medial or postposed *please*. This use of *liɣo* is not peculiar to Greek since it can be regarded as similar to what Brown and Levinson (1978: 144, 182) report for Tamil and Malagasy, where the words for *please* literally mean 'a little'.

It should be noted that the use of *liɣo* to modify both verbs and nouns in Greek is a conventionalized marker of politeness. It is so frequent that even children appear to be aware of this convention. A personal example from my notebook is perhaps most indicative. When a lady asked a waiter to bring some water saying *nero fernete liɣo?* 'water do you bring a little?', a young girl started laughing and commented 'why a little, we want a lot'. Her laughter, however, had betrayed that she knew very well that *liɣo* was used metaphorically, functioning as *please*, rather than literally.

In Greek, indefinite pronouns are related to this use of *liɣo*. In cases in which the elements modified are quantifiable entities, indefinite pronouns *kanenas* or *kanis* (masculine), *kamja* (feminine), *kanena* or *kana* (abbreviated slang form—neuter) with singular nouns only, and *tipote* or *tipota* 'any(thing)', can be used instead of *liɣo*. For example:

> katerina   vale   kamja   kaseta   [AN 1: 45]
> Katerina   put on   some   cassette

but,

> Niko   vale   liji   musiki   [NB]
> Niko   put on   a little   music
>
> exis   tipota   eljes?   kamja   sarðela? [KE 1: 11]
> do you have   any   olives? a   sardine?

Indefinite pronouns are used in requesting constructions in cases in which *liɣo* would yield grammatically unacceptable sentences, as well as in those in which *liɣo* and *tipota* are interchangeable. For instance, in the above example *exis tipota eljes . . .?* we could also have *exis lijes eljes?* 'do you have a few olives?', or even *exis kamja elja?* 'do you have an(y) olive?' All these indefinite pronouns work in a way similar to *liɣo*, and can also be followed by diminutivized nouns. Such collocations can also be replaced by diminutives. Their only difference from *liɣo* is that they have not been conventionalized to the same extent and are restricted to familiar informal contexts. For example:

> ðose ke   kanena   kariðaki   sta peðja   [KE 3: 11]
> give and   some   walnut-*dim.*   to the children (guys)

Nobody could seriously interpret this as a suggestion of offering one small walnut to a number of people. It is clear that such expressions serve the satisfaction of the positive politeness need of sharing, even if that is something extremely small.

There are a number of extremely common modifiers in English which are almost absent from Greek. These include *just, possibly, rather, perhaps, sort of*, and others. Most of these are adverbs or adverbials modifying verbs, and their function is to tentativize what speakers say, thus allowing them not to fully commit themselves to what they are saying. For example:

> I just wonder if you could help me.   [PL 2: 114]
>
> could I possibly borrow it for a day or two?   [Q 20: S 2]

The word *just* and *possibly* in the English examples cannot be rendered in Greek. It appears that there is no equivalent word which could be used here. However, when *just* means 'only', as for example,

> ... will you do just one thing for me? [SR 2: 117]

it can be rendered in Greek as *mono/monaχa* 'only'.

sas parakalo poli	pame	mazi	na tus ta δoso
please	(let's) go	together	that I give them these
monaχa	ke na tus	χeretiso	[KA 2: 148]
just (only)	and greet	them	

Here, however, the function of *just* is not so much to tentativize what the speaker says, but rather to emphasize it; thus, *just* seems to contribute necessary information for the correct understanding of the utterance.

Among the other modifiers, only the neuter adjective, *δinaton* 'possible' can be used with requests in Greek, while an adverb equivalent for *possibly* does not exist in this sense. It appears that *can* or *could* and *possibly* used together sound redundant in Greek; thus, whereas *if it would be possible* . . . can be translated as *an θa itan δinaton* . . ., there is no equivalent form for *could I possibly* . . .? What is, however, more frequently used is *θa su itan efkolo* . . ., meaning 'would it be easy for you . . .'; that is, *easy* rather than *possible* is preferred.

Such tentativizing modifiers are not frequently used in Greek and some of them do not even have one word translations. When used, they imply the speaker's concern for the addressee's ability or willingness to perform the action rather than the speaker's attempt to mitigate the impact of full commitment.

7.2.2.1.3 *Tag questions*   As has been pointed out earlier, the main mitigating device used with request constructions in Greek, except perhaps the very elaborate ones, is the use of diminutives and expressions meaning 'a little'. By contrast, in English requests are frequently attenuated with tag questions. The system of question tags is highly developed in English, and tags can take a variety of forms and perform a variety of functions.[6] The equally developed

---

[6] The literature on the subject is indicative. See Lakoff (1969 and 1975); Cattell (1973); among others.

system of modal verbs has perhaps contributed to such a formal variety of tags in English, which is not true of other languages, such as Greek, Hebrew (Blum-Kulka, 1982 and 1983) and Polish (Wierzbicka, 1985*a*). For example:

leave it here, will you? [PN 2: 127]

have a glance at these, won't you? [OR 3: 173]

One could imagine a number of alternative possibilities for the above tags, such as *can you?* or *can't you?* There is a tendency for tags to have the opposite polarity of the sentences they are attached to. With positive imperative constructions the flexibility seems to be greater, but as Wierzbicka (1986: 87) has pointed out, the force of each one of them is different. In Greek, on the other hand, the only possibility, if used at all in such contexts, would be *endaksi*, which means 'OK', a kind of token tag.

In most cases, English tags enable speakers to mitigate the force of the request by sounding more tentative and less committed to what they say. According to Lakoff (1977: 83), 'tags have the effect of hedging—protecting a speaker from the consequences of his speech acts'. Thus, in using tags, the speakers express their concern not to impose on the addressees and at the same time protect themselves from a possible refusal. Lakoff (1975: 16–17) claims that in general women use more question tags than men, exactly because this enables them to avoid commitment and thus conflict. She adds that tags also signify that the speakers are not really sure of themselves and might not even have views of their own, and thus are looking to the addressees for confirmation. Both of Lakoff's claims have been attacked on the grounds that women do not always use tags more often in all situations and also because tags can have other functions besides signalling lack of confidence.[7] Tannen (1990: 228) suggests that it seems more a matter of expectation and stereotyping rather than actual difference in the frequency of employing tags.

By contrast, token tags, occasionally used in Greek, invite the addressee's involvement and thus agreement and common ground. 'When token tag questions are tacked on to a presumptuous positively polite request . . . the results are basically still positive-politeness strategies, even though they make use of essentially

---

[7] See, for instance, Dubois and Crouch (1975); and Holmes (1986).

negative-politeness techniques to soften the presumption' (Brown and Levinson, 1978: 235). One naturally wonders why token tags should be seen as softening presumptions rather than simply as attracting the addressee's participation.

It therefore appears that although requests in both Greek and English are softened, this is achieved through different devices which clearly reflect different values. The importance of non-imposition and independence in English has contributed to the development of linguistic means through which such needs will be satisfied, whereas in Greek the significance of involvement and dependence has contributed to the development of means through which such needs are expressed. Brown and Levinson (1978: 113) acknowledge the use of diminutives as in-group identity markers and consider them to be characteristics of positive politeness since they are directed towards the addressee's positive face.

7.2.2.2 *Intensifiers*

A number of lexical items, mainly adverbs, are used with requests to intensify usually one item and consequently the utterance as a whole. Expressing one's feelings and emotions openly and even attacking the addressee's identity, appear to be less taboo in Greek than in English society; thus, whereas a number of intensifiers were found with requests in Greek, very few were found in English. The most common Greek intensifiers are given below.

The form *pja*, which is a temporal positive adverb meaning 'already', can be used with requests as a negative adverb meaning something like 'anymore', 'after all', or 'finally'. It usually intensifies negatively loaded utterances and implies impatience. It is often employed with imperative constructions and follows the imperative verb. For example:

> papse pja   na mas kanis ti meɣali
> stop after all to pretend that you are old (mature)
> ke tin eksipni   [KA 1: 67]
> and clever

However, what is used more frequently in the same sense is *epitelus*, which is more flexible in that it can occupy initial, medial, or final position in an utterance. Although it is usually used with imperatives, it can also occur with other constructions; for example:

epitelus, kirie, δe borume esto ke arγa na sistiθume?
finally, sir, can't we introduce ourselves even late?

[MR 2: 35]

papse epitelus na me taleporis me tis kaltses [MR 4: 74]
stop finally to bother me with the stockings

The form *ja* is a preposition, but it is very often used as an extra persuasive element, usually with imperatives or sometimes subjunctives. In English it can be rendered as *come on*. For example:

ja eksijise mu kalitera [Z 1: 48]
come on explain to me better

The form *ke* is a conjunction meaning 'and'. It is, however, sometimes used to intensify a request, even if nothing has been said before to which the request could be reasonably conjoined. For example:

ke fere to onomatolojio apo mesa [KE 3: 30]
and bring the name-list from inside (the other room)

It is as if there is a missing utterance from which only the conjunction has remained.

The form *e* occupies initial position and intensifies a request; for example:

e, proseχe nde[8] liγaki [KE 2: 89]
e, be careful (nde) a bit

This should be distinguished from the token tag *e* 'OK' which follows a request and seeks, or presupposes, the agreement of the addressee.

The lexical items *ande* and *ainde* are alternative forms of a semantically void exclamation, usually prompting the addressee for action. For example:

ande re aristo, kunisu [E 4: 147]
come on (re) Aristo, move

---

[8] *nde* is a semantically empty, untranslatable intensifier. For a discussion of its pragmatic functions, see Tsochatzides (1986).

ande	pame!	[KA 2: 185]
come on (let's)	go!	

The lexical item *tulaχiston* 'at least' is used with requests to express acceptance of partial satisfaction of what could have been a more threatening request. For example:

tulaχiston,	kirie,	δen borite	na svisete	ta fota?
at least,	sir,	can't you	turn off	the lights?

[MR 2: 42]

The lexical item *lipon* literally means 'then', 'therefore', 'so'. It implies that there is a prior agreement and that a conclusion is about to be drawn. It can be used with requests when there is no such prior agreement, but when it is simply the intention of the speaker to present it as such, thus pressurizing the addressee to comply with the request. For example:

δimitri,	ela	lipon	[KA 3: 213]
Demitri,	come on	then	

lipon	sikoθite	[KE 3: 89]
so	get up	

ke eχo	ke sena	ke δe	voiθas	kaθolu!	voiθise me
and I have	and you	and don't	help	at all!	help me

lipon	na spaso	tin klosti	[S 1: 9]
then	to break	the thread	

Avoiding disagreement is a positive politeness strategy. What is involved here is not real agreement, but rather pseudo-agreement or an implication that the addressee should have known better. Speakers use such items because 'by pointing to a *fake* prior agreement they call upon the cooperative agreement associations' (Brown and Levinson, 1978:120). The items *then* and *so* can have similar functions in English (ibid.), as for instance:

give us a tenner then	[B 1: 113]

The form *ela* is the imperative of the verb *erχome* 'come'. It is often used with requests, both in the singular *ela* and the plural *elate*, in the sense of 'come on'. Used by itself, it is usually negatively loaded, but reduplicated or followed by *tora* 'now', it is used in emotionally positive situations indicating the speaker's concern for the addressee.

For example:

ela	maki	kofto	[MR 6: 125]
come on	Maki	stop it	

ela	tora	maritsa,	jati kles?	[MN 1: 55]
come on	now	Maritsa,	why are you crying?	

ela,	ela	stamata	tora . . .	[MN 1: 70]
come on,	come on	stop	now . . . [crying]	

Intensifiers found in English are *come on* and *at once*. For example:

come on, give us a hand. Give us a hand here.   [A 1: 199]

stop that at once!   [NB]

There are also intensifying items which over-represent reality. In English, these are usually adverbs such as *absolutely* and *terribly*, whereas in Greek they are phrases with nouns. For example:

θarθis kamja fora?   [KA 1: 30]
are you ever going to come?

Such items, however, are not common with requests.

Some lexical intensifiers, that is, words or phrases, can also be used to strengthen the force of a request. These include curses, derogatory alternatives of common words, and other fixed expressions, such as *for god's sake* or *pros θeu* (meaning the same) used mainly in tense situations to indicate anxiety or anger. For example:

pros θeu,	mi fonazete	[Z 3: 19]
for god's sake,	don't shout	

klisto	afto to rimaδi	[AN 1: 37]
turn off	this wreck (here it refers to the radio)	

ena tsiɣaro	anaθema sas . . .!	[KA 3: 222]
(give me) a cigarette	to hell with you . . .!	

oh! give it to him, Jimmy, for heaven's sake!   [OS 1: 11]

don't bloody well keep on about it   [B 2: 58]

drink that tea and clear off   [OR 1: 35]

In Greek, some of these expressions are used among friends as an indication of familiarity and closeness, although many people consider them to be impolite or even rude. This, however, is not a specifically Greek way of emphasizing solidarity, because as Brown and Levinson (1978: 234) point out, in intimate relations the danger of face threats is assumed to be minimal. 'This gives rise to the use of bald-on-record insults or jokes as a way of asserting such intimacy. Hence, we get conventionalized (ritualized) insults as a mechanism for stressing solidarity.'

Generally speaking, it appears that English speakers use relatively few intensifiers with requests, although they employ many softeners. These soften the impact of the request in that they allow the speakers to sound more tentative and less committed to what they are saying. It is important for the English speaker to be very careful not to attack or threaten the addressee. By contrast, in Greek many more intensifiers are used and the mitigators employed are of a different kind. These enable the Greek speaker to show familiarity and informality rather than tentativeness.

7.2.3 Fillers

Yet another form of internal modification are fillers, optional lexical items or simply 'noises' produced by speakers to fill in the gaps occurring in discourse. They are highly formulaic and mostly semantically void in that although they have a certain literal meaning, they do not retain it when used as fillers. Their function is socio-pragmatic rather than semantic. They save interactants from the embarrassment of lengthy gaps and the uneasiness of expressing something directly which may be thought of as unpalatable by the addressee. They also function as attempts to make utterances more vivid by involving the addressee. Edmondson (1981: 153) calls such elements 'fumbles'. Fumbles or fillers are not characteristic of requests only, but of interaction as a whole. The ones which are more likely to occur with requests are (*a*) hesitators, (*b*) cajolers, (*c*) appealers, and (*d*) attention-getters (see Edmondson, 1981; Kasper, 1979; and House and Kasper, 1981).

7.2.3.1 Hesitators

Hesitators occur when the speaker is uncertain of the impact of a request on the addressee. This real or conventional concern can be expressed by employing various means of hesitation, such as simple stuttering, repetition, or a combination of the two.

Impressionistically, hesitation-stuttering is more common in English than in Greek. A kind of hesitation can also be achieved by repetition. Repetition involves reiteration of words or phrases, or even their substitution with synonymous expressions.

> . . . perhaps—perhaps you don't want to waste your time coming here any more? [R 1: 65]

> θeoni . . .   mipos . . .   mipos   eχume
> Theoni . . . do we happen . . . do we happen to have
> paγakja? [MT 2: 48]
> ice-cubes?

The words repeated may convey this kind of uncertainty, as in the requests above, which are, furthermore, realized indirectly.

7.2.3.2 *Cajolers*

Cajolers are addressee-orientated internal modifiers, in that they function as attempts by speakers to make things clearer for the addressees and invite them, at least metaphorically, to participate in the speech act. Examples of cajolers include *you know*,[9] *you see*, *I mean* in English, and *ke pu les* 'and as you say', *katalaves* 'you understand', *kseris* 'you know', *vlepis* 'you see' in Greek. The only one which is found with requests in Greek is *kseris* 'you know'. For example:

> kses,[10]   etsi liγo   alafroma piso [KE 2: 87]
> you know,   just a bit off the back

Edmondson (1981: 155) includes *please* in the cajolers, but I will consider it separately because in Greek the equivalent, *parakalo*, is a full verb which can be conjugated and receive subject and object, rather than an uninflected lexical item, and can also be used performatively.

7.2.3.3 *Appealers*

Appealers are addressee-orientated modifiers which are used by the speaker at the end of a sentence as an appeal for the addressee's

---

[9] For a detailed discussion of the distribution and functions of the pragmatic expression *you know*, see Holmes (1986).

[10] *kses* is a slang, abbreviated form of *kseris* 'you know'.

participation. They point to some kind of prior pseudo-agreement between the participants and attempt to elicit a kind of promise from the addressee, at least metaphorically, that he or she will agree to perform the act. Examples of appealers are *OK* and *right* in English, and *endaksi* 'OK', *etsi* 'all right', and *e* 'what did you say?', 'what do you say to this?', or 'OK' (intonation differentiates the various meanings). Further examples of appealers are *simfoni* 'agreed' and *akuses* 'did you hear' in Greek. Most question tags in Greek function as appealers. Examples are:

so I must ask you to go. OK?   [PL 2: 110]

θa mu kanis   ti χari   se parakalo, na min tus
will you do me   the favour   please   not to
ksanapis   na 'rθun,   akuses?   [Z 1: 13]
say-again to them   to come,   did you hear?

svista,   etsi?   [KE 2: 88]
razor cut,   all right?

. . . ela   pjes   ena δaχtilaki.   ena mono omos, e?
. . . come on   drink   one drop.   Just one though, OK?
                                                       [AN 1: 9]

Appealers appear to be more frequently employed in Greek than in English, perhaps because they also function as kinds of token tags and intensifiers.

7.2.3.4 Attention-getters

Attention-getters, as their name suggests, are devices used to attract the addressee's attention, literally or figuratively, before the actual request is launched. When used metaphorically they imply the speaker's concern for a pleasant, harmonious encounter.

Attention-getters fall into three main categories, (*a*) formulaic entreaties, (*b*) formulaic greetings, and (*c*) imperative constructions. Formulaic entreaties are attempts by the speaker to attract the attention of the addressee and simultaneously apologize for the intrusion. Imperatives are acceptable in English in this function, whereas Greek usually uses present tense constructions and nouns. Examples are:

excuse me, which is the way to the ladies?   [PL 1: 21]

siɣnomi,   to pentaɣono itan afto
forgiveness,   was it the bus to Pentagono
pu perase?   [NB]
which has gone by?

Formulaic greetings such as *hello* can be used before the expression
of the actual request. They are attempts to show the addressee that
besides the request that is going to follow, the speaker is interested
in a harmonious, social encounter.

Imperative constructions, mainly with verbs of perception which
do not retain their literal meaning, such as *hear/listen* and *look* and
the verb *perimeno* 'wait' and *stekome* 'stop and wait' can be used to
attract the attention of addressee and involve them more in the
request which follows. For example:

wait a minute, listen to me. Listen ...   [R 1: 14]

kita   min to pandrepsis   [KE 1: 22]
look (be careful)   don't break it

This function is also fulfilled by the idiomatic expression *pu 'se*,
contracted form of *pu ise* meaning 'where are you?' For example:

... ke pu 'se,   proseҳe   min ti strapatsaris
... and where are you,   be careful not to damage it
                                                   [E 1: 11]

On the issue of fillers, Mackridge (1985: 342) observes that
generally speaking, Greeks tend to be eloquent, although many of
them use 'fillers' which have little or no semantic content, such as
na pume 'let's say', *katalaves?* 'did you understand', *kseris* 'you
know', *vlepis* 'you see', and *etsi* 'thus', which are used when the
speaker is trying to think, as well as *e*, *em*, *a*, *ts*, and *m*, which are
employed when the speaker is hesitating.

7.3 EXTERNAL MODIFICATION

In the case of external modification we do not usually have lexical
items modifying one word of the request, but optional clauses
which soften or emphasize the force of the whole request in some
way or other. Most external modifiers are means by which the
speaker tries to elicit the addressee's co-operation to support the
actual request. They fall into two groups: commitment-seeking
devices and reinforcing devices.

7.3.1 *Commitment-seeking devices*

Before uttering a request, the speaker may want to check whether or not to go ahead and express a desire. In other words, the speaker wants to ensure that certain conditions hold for the successful fulfilment of the request, and to get some kind of commitment that the addressee is willing to perform the task requested. These are what Edmondson (1981) calls 'pre-exchanges'. He says that pre-exchanges (parallel to pre-sequences in the ethnomethodological literature), 'are defined such that the *outcome* of such an exchange directly leads to the initiation of a following Head (or other) exchange' (ibid. 100), in this case of the request. Such pre-exchanges usually take the form of questions such as *will you do me a favour?* or *θa mu kanis mja χari?* 'will you do me a favour?', or *could I ask you something?* or *na su zitiso kati?* 'to ask for something from you?' Pre-exchanges such as *boro na kano mia erotisi?* 'could I ask a question?' or *δe mu lete?* 'don't you tell me?', 'could I ask', can precede requests for information in Greek, but are rather uncommon in English.

Such pre-requests do not state what will be requested but oblige the addressee to respond either positively or, less frequently, negatively. Positive responses place the speaker on safer ground to perform the request and increase expectations that it will be successful. Speakers do not usually expect negative responses to such pre-requests, unless as a joke or for some serious reason which is often stated and justified by the addressee. If addressees do not want to commit themselves, they can question the pre-request, asking for the request proper before committing themselves. The fact that speakers do not usually expect a negative answer from addressees has had two important consequences. First, such pre-requests have become conventionalized and sometimes do not constitute a separate move on the part of the speaker that entails a response from the addressee. For instance, instead of waiting for an answer to a pre-request, the speaker may embellish the request with a pre-posed or post-posed phrase such as *do me a favour*, as in the following examples:

> . . . I wondered if you could do me a favour and pick it up for me? [Q 19: S 3]

kane mu ti χari,   se parakalo,   na perasis   na ton paris
do me the favour,   please,   to go by   and get it
                                          [Q 3: S 4]

This conventionalized usage does not always mitigate the request; it
can also intensify its force, as for example:

do me a favour. Just shut up for one minute about Carol,
would you?   [A 1: 163]

na mu   kanis ti χari   ke   n'afisis   ti γria   isiχi . . .
do me   the favour   and   leave   the old woman alone . . .
                                               [Z 1: 35]

Secondly, sometimes such pre-requests can be handled as requests if
the context is such that the addressee can guess what the likely
request is going to be. This gives rise to non-conventional indirect
requests. For instance, Sue, who was sunbathing, turns over and
says to Pauline *do me a favour* and Pauline starts rubbing sun-tan
lotion on Sue [PG 1: 95].

Although this device is used in both languages, in English it
appears to be used at all levels of social distance irrespective of the
degree of imposition, whereas in Greek it is mainly used when there
is greater social distance and the imposition is assumed to be
higher. When used in Greek in cases in which familiarity exists, it
sounds more like begging.

Of course, what the degree of imposition is for any act is
culturally determined. In a culture where social distance pre-
dominates we would expect many more acts to be regarded as
heavier impositions than in cultures where closeness is valued more
and people feel freer to ask for and perform favours.

7.3.2 *Reinforcing devices*

Edmondson (1981) calls these devices 'supportive moves' and
subdivides them into grounders, expanders, and disarmers. What is
interesting about such devices is that they can function in two
contrasting ways; that is, they can support the central move and
thus mitigate the impact of the request, but they can also intensify
its force. This is especially true of grounders which can be
explanations, but can also be explanatory promises or even threats.

7.3.2.1 Grounders

Grounders are usually clauses which can either precede or follow a request and give reasons or justifications for the act requested. Grounders themselves can be accompanied by further explanations or justifications; for example:

> ... well come on—hurry up—I'm dead excited. I've never seen a live play before. [R 1: 38]

Grounders contribute to a harmonious encounter in that the speaker, by giving reasons for a request, expects the addressee to be more understanding and willing to co-operate. For example:

> ... bring my keys. I want to undo my cases [B 1: 3]
>
> kiria meri! kiria meri! petraki! χamiloste, sas parakalo
> Mrs Mary! Mrs Mary! Petraki! Turn down, please
> tin tileorasi ine aδjaθetos o andras mu! [AN 1: 8]
> the television my husband doesn't feel very well!

Such explanations can also be associated with 'white lies', which are used, when the speaker does not want to state the truth since it may threaten the addressee's face (Brown and Levinson, 1978: 120). 'Greeks believe that face-saving lies are highly desirable and at any rate most acceptable' (Triandis *et al.*, 1972: 224). In the above Greek example, this is actually the case because after the wife had finished asking the neighbours to turn the TV down, the irate husband says γaiδurja! δen eχo tipota! aku aδjaθetos 'donkeys! I don't have anything (I feel well)! listen not feeling well'.

If a grounder precedes a request, it might also imply tentativeness and difficulty in making the actual request. For example:

> ... because we do find ourselves in a little difficulty and we wondered if you could ... give us a lift to this wedding tomorrow. [PL 2: 77]

Although my approach to data in this work is qualitative rather than quantitative, the large number of requests which have been examined appear to justify a tentative generalization that grounders are more common in Greek. One situation (see Appendix II/2, S. 4), in which informants had to ask their mother to buy a magazine for them, since she was going out, is quite telling in respect of my own personal preference as a Greek. A number of Greeks (10 out of 60) requested her to do so because they could not go out themselves for some reason. In the same situation, none of the English informants used any justification for the request. The reason for this difference might have been the fact that in the description of the situation in Greek, I mentioned that the requesters were busy and could not gò out, information which I accidentally omitted from the description of the English situation. It might be argued that this gave an incentive to the Greeks to use such a justification for the request. Whether or not this was so is irrelevant, but what is significant is the fact that in my attempt to render the situation in the two languages as clearly as possible, an unconscious and habitual communicative strategy—the need for explanation in Greek—manifested itself even in my instructions.

In another situation (see Appendix II/2, S. 3), informants had to ask a friend to collect their ticket from the travel agent. In this case, the reason—that they were very busy—was given in both Greek and English. Only a few Greeks (4 out of 60) mentioned the reason, but none of the English did.

Although these findings may be statistically insignificant, there is also independent evidence that Greeks tend to employ more grounders. Marmaridou (1987), comparing the Greek and English announcements delivered on board an Olympic Airways aircraft, a situation where extreme semantic and structural identity would be expected, noticed very interesting differences. One of these was the explicit justification in some Greek announcements which was absent from the English equivalents. One of the examples she cites is the following. (The italic part is the justification, which is missing from the announcement in English.)

> Ladies and gentlemen, you are kindly requested to remain seated while cabin attendants take passenger count. Thank you.
>
> kiries   ke   kirii   *ja na mi jinun laθi*
> ladies   and   gentlemen   so that no mistakes take place
> *ke kaθisterisi i anaχorisi mas*   tora   pu   to pliroma
> and delay   our departure   now   that   the crew
> asχolite   me tin katametrisi,   parakalume
> are occupied   with the count,   we request you

[KA 2: 39]

na minete kaθizmeni stis θesis sas. efχaristo
to remain seated   in your seats. I thank you

She concludes that this need for explicit justification in Greek might imply that performing a request in Greek without overt justification would violate the positive politeness strategy of conveying that the speaker and the addressee are co-operators, whereas in English such explicit information could be perceived as an imposition on the addressee and thus a face-threatening activity.

Brown and Levinson (1978) say that asking for or giving reasons for a speech act is a positive politeness strategy. If, then, this is indeed the case, that Greeks employ more grounders, it serves as additional support for the hypothesis that Greek culture is a positive politeness culture.

7.3.2.2 Disarmers

I use this term in a broader sense than that in which it has been used in the relevant literature, since there is no term which covers all the external modifying devices which disarm addressees from the possibility of a refusal, or induce them to do something. These can be complimenting phrases, entreaties, or formulaic promises, and, in general, phrases which express the speakers' awareness and concern that the requests might be an imposition on the addressees. Although all these phrases are optional, usually one or even two of them co-occur without any fixed order and can occur in initial or final positions. The feature they all share is that they indirectly and conventionally limit the addressees' freedom to decide by putting gentle pressure on them to comply with the request and thus not to lose face by being uncooperative. For example:

keti! . . .   θa χorepsis   ki apopse,   opos
Kate! . . .   will you dance tonight, too, in the way that
monaχa   esi χorevis?   [KA 2: 39]
only   you can dance?

I don't want to bother you, but is there somewhere we can go?   [PL 1: 32]

without your help I have very little hope of locating her

[PL 2: 110]

if you've got the time, could you manage to pop in for me
please   [Q 10: S 3]
. . . I'd appreciate it if while you are buying some stamps, you
would get me some as well   [Q 12: S 6]

A variety of clauses can function in this way in both languages. 'If'
clauses are perhaps the most common. The notion of possibility
they indicate makes the addressees feel good that they are not
imposed on and allows the speakers to appear considerate.

7.3.2.3 *Expanders*

Repetition is usually seen as a weakness in discourse and people try
to avoid or justify it with expressions like *have I told you this
before?* or *once again*, and so on. It does, however, serve a variety
of functions in language and is used, for example, to create
vividness and/or to indicate tentativeness. Furthermore, 'the stronger
the emotive urge in the speaker, the greater the likelihood of
repetition, which is usually calculated to have a greater effect on the
interlocutor than a single occurrence of the request' (Persson, 1974:
89).

Speakers can repeat their words identically, expand on them by
adding further elements, or use synonymous expressions. In
examining requests for action, Labov and Fanshel (1977: 214) have
observed that 'if a request is repeated in exactly the same words, the
action is normally heard as a sharp criticism'. For example:

ena lefto.	ena lefto	na to skefto.	afiste me
one minute.	one minute	to think about it.	Let me
na to skefto			[KE 3: 100]
think about it.			

aleko ti somba.	svise	ti somba.	[KE 3: 72]
Aleko the stove.	Turn off	the stove.	

don't touch me! . . . Just leave me alone!   [SR 2: 100]

I just would like, if you don't mind, if I could, . . . I'd like to
spend the night here. Just tonight. Stay here.   [PL 2: 105]

Repeated utterances may occur in the same move, or follow the
addressee's response. However, expansion is a feature of consecutive
turns rather than single acts. The addressee may repeat part or all of

the speaker's utterance along with his or her own contribution. Repetition can be used to stress agreement between interactants and is a positive politeness device according to Brown and Levinson (1987: 112).

7.3.2.4 *Please*

Having discussed most of the internal and external modifiers, let us move on to the examination of *please* and its approximate Greek equivalent *parakalo*, possibly the commonest and most significant modifier in requests. Both in Greek and in English, these appear to have escaped close study because they have been assumed to be the most transparent politeness markers. In other words, they are seen as softening the imposition entailed by the verbal act. For example:

> Make me a cup of coffee, please   [NB]
>
> Could you pass these round, please   [NB]

However, *please* can also appear in cases in which the speaker does not care to sound courteous, as for instance, *oh, why, don't you shut up, please!* We can also have *please* in cases of begging; for example:

> [among sisters]
> I need you! Please believe me! . . . Please. Carol. Don't let me go.   [SR 2: 147]

Thus, besides its conventional politeness use, *please* seems to be found in emotionally loaded situations, cases in which it is not at all clear that it is an indication of politeness.

What is noteworthy is that the distribution of *please* cannot be explained on purely syntactic or even semantic grounds. Quirk *et al.* (1972: 470) include *please* in a small group of adverbs they call 'formulaic adjuncts'. Although it functions as such in many respects, its status appears to be problematic in that it cannot be modified. It is flexible to co-occur with imperative, interrogative, and affirmative constructions (Stubbs, 1983: 72) and also appears to be closely associated with simple present and future tenses. Furthermore, its presence is not restricted by the presence of other politeness markers and its meaning does not contribute to the content of the utterance. On the other hand, its distribution seems to be restricted in terms of the speech act in which it can appear. Although it can freely co-occur with utterances which may be interpreted as requests, it cannot be employed with statements, promises, threats, invitations, etc. (Stubbs, 1983: 72).

As has been noted by Searle (1975: 68), among others, the insertion of *please* 'explicitly and literally marks the primary illocutionary point of the utterance as directive', although the literal meaning of the rest of the utterance may not be a directive. Similarly, Bach and Harnish (1982: 201) observe that inserting *please* in sentences which are simply used to ask questions or make statements makes no sense and renders them ungrammatical and add that 'it is not clear whether "please" is itself a directive force-indicating device or whether it merely cooccurs with something that is' (ibid. 188).

The thrust of these observations is that in ambiguous cases, *please* enables the addressee to infer correctly whether the utterance is meant to be a request or a mere question. For example, *can you lift the parcel?* can be ambiguous: it may be a literal question about the ability of the addressee to lift the parcel or a request to do so. With a pre-verbal or post-sentential *please*, however, it becomes an unambiguous request. However, as Stubbs (1983: 72), drawing upon Butler, observes, 'there is a gradient of restriction on the distribution of *please*, according to the directness or opacity of the speech act performed'.

Similarly, Searle (1975) claims that the more conventional the requesting construction the more readily it accepts *please*. In other words, if a great deal of inference is needed to interpret the utterance as a request, the use of *please* will be more restricted even positionally. Ervin-Tripp (1976: 48) notes that 'preposed "please" can appear with any directive, as an attention-getter and an apology for interruption. Postposed and medial "please" seem to be limited to obvious directives, including conventional or routinized hints and requests.' By contrast, House (1989: 105) claims that hints do not accept *please* because the combination of the two contributes to a self-contradictory strategy since the speaker chooses, on the one hand, an off-record device in order to enable the addressee to decide on its interpretation and, on the other, marks the utterance as a request by using *please*.

Despite arguments attributing the English *please* exclusively to requests, it seems that it can be used, though marginally, with some offers and invitations as in *come in, please,* and as a positive response to offers or even requests,[11] as for example:

A: would you like more coffee?
B: please

A: could I have your pen?
B: please (do)

In Greek, the rough equivalent *parakalo* is a full verb. It can mean 'supplicate', 'request', 'implore', 'entreat', or even 'insist', and so on. This means that it is functionally more flexible than the English *please* and not necessarily restricted to transparent requests. It is frequently preceded by the weak form of the personal pronoun (*se:* 2nd person singular, or *sas:* 2nd person plural) as its object and can be followed by the intensifier *poli* 'very', which can itself be modified by *para*, as *para poli* 'very much'. Therefore, it can easily be used as a separate clause and as a separate tone group. When *parakalo* is used by itself, it is frequently an elliptical form of an underlying clause; for example, the response *parakalo* to someone knocking on a door means 'come in please'. Similarly, on the phone the answerer's possible response, *parakalo*, means 'speak please'. The full form *lejete parakalo* 'say (pl.) please' is also possible.

The pronominal object is not grammatically essential but gives the utterance a touch of familiarity since the marker is mainly used in cases in which there is social distance. Without this object it sounds rather abrupt and is used more conventionally as in *ti ora eçete, parakalo?* or *ti ora eçete, sas parakalo?* both meaning 'what's the time, please?'

Because of its brevity, it is used on signs in the plural form, cases in which the addressee is obviously not a single individual. For example:

parakalume   min kapnizete
please (pl.)   do not smoke

The verb *parakalo* can be used to report requests, as for instance in *ton parakalesa na mu ðanisi to vivlio tu* 'I kindly asked him to lend me his book', and can occur in any tense in either the singular or the

---

[11] House (1989: 97) claims that such a response is actually a request for action.

plural. It is also frequently used as an overt performative in formal situations; for example:

> [to somebody superior]
> . . . θa sas parakalusa,   ean δen to χrisimopiite   na
> . . . would you please,   if you aren't using it   to
> mu to δanisete   [Q 48: S 2]
> lend it to me

The fact that *parakalo* can be used to report requests and also as a performative means that it can be part of the written medium not just of the spoken one, as is the case with its English equivalent. The positional flexibility of *parakalo* is roughly the same as that of *please*.

However, the question worth examining is the extent to which *parakalo* differentiates between requesting and non-requesting constructions. It seems that although it is mainly used in utterances with requesting force, it can also occur with utterances which are not requests. Since almost any question is a request for information, *parakalo* can be pre-posed or post-posed meaning 'please tell me/ us'; that is, it is an elliptical clause, functioning as a modifier to the question for information. For example:

> ti eχete diθi   parakalo?   [MN 5: 113]
> what are you dressed up as   please?

Such constructions in Greek are used when there is social distance. For instance, a shop assistant or waiter may say something like *ti θa θelate parakalo?* 'what would you want please?' or *ti θa parete parakalo?* 'what will you take (have) please?'

The elliptical usage of *parakalo* can be found with assertions, too.

> sas parakalo,   ime apolitos simfonos   [Z 3: 29]
> please, (don't go on)   I absolutely agree
>
> parakalo,   en katalaveno   ti enoite [Z 3: 26]
> please, (excuse me)   I don't understand what you mean

In many cases *parakalo* is itself the request, and what follows is its justification. It can be used either to avoid the repetition of the actual request, or to imply that it can be easily inferred from the context. For example:

se parakalo . . .   δe mu aresi na vlepo tus andres
please (stop it) . . . I don't like seeing   men
na kanun jimnastiki   [MR 4: 73]
exercise

One clear difference in the use of *parakalo* versus *please* is
that *parakalo* is also an appropriate response to thanking and
apologizing expressions, as in:

A: efχaristo   poli!
   thanks   a lot!
B: parakalo,   δen itan tipota
   please,   it was nothing

In Greek, *parakalo* is also used in various slang, jocular, and/or
ironical expressions. For example:

. . . ke ti lei parakalo o vagos?   [E 4: 151]
. . . and what does Vagos have to say please?

ma   ti '   lete   parakalo   [NB]
but what   are you talking about   please

. . . ke jati,   parakalo?   [MN 3: 33]
. . . and why,   please? ('if I may ask?')

The combination of *parakalo* with *jati* 'why' can be heard as a
complaint.

Parakalo can also mean 'if you can believe it', as is the case with
if you please in English; for example:

. . . ke parakalo,   me χartziliki
. . . and please [can you believe it]   with cash
pu mazeva   tris mines prin   [P 2: 75]
I have been saving up   for three months

eksinda xiljaδes   parakalo   [P 2: 76]
sixty thousand   please [if you can believe it]

It is also used as an attention-getter in cases in which *excuse me* and
less frequently *please* is used in English. This perhaps indicates that
in English you sound more polite if you initiate your request with
an apology for the intrusion, whereas in Greek a more immediate
requesting element is more common. For example:

[knocking at a ticket box]
parakalo! . . . kanis.   bravo eksipiretisi [MT 1: 77]
please! . . .   nobody (here). such very good service

. . . sas parakalo,   mipos kserete . . .?   [MT 1: 78]
. . . please,   do you perhaps know . . .?

In Greek *parakalo* cannot be used in the sense of 'satisfy', as is the case in English, as for instance in *he is difficult to please* or in the expression *please yourself*. This is because in these cases *please* is used in its literal sense of 'pleasing', whereas the literal meaning of *parakalo* is to 'request formally'.

From the above discussion it becomes clear that *parakalo* and *please* are not equivalents. In an attempt to examine the similarities and differences between them, when used with requests, I examined their occurrence in my data. This marker was found on the whole slightly more in my Greek data than in the English. In the Greek discourse completion tests (see Appendix II/2), *parakalo* was employed in 94 out of 360 requests (26.11 per cent), while the English used *please* only in 67 out of 300 requests (22.33 per cent). Similarly *parakalo* was employed in 119 out of 760 requests (15.65 per cent) collected from Greek plays, and *please* in 72 out of 490 requests (14.69 per cent) collected from English plays. Furthermore, *parakalo* was interspersed in the constructions, whereas in English *please* tended to be utterance-final.

The situational pattern of *parakalo* and *please* in the requests elicited by means of discourse completion tests appears to be roughly the same, both being used less frequently with friends and relatives, except mothers. The mother who was asked to buy something for the speaker (see Appendix II/2, S. 4) received by far the most *please* expressions in English, and even more so in Greek: 30 out of 60 requests (50 per cent) in Greek, and 20 out of 50 requests (40 per cent) in English. By contrast, in Greek it was the subordinates who received the most *parakalo* expressions – in 34 out of 60 requests (56.6 per cent). In English the subordinates received *please* in only 14 out of 50 requests (28 per cent). The superior from whom the participants had to ask to borrow a book (see Appendix II/2, S. 2) received a fair number of *please* expressions in English, but comparatively fewer in Greek. Thus, Greek superiors received *parakalo* in 11 out of 60 requests

(18.3 per cent), whereas English superiors received *please* in 14 out of 50 requests (28 per cent). All this is illustrated in Table 7.1.

The findings are interesting, although at first sight they appear odd. Greeks are often considered to be less polite than the English, and yet evidence from two independent sources shows that they use *parakalo* more often than the English use *please*. Politeness obviously means much more than the mere appearance of *please* in a construction. Other elements in the utterance or changes in the structure are more decisive in assigning higher levels of politeness or formality, since *please* is very often used conventionally. However, the extent of conventionalization cannot be determined independently of the social and situational context of the utterance. This issue definitely deserves further investigation but it seems that what is highly conventionalized is not appropriate to indicate higher levels of politeness nor to express the kind of politeness expected in in-group encounters. In other words, the determining factors seem to be a relative social distance between interactants and a requested task falling, to a certain extent, beyond the normal everyday tasks people perform for each other easily. These tentative assumptions seem to explain, first, the relatively low percentage of this marker in my data as a whole, since most situations depicted

TABLE 7.1 *Frequency and percentage of occurrence of* please/parakalo *in elicited requests from 6 situations sampling 50 English and 60 Greek informants*

Situation	English		Greeks	
	No.	%	No.	%
Request to a close friend for food	4	8.0	3	5.0
Request to borrow superior's book	14	28.0	11	18.3
Request to a close friend to collect ticket	7	14.0	8	13.3
Request to mother to buy magazines	20	40.0	30	50.0
Request to brother/sister to lend shirt/blouse	8	16.0	8	13.3
Request to subordinate to buy something	14	28.0	34	56.6

did not exhibit a combination of these two features, and secondly, the scarcity of *please* expressions among friends and relatives, except mothers, on the one hand, and towards a superior, on the other.

The most interesting exception to the above assumption is that of mothers. Mothers stood out from all others in receiving the highest amount of *please* expressions in English and the second highest in Greek (which was still higher than that received in English). This may be due to the fact that, despite the lack of social distance, asking the mother to buy something for the speaker is seen as being beyond the mother's duties, considering her age, too. Other more formal devices would have sounded distancing and less appropriate, so *please* appeared to function better. It is also noteworthy that many English informants offered the mother the money for the goods requested, thus mitigating the impact of what was requested, whereas only one Greek did so. It is interesting to note that in this case, the person's mother had actually died when he was a baby and, consequently, he had never experienced a real mother–son relationship, and the situation was, therefore, hypothetical for him.

The difference found in the frequency of *parakalo* and *please* towards the superior is not surprising. Situations involving teachers and students in Greece require higher levels of formality, and lending books falls outside the teacher's duties to a greater extent. These social considerations along with the facility of language to indicate formality through the use of plural to single addressees render *parakalo* less necessary than *please* in English. Furthermore, in most cases where *parakalo* was employed it was used as a performative verb, a device which contributes to the necessary formality.

However, in requesting subordinates, a striking difference is observed in the use of *parakalo*, *please*: 56.6 per cent in Greek compared to 28 per cent in English, respectively. This high percentage can be accounted for by the relative social distance between interactants, whereas the difference between the two societies seems to have a different source. It may be related to findings reported elsewhere (see section 3.4), concerning the use of formal pronouns observed in Greek; that is, that nowadays formal plural forms toward a single addressee are frequently used downwards in the social scale.

From this brief account it becomes clear that *please* and *parakalo* are not equivalents. Their function is still poorly understood despite the fact that they are considered to be the most transparent markers of politeness, assumptions which need further investigation.

7.4 CONCLUDING REMARKS

It is commonly accepted that constructions do not function independently of their modification. Thus, I have also tried to examine the types of internal and external modifications and their contribution to the force of requests. It should be noted that most of these modifiers are not restricted to requests, but can be employed with other speech acts.

Two general observations concerning internal modification are derived from the examination of the data: the kind of modification favoured in the two languages is not only different but also contributes to the elaboration of English requests. The first observation concerns the differential preference of mitigating and/ or intensifying modifiers, and the second, mainly what I have called openers.

Openers appear to be an integral part of most requests in English. By contrast, their use in Greek appears to be more limited to cases in which they retain their literal meaning; this difference also contributes to a more straightforward realization of requests in Greek. The tense and aspect of these openers can vary in English and may or may not include a modal. Openers are directed towards the perlocution, that is, the effect that the utterance will have on the addressee, rather than towards the illocution, that is, the act itself. They enable one to sound vague, with diminished commitment to what one is saying, distancing oneself, in a way, from the request itself. The major difference found between Greek and English openers is the possibility of a negative realization in English; for instance, *I don't think* or *I don't suppose*. These were encountered even with requests towards friends and family members. This kind of formulation is absent from Greek.

Thus, clearly both the constructions used and their modification contribute to greater elaboration and formality in English. If such elaborate constructions are employed in Greek in cases in which there is familiarity, they imply a breach in the relationship and may be questioned. The notion of what constitutes the appropriate distance is itself differentially valued in the two cultures (see section 2.5.1). Thus, for example, in the situation (Appendix II/2, S. 1) where informants had to ask a friend to give them something to eat because they were hungry, although very few informants, both Greek and English, replied that they would never ask for food, no matter how hungry they were, on the whole Greek requests were less elaborate and in the singular with the prevailing type of something like *do you have anything to nibble?* This is in accord with the point made earlier (see section 6.1) that food-sharing indicates intimacy and is thus linked to informal language. By contrast, English requests tended to be a lot more tentative and elaborate.

The other observation concerning internal modification has to do with the form of modification which is most prolific in each language. Most modification in English is achieved by means of mitigators, which tentativize the request and thus its impact on the addressee. The most common English modifiers of this kind, frequently used with requests, are *just* and *possibly* to modify verbs, and question tags. In contrast to this tentativizing modification, which is rarely used in Greek, Greek utilizes diminutives extensively to indicate smallness and thus endearment and closeness. These are so frequently employed that they sometimes sound amusing to non-native ears. Intensifiers, on the other hand, which reinforce the request and make it sound more like a demand, are extremely rare in English, apart from cases of tension. By contrast, Greek employs more intensifiers.

Does this then mean that Greeks are less polite and less considerate of other people than the English? This would perhaps be the case if politeness depended entirely on the kind and number of words in the utterance, that is, its elaboration, but obviously this cannot be the case. On the one hand, intensifiers can also indicate an attempt by a committed speaker to avoid possible disagreement. As has already been mentioned, most intensifying items used in this way lose their literal meanings and acquire strong exhortative functions. On the other hand, elaboration may indicate formality but not necessarily politeness, and clearly these two concepts are not synonymous. Elaborate realizations are apparently closely related to one kind of politeness—negative politeness. Structures by themselves are not inherently polite or impolite, as has been pointed out elsewhere, and this would also appear to be true of their modification. Both the structures and their modification acquire their politeness index within a specific culture.

As regards external modification, the main difference between Greek and English seems to be the Greek tendency to give reasons for the requests more frequently than in English, which is a feature of positive politeness. What is essential in understanding this differential choice among the devices available in the two languages is that different social norms and values bring about different conventionalized patterns for the realization of speech acts in each language.

The best judges of whether an encounter is impolite or not are the native participants, who share, to a great extent, deeply ingrained social norms and values. Non-native participants will base their judgements on their own cultural values of what is polite, acceptable behaviour; thus, misjudgements are likely to arise. Because English culture values distance, intruding into an interlocutor's territory is something of a cultural taboo. Consequently, these distancing devices enable English speakers to sound safely vague and addressees to feel that that are not being imposed upon.

Greek culture, on the other hand, values intimacy. Intrusion into an interlocutor's territory is not taboo, or perhaps it is more accurate to say that intrusion is defined differently. Consequently, devices which emphasize this closeness are considered polite. This contention is again supported by evidence from my data. Although available in the language, distancing devices, have not been conventionalized to the same extent as they have in English. They are mostly employed asymmetrically, that is, upwards when the status of the interactants is different and perhaps when the weightiness of the imposition on the addressee is thought to be great. But here again the socially determined rights and obligations of the interactants are important factors which enter into such considerations.

8

Conclusions

In this work, an attempt has been made to investigate what is perhaps the most basic ingredient of successful interpersonal communication – politeness. Despite its significance and the recent plethora of relevant publications, politeness still remains an issue worthy of further investigation.

The main claim made here concerning the politeness orientation of the two societies seems to be further reinforced if one looks at the manifestations of other speech acts and of linguistic devices in general. To this end, other supportive evidence of this nature is referred to briefly in the following section.

8.1   FURTHER SUPPORTIVE EVIDENCE

Another positive politeness strategy is to intensify interest to the addressee. This can be achieved by making a good story. Linguistic devices which contribute to such an effect are the 'vivid present' and the use of direct rather than indirect reported speech (Brown and Levinson, 1978: 111–12). Tannen (1983: 359), in her analysis of a number of Greek narratives, reports that they were found 'very vivid' and points out that 'this impression seems simply to reflect a phenomenon frequently observed, and supported by folk wisdom, that Greeks are good storytellers'. She adds that the linguistic features which contribute to this impression are, among others, 'direct quotation in reported speech' and 'historical present verbs'. She further suggests that such linguistic features contribute to a sense of involvement; in other words, they reflect positive politeness values.

An off-record device closely related to positive politeness is the use of rhetorical questions (Brown and Levinson, 1987: 223, 251). 'One particular characteristic of MG [Modern Greek] spoken style is the very frequent use of interrogative sentences as rhetorical questions . . . often as responses to other questions' (Mackridge, 1985: 341). This, however, is not the only function performed by rhetorical questions. Very frequently they are used instead of statements. In other words, they are not information-seeking devices since they do not really require or receive any answers. They are employed by speakers in an attempt to make their contribution more vivid and interesting by provoking the addressees' more active involvement, a strategy which is clearly characteristic of positive politeness.

Furthermore, Marmaridou (1987) has noted very interesting linguistic differences in the Greek and English announcements to passengers on board Olympic Airways aircraft. Since the setting is identical, one might reasonably expect identical patterns, and yet this is not the case. The differences noticed, such as more explanations and fewer passive constructions in the Greek data, clearly reflect the positive politeness orientation of Greek society. More generally her English data appear to be clear manifestations of the negative politeness strategy 'state the FTA as a general rule', examples of which 'proliferate in airline-ese' (Brown and Levinson, 1978: 211–12). This strategy, which is closely related to indirectness, seems to be almost absent from her Greek data, which are more direct and addressee-orientated rather than indirect and setting-orientated. For instance, one of her examples is: 'Ladies and Gentlemen, if there is a doctor *on board*, kindly contact the Chief Cabin Crew', whereas the equivalent Greek announcement is 'Ladies and Gentlemen, if there is a doctor *among the passengers*, s/he is asked . . .'.

Further evidence emerged from my own research (Sifianou, 1989) into differences in telephone call openings in England and Greece. Here, too, the strategies preferred in the two cultures reflect the different politeness orientations of the two societies. In England and in France (Godard, 1977) overt self-identification of the participants and recitation of telephone numbers constitute appropriate, polite behaviour in telephonic interactions. In Greece, on the other hand, overt self-identification on the telephone is the exception rather than the rule. Even if callers identify themselves, there is hardly ever reciprocation. Furthermore, recitation of telephone numbers is rather unimaginable in a Greek context. The preference for recognition rather than overt self-identification is a positive politeness device, because as Brown and Levinson (1987: 39) point out, 'the preference for recognition without overt self-identification on the telephone can be attributed to the deleterious positive-face implications of failure of immediate recognition (like name forgetting)'. More generally, the telephone is seen as an instrument for conducting business or business-like affairs in England, which explains the formality in the language used, whereas in Greece it is seen more as an instrument for maintaining or enhancing interpersonal relationships, this explaining the informality in the language used. Social calls to exchange news or simply to chat with friends and close relatives are far more common in Greece than in England. On the other hand, Greeks do not rely on the telephone to sort out dealings with offices, stores, and so on, as frequently as the English do. Such differences can very easily lead to unfavourable judgements: see Tannen, 1984*b* quoting Kitroeff's article on instances of Greek telephonic behaviour. Here, she observes that Kitroeff assumes that his concept and strategies of politeness are universal, in spite of the fact that he had lived in Greece for twenty-five years. Therefore, since his expectations of polite telephonic behaviour are not met, he light-heartedly infers that politeness is inherent in the common telephone openings in most countries, except Greece.

Thus, even these cursory observations seem to provide additional support for a general positive politeness orientation of Greek society, an issue which has by no means been exhausted. Consequently, before summarizing our findings, I would like to address myself briefly to two areas in which the implications of this study may be of considerable significance, viz. language teaching and learning and future research.

8.2   IMPLICATIONS FOR LANGUAGE LEARNING AND TEACHING

It is widely acknowledged that adequate knowledge of subtle grammatical distinctions and lexical nuances will enable the foreign language learner to speak with greater linguistic accuracy and to understand information explicitly stated, but not necessarily to speak appropriately and understand exactly what is meant or implied in specific contexts. Getting the right message across is not always easy even within the same culture, because there are certain social and personal differences even among individuals; after all, 'the style is the man'. The problems, however, can become more serious when people from different cultures come into contact. Consequently, findings of sociolinguistic research should be of prime concern and considerable value to educators and foreign language teachers and perhaps more generally to anybody interested in becoming a successful communicator in another language. Communication difficulties due to lack of linguistic competence can be easily detected and are not associated with the non-native speaker's politeness, whereas the source of communication problems arising from different cultural assumptions and expectations, about what is appropriate linguistic behaviour, cannot be easily detected and will most probably be associated with the speaker's politeness, or rather with the lack of it. The main reason for this discrepancy seems to derive from the fact that native speakers not only develop linguistic competence through acquisition and learning but also acquire a sociolinguistic competence of which they are largely unaware. The latter type of competence is greatly determined by culturally bound interpretations of norms regarding, for example, the status and power of individuals or groups, or interpretations of freedom, harmony, generosity, politeness, etc. These norms and values are reflected in the linguistic structure and can affect upper-level discourse phenomena, such as discourse organization in general, or discourse strategies for requesting, apologizing, and disagreeing, or even lower-level phenomena such as back channel cues and fillers. It is worth noting here that even languages such as English, which are associated with a number of societies, reflect different values when used by different peoples.

In spite of the growing concern for the importance of integrating sociolinguistic findings in foreign language education, particularly in respect of curriculum and syllabus development but also for the purpose of classroom interaction for the development of communicative competence, more research needs to be undertaken.[1] Foreign language educators are expected to aim at providing learners not only with linguistic competence but also with communicative competence[2] which will enable the non-native speaker to select those grammatically correct expressions which are

---

[1] See Larsen-Freeman (1980); Loveday, (1982); Ribeiro-Pedro (1981); Sinclair and Coulthard (1978); Wolfson and Judd (1983); Thomas (1983); Valdes (1986); Yalden (1983) among others.

[2] For a review of the development of the concept of 'communicative competence', see Hymes (1985).

also appropriate in the specific situation (Gumperz, 1970: 205). The expression of politeness clearly falls within the speaker's communicative rather than linguistic competence, although the latter is a necessary prerequisite.

As a result, the burden placed upon foreign language educators has greatly increased since they are put in a very delicate position by not being justified in teaching the linguistic system without considering the socio-cultural system in which it is used. Thus, it becomes imperative to design appropriate materials and to provide foreign language teachers with the relevant training. The basis of such materials and training lies in insights gained from sociolinguistic research (see also Dendrinos, 1985 and Papaefthymiou-Lytra, 1990).

Extensive research into universal principles and cultural particulars of interaction will shed considerable light on and give insights into what it is that learners actually need to know along with their knowledge of the grammar of the foreign language in order to become successful interactants in the target language (Dendrinos, 1986). Furthermore, research into such areas will enable foreign language teachers to predict whether learners' errors are the result of their transfer of native strategies or of inadequate learning of the strategies of the target language.

The concept of politeness in a broad sense, meaning appropriate behaviour according to expected norms, is central to our better understanding of the norms of social interaction. Thus, knowledge of the cultural norms which underlie and determine surface forms seems indispensable to the acquisition of socio-cultural awareness in the foreign language. Failure to grasp such differences as well as failure to appreciate the different conventions which govern politeness strategies can lead to serious misjudgements and mis-understandings (see also Papaefthymiou-Lytra, 1987a).

There is also another issue which complicates the situation further. Cultural norms are so deeply ingrained in everybody that not only are they resistant to change but also, because they appear to be so natural, reasonable, and universal, it becomes extremely difficult to realize and make others realize that they are culture-specific and that other norms exist which are equally reasonable. It is perhaps for this reason that it is much more difficult, if at all possible, for adults to acquire different norms (Thomas, 1983: 110). For example, Tannen (1982: 229) reports an interesting case of a professional man of Greek origin living in the USA. He was occasionally bewildered by the fact that he was more indirect than most Americans. He had inherited this Greek characteristic although he did not speak any Greek.

Given the lack of research in the area of socio-cultural competence, we can only make some tentative suggestions at this stage which may be of value to both foreign language educators and learners. When the native teacher has a culturally heterogeneous group of learners, the issues involved are different and should be tackled in different ways. I shall, therefore, focus on cases in which both the foreign language instructor and the students share the same socio-cultural background.

Research concerning politeness phenomena has attracted a great deal of interest in recent years and justifiably so, since politeness is basic to social interaction and is an integral part of the socio-cultural system. Among the aspects and manifestations of politeness which have been explored, the area of requesting occupies a prominent position. This, of course, does not mean that this area has been exhausted; on the contrary, much more has to be done. On the other hand, some valuable insights are available and should be incorporated into textbooks and teachers' manuals. The informed teacher can thus have a base from which to start explaining, expanding, and sensitizing students on issues of appropriate interaction.

Requests are very frequent in daily encounters, outside and inside the classroom, perhaps more so in Greek than in English. In addition to differences observed in the concept of requesting in the two societies (see section 5.3), the interest in requests also lies in the fact that they manifest a wide variety of both constructions and lexical alternatives reflecting differing values. Thus, for instance, a Greek learner may use an imperative or a direct construction for a request where a native English speaker would find an indirect construction more appropriate. Problems can also arise from the inappropriate use of modals, terms of address, diminutives, and so on. For instance, the elaborate system of modals in English (see section 6.2.1) may puzzle the Greek learner, who will tend to generalize and use *must* to express obligation in most contexts. The lack of a title plus first name (TFN) form of address in English will force the Greek learner either to transfer this form from Greek or choose inappropriately between a title plus last name (TLN) or simply a first name term of address (FN) (see section 3.5). Thus, instead of addressing a non-intimate neighbour, for instance, as 'Mr Jones' he may say either 'Mr Bill' or simply 'Bill'. Similar failure can also arise from different assessments of the status or the social distance between interlocutors. For instance, a Greek learner, even if encouraged to do so, would find it a lot more difficult to address the teacher by first name than would be the case in England, especially in a university context, since the teacher as a rule is seen as having a higher status in Greece. Relaxing this convention may lead the student to assume that the social distance has been decreased and, consequently, that such a teacher may be approached and asked for various kinds of favours which assume a closer relationship. The lack of a rich system of diminutives in English, when compared to Greek, one of whose functions is to soften the force of imperative requests (see section 7.2.2.1.1) may lead the learner to use an English imperative request without any mitigating device, since the diminutivized form cannot be rendered. One could add numerous examples which can cause such un-intentional appropriateness errors, but my main aim here has been to point out some possible ways of overcoming such problems.

Giving lists of alternatives for drills and memorization and endless admonitions as to what is correct and polite can only demoralize the learner and thus defeat the original purpose. In any case, there is considerable variation in the degree of socio-cultural competence even within the same community; there is not just one way of behaving appropriately. How do we then go about trying to develop this competence without risking results entirely opposite to those intended? First of all, non-native teachers, using appropriate materials should consciously and conscientiously try to present an appropriate model for students to imitate. Secondly, they should be alert to instances from interactions in the classroom which can be commented upon, exemplified, and perhaps drilled. These should include both felicitous and infelicitous occurrences. Praise of specific successful attempts will function not only as a reward for the success of the attempt but also as an explicit demonstration of what is expected. On the other hand, if the students employ an imperative construction for a request and the teachers feel that this is rather inappropriate in the specific context, they can invite the class to give alternative possibilities.

Furthermore, occasions will arise in which students use an

inappropriate or mother-tongue construction to apologize, thank, compliment, offer, etc., or perhaps omit such verbal behaviour altogether in a context in which it is required. The teacher should pick up and exploit all these instances, but of course with discretion and sensitivity. Such opportunities may prove rare, but provide means for natural exchanges which cannot be left unexploited.[3]

Generally speaking, however, the kind of interaction which naturally takes place in a classroom is rather different from what happens in society at large. Thus, the teacher aided by appropriate materials will have to design real-life situations and have students role-play them (Dendrinos, 1988). If these are carefully selected to depict everyday life, they can lead to interesting discussions.

Class discussions can also be motivated by available teaching materials. The teacher can pick out all sorts of points which may differ from the native culture. These can include topics which may be considered taboo; structures functioning in different ways; equivalent lexical items which may appear redundant, meaningless, or misplaced; and fixed expressions which, when rendered into another language, will not be appropriate for the same function. Many textbooks, in illustrating instructions for instance, present the procedure that should be followed to use a public telephone in England. This is an excellent opportunity for the teacher to expand on the discourse considered appropriate. What are the expected opening exchanges? Is overt self-identification always necessary? More general aspects of cultural assumptions and knowledge of the world should also be brought up, for instance, personal aspects which can or cannot be freely inquired about, such as income and marital status.

Other sources of invaluable cultural information are newspapers and magazines, and, of course, radio and television. The presentation of a certain news item, an advertisement, an interview, and so on, can serve as the basis for comparisons which may lead to cultural insights. Students should be encouraged to contribute their own views and explanations on elements they find odd, irrelevant, or simply different. Great care and awareness of the issues involved are obviously needed on the part of the teacher in tackling such comparisons so that undesirable value judgements are avoided or are pointed out as such (Papaefthymiou-Lytra, 1987*b*).

---

[3] See Papaefthymiou-Lytra (1990), for practical applications.

Films and literature, especially plays, can also serve as an excellent, interesting source of cultural information (Valdes, 1986). Good playwrights, more than textbook writers, depict their socio-cultural milieu. The students can be encouraged to read, improvise, and even perform plays. Thus, apart from all other benefits of reading, they will be enabled to discover or pinpoint a variety of cultural aspects in natural contexts. Such knowledge will not only facilitate effective cross-cultural communication, but will also increase their understanding of their own culture and language in a most enjoyable way.

These are just a few examples of what can be done in a class to increase the students' awareness of the variety of the issues involved in politeness and to help them improve their communicative performance in the target language. One may wonder what the ultimate goal of such a concerted effort would be if one cannot really escape from one's own culture. The aspiration is not for the students to abandon their cultural identity and conform to other cultural norms. Foreign language educators should aim only at assisting students in becoming aware of the different ways of behaving both verbally and non-verbally. Such awareness does not mean that cultural differences will necessarily be reduced. It simply means that students will be furnished with adequate knowledge which will facilitate their understanding of these cultural differences and thus help them increase their flexibility towards and tolerance of cross-cultural variation. Even if learners are not prepared to conform to other norms when interacting with foreigners because they still find such norms odd or exaggerated, they will at least be capable of identifying the sources of possible problems. Consequently, fluent, non-native speakers will be enabled to avoid appearing impolite, hypocritical, or ironical, and also to make less biased judgements of others because they will have gained the ability to grasp the true significance of what they hear, and, therefore, to behave accordingly. As Thomas (1983: 96) points out, the teacher's job is not to enforce Anglo-Saxon standards, but only to prevent students from unintentionally appearing rude or subservient.

Possible resistance to conformity to the socio-cultural norms underlying the target linguistic system is but one side of the coin, the other being more positive. The Greek learner, being brought up in a more or less homogeneous socio-cultural environment, comes to class unaware of the possibility of cross-cultural differences, except possibly for stereotypes. Once properly sensitized, a student will most probably be willing to try to acquire the complete system of the target language rather than simply its linguistic aspect. Similarly, Thomas (1983: 103) contends that in so far as the learner 'is prepared to learn the language at all, s/he is usually willing, if not able, to try to conform to the pragmalinguistic norms of the target language'.

Language and culture are intricately interrelated. Evidence for this is the fact that when the cultural system changes, the linguistic system is influenced as well, and vice versa. Certain features of linguistic structure, such as honorifics or diminutives, appear to reflect cultural aspects directly; others do so indirectly. Thus, modern language teachers cannot ignore the social structure and the cultural values of the society in which the language is used. They cannot teach the one successfully apart from the other because on the one hand, they will be doing their students the service of teaching them a different code with which to communicate, but on the other, they will be doing them the disservice of reducing the possibilities of successful, satisfying, and harmonious communication. Even if this is not considered to be a challenge in its own right, sensitization with cross-cultural issues will increase one's understanding of the deep interrelationship of one's own language and culture and will, consequently, lead to broad-mindedness and tolerance of practices different from one's own. This reason alone points to the importance of further research into cross-cultural issues, which is briefly discussed in the next section.

8.3   IMPLICATIONS FOR FUTURE RESEARCH

Thorough investigation and awareness of how people use language in their daily lives should help to improve both intercultural and intracultural communication and understanding. These are significant reasons for pursuing further research in this area. Politeness phenomena go to the very foundations of social life and are reflected in all levels of language. Thus, they are of interest to both scholars and laymen who are concerned with finding out more about what contributes to the success or failure of our everyday interactions and what it is that strains and breaks or creates and improves social relationships.

Until fairly recently, our knowledge regarding processes of interaction and behaviour in general across cultures has been largely anecdotal, consisting mainly of observations and personal experiences of visitors with different cultural backgrounds. These observations have led to various persistent positive and negative stereotypes, which are worth investigating since they may point to problem areas. The recent development of the variety of approaches to language study outside the transformational models has brought interaction and politeness phenomena to the centre of scholars' concern. Initial scattered attempts generated a plethora of publications within a variety of fields, especially after the reissue of Brown and Levinson's extended essay in 1987. Lakoff's (1973) rule-based approach has been shown to be brief and inadequate to account for politeness phenomena universally. On the other hand, Leech's detailed model appears to be a rather theoretical construct mainly dealing with 'absolute' politeness. The most extensive, independent theory of politeness is found in Brown and Levinson's work. Being so extensive, covering a wide variety of aspects ranging from higher-level linguistic phenomena to minute details, it offers a useful tool for the study of interaction. Their findings have been both supported and refuted by subsequent research. Nevertheless, their detailed discussion still remains highly intriguing and provides flexible means for cross-cultural and intracultural research.

It has been suggested elsewhere that it may not be unreasonable to assume that societies which have been stereotyped as less polite most probably exhibit a positive politeness orientation, whereas societies which have been stereotyped as more polite most probably exhibit a negative politeness orientation. This may be a consequence of the very simple fact that the overtly marked formality, which is encapsulated in negative politeness devices, is what we readily conjure up when we try to measure the degree of politeness in utterances or in behaviour generally.

However, in contrast to earlier works attributing a negative politeness orientation to Chinese (Young, 1982) and Japanese (Brown and Levinson, 1978: 250) cultures, more recent research (Gu, 1990; Matsumoto, 1988) challenge these assumptions and claim that Brown and Levinson's model based on two distinct aspects of face cannot adequately account for politeness phenomena in these cultures. These observations suggest that the deference component may need reconsideration. It may be the case that the concepts of 'deference' and 'formality' in oriental cultures differ from those in Western societies. However, to my knowledge, the solidarity politeness component has not been shown so far to present any similar problems. On the contrary, research on a variety of cultures has identified a number of positive politeness strategies to be prevalent in daily encounters. A tentative reservation relates to the 'seek agreement' and 'avoid disagreement' strategies which intuitively appear to be unlikely positive politeness devices.

It should be noted here that even if some societies have the same politeness orientation, they will not exhibit identical preferences of strategies, since this orientation is relative rather than absolute. This similarity of orientation deserves further investigation because it may contribute to a better understanding of as yet unsuspected similarities and differences, which may provide scholars with a more secure basis for claims of universality of politeness principles. Furthermore, the use that societies make of off-record strategies is decisive, because it seems that such devices can function in at least two ways: they can be perceived and interpreted either as positive politeness devices offering addressees opportunities to be of help, or as negative politeness devices enabling speakers to minimize impositions. Off-recordness and its relation to indirectness is worthy of further investigation because it is quite intricate and rather poorly understood. As it stands, it leaves ample room for doubts as to whether Brown and Levinson (1987: 20) are correct in insisting, in spite of counter-arguments, that there is an intrinsic ranking of their politeness strategies. On the one hand, one could be easily trapped into assuming that societies having a more positive politeness orientation are less polite than those having a more negative politeness orientation. It would be fatuous even to think that there is the possibility of some peoples being more polite than others. What is possible is a differential preference of formality, which indicates the need for examination of the relationship between formality and politeness, and more generally of the relationship between politeness and courtesy, tact, generosity, etc. On the other hand, the position of off-recordness in societies is unclear, as is the claim which attributes higher degrees of politeness to off-record constructions.

Consequently, despite any shortcomings, Brown and Levinson's theory still remains an extensive and flexible model which can serve as a springboard for cross-cultural comparisons and contrasts for

many years to come. Such research may include a wide variety of
cultures and linguistic systems, going down to the minutiae of
linguistic phenomena which may even escape strict linguistic
interpretation. For instance, in Greek there is a pronoun *mu* which
can be inserted optionally in certain constructions, such as *ti mu
kanis* literally meaning 'what are you doing *for me*' used as a
greeting in the sense of 'how are you'. The use of this element
cannot be explained in terms of grammar, as it is neither the subject
nor the object of the construction. It is simply an element with the
pragmatic function of indicating a certain closeness in the relationship and cannot be rendered in English. This may seem a small
inconsequential difference which, however, points to the more
general and important issue of the interrelationship of language and
culture.

Therefore, more cross-cultural research seems to be necessary to
explain differences in a wide variety of broad and specific linguistic
aspects, embracing spoken and written discourse organization,
topics which can or cannot be publicly brought up, which questions
can be freely asked of whom and by whom, names and manifestations
of speech acts, and a variety of other issues which may crop up in
the process but which have been unsuspected so far. All these
should be seen within the value system and the experiences and
beliefs—religious, political, or otherwise—of the communities
under study, areas which have received relatively little attention so
far. Their significance, however, should not be ignored, as they
penetrate the linguistic domain in intricate and inconspicuous
ways. If, for instance, a society places a high priority on linguistic
sincerity, it will not be surprising to find that these people will
prefer direct to indirect constructions, as Blum-Kulka (1987: 145)
reports for speakers of Hebrew. It has been reported that some
cultures are more tolerant of direct lying, for various reasons, than
others who prefer a more indirect kind. Such a difference will
obviously be reflected in their linguistic codes. What should be
borne in mind, as Thomas (1983: 106) points out, is that when we
talk about cultural values in linguistics, we are not referring to any
'moral or spiritual qualities', but only to 'the linguistic encoding of
certain attitudes and values'.

The need for cross-cultural research becomes more conspicuous
nowadays when contact on all levels between people from different
backgrounds has increased and will go on increasing. English, being

spoken by millions of people as first, second, or foreign language, has received considerable attention from scholars. It has been taken for granted, to a great extent, that pragmatic features of English in particular must characterize any other language, simply because they are 'natural' and 'reasonable'. This has led to a degree of ethnocentricity in most accounts and surprisingly ignores the fact that even native English speakers from different cultural backgrounds can have communication problems, obviously not because of the linguistic code, but because of the culturally specific expectations of what is appropriate in a specific context. For example, an interesting difference which may cause problems when Americans interact with Australians is reported by Smith (1987*b*: 2). She says, quoting Renwick, that 'Americans tend to like people who agree with them. Australians are more apt to be interested in a person who disagrees with them; disagreement is a basis for a lively conversation. Americans assume that if someone agrees with them, that person likes them; disagreement implies rejection.'

It has also been taken for granted or somehow implicitly assumed that the burden for the success of cross-cultural encounters lies with non-native speakers of English. Any failure is usually their responsibility, because they were misunderstood or led their interlocutors to misunderstand by not expressing themselves appropriately. This should not be taken to imply any intentional denigration; it only points to the importance of recognition by both native and non-native speakers that variant conventions do exist which are as 'natural' and 'reasonable' as their own.

Thus, work which has been done on English could be used as a starting point for further research on what happens in other cultural and linguistic systems. If a wide variety and number of societies are investigated, then more objective results will be guaranteed.

In conclusion, it should be noted that such findings should not be confined to academic books and periodicals. In addition to language teachers and educationalists in general, the general public should be made aware of such findings. Their need is no less serious than that of scholars and educators. They may have been equally puzzled and embarrassed on occasions and they may have been faced with unpleasant situations they were not able to understand. Thus, their desire to communicate effectively should not be underrated. In any case, only in this way will the necessary sensitization towards cross-cultural issues infiltrate societies and cease to remain the prerogative of the few.

8.4   FINAL CONCLUDING REMARKS

Human beings are assumed to have basic universal needs which partly motivate communication. The success or failure of communication itself greatly depends on the understanding and use of the appropriate politeness principles. Although individuals may have their own personal styles of communication, personal values reflect group values to a great extent. This explains why we can make generalizations, both positive and negative auto- and hetero-stereotyping.

One motivation for this work is the observation that the concept and patterns of polite behaviour and, consequently, the expectations of the interactants involved differ from culture to culture. To account for these differences between Greece and England, the theoretical model proposed by Brown and Levinson (1978, 1987) was used extensively, concentrating mainly on their dichotomy between positive and negative politeness, in other words, between familiar, friendly 'solidarity politeness' and formal 'deference politeness'. Although it is preposterous to see this distinction as absolute, in a relative sense, it can shed considerable light on differences observed in various societies.

My hypothesis has been that the major difference concerning the Greek and the English systems of politeness is a matter of orientation rather than degree—more negative politeness orientation in England and more positive politeness orientation in Greece. This is not surprising if we bear in mind the importance Greeks attach to the in-group/out-group distinction, which entails closer relationships and thus less formality among people who belong to the same in-group. For these people the functional significance of closer ties is obvious. 'It is easier to survive in a highly competitive world as a member of a group of people who cooperate and help one another' (Triandis and Vassiliou, 1972: 305). Since 'social structure informs and determines interaction and . . . interaction creates or recreates social structure' (Brown and Levinson, 1978: 245–6) the differences observed seem to fall into place.

Although the approach to data has been qualitative rather than quantitative, the large amount and great variety of data examined from both languages has made certain generalizations possible. The first observation is that the notion of politeness itself is construed differently in the two societies—broader in Greece, narrower in England. This finding is in accord with Brown and Levinson's observation that positive politeness is less focused and less specific than negative politeness. This obviously leads to both different expectations of what polite behaviour is and different verbal and non-verbal realizations of politeness, partly justifying my hypothesis.

Further and more extensive justification has resulted from the analysis and interpretation of the actual manifestations of requests in everyday encounters. At first sight, both languages appear to afford their speakers very similar constructions for performing requests, yet there are significant differences in terms of both structures and their modification. It is these differences, such as the flexibility to use indicative constructions to request, which are revealing. The structural similarities between these languages will undoubtedly facilitate people's communication, but even these cannot guarantee appropriate results. And clearly it is this appropriateness which causes most misunderstandings, embarrassment, and sometimes hard feelings, as everybody who has tried to communicate in a foreign language knows all too well.

Within the set of grammatically possible structures, there is a subset of conventionalized ones for specific contexts, which vary from language to language. An illustration of this is that present indicative constructions are frequent conventional means of requesting in Greek, whereas it is mainly ability questions which serve this purpose in English. By contrast, such questions work more successfully as questions about one's ability to do the act, rather than as requests to perform it in French and Russian (Thomas, 1983: 97). All this is indispensable knowledge for every speaker who aspires not just to communicate, but to communicate appropriately and successfully in a foreign language, especially since choice among variants is so frequently attributed not only to degrees of politeness but also to mental ability. In the same way lexical items and their nuances will be expanded or restricted to cover the needs of each particular community. Thus, for instance, the fact that the breadth of the term *request* cannot be rendered by a single lexical item in Greek is indicative of a differential conception of the speech act as a whole.

Which forms will be selected and conventionalized in a language largely depends on the cultural values of that linguistic community. For instance, it could be argued that although modals are flexible means for encoding distancing in the past or future, this cannot be achieved by means of the present tense. Socio-cultural norms and values underlie the tacit agreement among native speakers as to which forms are conventionalized, which forms carry what degree and what kind of politeness, and when, where, and by whom they can be successfully used. As Hudson (1980: 119) has pointed out, 'different norms for speech in different societies can often be explained by reference to other aspects of their culture and cannot, therefore, be satisfactorily studied in isolation'. A case in point is the required degree of indirectness in directives. The preference for conventional indirectness and elaboration in English reflects the need for independence and may well have sprung from the abolition of the singular/plural distinction. Thus, formality had to be expressed by other linguistic means, and elaboration was a convenient solution. The fact that this kind of elaboration and indirectness is not only used on formal occasions but prevails in everyday informal encounters as well does not invalidate the above claim. It further reinforces it, because, since the plural *you* was chosen and established as the only possible second person address form, it is not unreasonable to suggest that the same reasons underlie the preference and conventionalization of more elaborate forms at the expense of simple, more direct ones.

In Greek, on the other hand, elaboration is not necessary to the same extent, since the singular/plural distinction facilitates the manifestation of formality. Thus, simple yes–no questions are more frequently employed as requests than more elaborate, indirect ones; and imperatives exhibiting a wider flexibility as far as number, aspect, and even person are concerned are used as appropriate requesting devices by native speakers. This cannot be unrelated to the general ethos of Greek society which allows more directness than English society. To be reserved and distant and to avoid expressing feelings and emotions are not usually approved cultural principles in Greece.

Conversational strategies—and conventional indirectness is one of them—have very often been explained in terms of a universal natural logic. Brown and Levinson contend that the reasoning behind indirectness lies in universal principles, although they also point out that the use of these principles differs systematically across and within cultures. This is a valid observation because otherwise people whose speech norms do not rely so heavily on indirect constructions to perform requests would be condemned not only as impolite but also as not sharing what is thought of as universal, natural logic. It should be borne in mind that besides universal, natural logic, there is also what Gumperz (1982*a*: 182) has called 'cultural logic'.

A thorough investigation of politeness strategies should also include a close examination of the kinds of modification that are present in requests. Here, too, the differences in my data between Greek and English were revealing. Most types of modification found in English contributed to elaboration, and generally enabled the speaker to sound more tentative and less sure of the outcome; for instance, openers, tags, downtoners, and so on. By contrast, in Greek the softeners were of a different kind; for instance, diminutives and other modifiers with a similar force. Such modifiers do not enable the speaker to sound more tentative and uncertain, but reinforce a picture of closeness. Intensifiers, most of which cannot even be rendered in English, were also frequent in Greek. Terms of address were also found to be more frequently used in Greek than in English. These, together with diminutives, constitute in-group identity markers, which are features of positive politeness. Greeks were also found to give reasons for their requests more frequently than the English, which is yet another characteristic of positive politeness.

The conclusion that can be arrived at from the investigation of both the conventionalized request patterns and the preferences for modification in the two languages is that Greeks tend to prefer more positive politeness strategies, such as in-group markers, more direct patterns and in general devices which can be seen as attempts to include the addressee in the activity. They also tend to use constructions which sound more optimistic about the outcome of the request; for instance, they use imperatives, but avoid negative requesting constructions. The English, on the other hand, seem to prefer negative politeness devices as far as both structures and modifications are concerned. Conventional indirectness, the chief characteristic of negative politeness, is equated with politeness, and this together with the preferred modification contribute to the elaboration of the structure and the tentativeness of the message.

Pessimism expressed by means of negative constructions is also frequent. Linguistic pessimism versus linguistic optimism is perhaps the major difference between positive politeness and negative politeness societies (Brown and Levinson, 1978: 131).

I hope it has become clear that despite the similarities the conception and manifestations of politeness are essentially different in the two societies. Consequently, judgements concerning the other culture based on one's culturally determined conception are bound to be biased and misleading. People usually express themselves in a natural, polite way, conforming to social expectations including those of the addressee.[4] If an utterance does not satisfy the addressee's expectations, then this deviation gives rise to judgements concerning the politeness of the utterance and the speaker. This does not usually happen in encounters among fellow natives, but it is more common when the participants have different socio-cultural backgrounds and thus different expectations.

The English, being from a more negative politeness society, where politeness is very closely related to formality, may consider Greeks to be too friendly and impolite. By the same token, Greeks, being from a more positive politeness society, may judge the English as too formal and distant and perhaps hypocritical rather than polite. If the speaker is perceived to be too polite, the addressee may be insulted, which will also be the case if the speaker is perceived to be too friendly (see Brown and Levinson, 1978: 235).

Thus, clearly, cultures cannot be reasonably and objectively assessed as more or less polite than others, but polite in different ways, or 'appealing to different forms of politeness' (Thomas, 1983: 98). This also explains why some Greeks find their compatriots impolite. Besides those who have aspirations for social advancement and feel that this can be partly achieved by imitating foreign or socially higher ways of behaviour, there are also those who, most probably under foreign influence for various reasons such as having lived abroad for a long time, have changed their views and expectations of what polite behaviour is. Perhaps more importantly, the fact that Greeks construe politeness as a wider,

---

[4] For a fuller discussion of the important role that the native listener's expectations play for the successful interpretation of speech acts in native/non-native encounters and their relation to politeness, see Ervin-Tripp (1976), Tannen (1984*a*); Hackman (1977).

more inclusive concept than the English has led to a greater diversity of opinions concerning the degree of politeness of other Greeks.

Thus, although this work is by no means exhaustive, I hope that it has been demonstrated that the observed differences in the two cultures reflect differences in the conception and realization of politeness rather than differences in the degree of politeness. This knowledge is, I believe, indispensable for improving intercultural understanding and appreciation of values and attitudes that differ from our own.

APPENDIX I
Plays Used as Data

A. GREEK PLAYS

ANAGNOSTAKI, LOULA
AN 1   1. I KASETA (The Cassette), 1–106 (unpublished).

EFTHEMIADES, MITSOS
E 1   1. FONIAS (The Murderer), Theatrika 2: 9–99 (Athens: Asteri, 1981).
E 2   2. O FONDAS (Fondas), Theatrika 1: 81–105 (Athens: Asteri, 1981).
E 3   3. TO IPOSTEGO (The Shelter), Theatrika 1: 110–29 (Athens: Asteri, 1981).
E 4   4. PSOFJI KORJI (Dead Bed-bugs), Theatrika 1: 133–62 (Athens: Asteri, 1981).

KAMBANELLIS, IAKOVOS
KA 1   1. EVDOMI MERA TIS DIMIOURGIAS (The Seventh Day of Creation), Theatro 1: 21–87 (Athens: Kedros, 1978).
KA 2   2. I AVLI TON THAVMATON (The Courtyard of Miracles), Theatro 1: 96–187 (Athens: Kedros, 1978).
KA 3   3. I ILIKIA TIS NICHTAS (The Age of Night), Theatro 1: 197–276 (Athens: Kedros 1978).

KEHAIDIS, DEMITRIS
KE 1   1. I VERA (The Wedding Ring), 9–55 (Athens: Ermis, 1984).
KE 2   2. TO TAVLI (The Backgammon), Theatro 1: 59–114 (Athens: Ermis, 1984).

—— and HAVIARA, E.
KE 3   3. DAFNES KE PIKRODAFNES (Laurels and Bitter Laurels), Theatro 3: 9–108 (Athens: Ermis, 1980).

MANIOTIS, GEORGE
MN 1   1. TO MATS (The Match), 9–83, 2nd edn. (Athens: Kedros, 1978).
MN 2   2. PATHIMATA (Misfortunes), 11–69, 2nd edn. (Athens: Kedros, 1976).
MN 3   3. PROINI SINOMILIA (Morning Chat), in TA PARASITA (Interference), 31–61 (Athens: Kedros, 1983).
MN 4   4. TO PECHNIDI TON CHRISTOUGENON (Christmas Game), in TA PARASITA (Interference), 63–110 (Athens: Kedros, 1983).

MN 5   5. TO KINIGI TOU THISAVROU (Treasure Hunt), in TA
        PARASITA (Intereference), 111–58 (Athens: Kedros, 1983).

MN 6   6. EORTASTIKO PROGRAMA (Festive Programme), in TA
        PARASITA (Interference), 159–80 (Athens: Kedros, 1983).

MN 7   7. MISTIRIO STO PANEPISTIMIO (Mystery in the University),
        in TA PARASITA (Interference), 181–233 (Athens: Kedros,
        1983).

MOURSELAS, KOSTAS

MR 1   1. ENIDRIO (Aquarium), 11–116 (Athens: Kedros, n.d.).

MR 2   2. I KIRIA DEN PENTHI (The Lady Doesn't Mourn), in
        Selected Short Plays, 9–47 (Athens: Estia, 1984).

MR 3   3. TO DIKANO (The Double-barrelled Shot Gun), in *Selected
        Short Plays*, 51–69 (Athens: Estia, 1984).

MR 4   4. TO ROLOI (The Clock), in *Selected Short Plays*, 71–102
        (Athens: Estia, 1984).

MR 5   5. DIAKOPI REVMATOS (Power Failure), in *Selected Short
        Plays*, 103–118 (Athens: Estia, 1984).

MR 6   6. I MEGALI KOBINA (The Big Deal), in *Selected Short Plays*,
        119–28 (Athens: Estia, 1984).

MR 7   7. I BOUHARA (The Bouhara Carpet), in *Selected Short Plays*,
        129–41 (Athens: Estia, 1984).

MR 8   8. GRAFIO ME THEA PROS TIN PLATIA SINTAGMATOS
        (Office Overlooking Syntagma Square), in *Selected Short
        Plays*, 143–55 (Athens: Estia, 1984).

MATESIS, PAVLOS

MT 1   1. O STATHMOS (The Station), 73–103 (Athens: Dodoni,
        n.d.).

MT 2   2. TO FANDASMA TOU KIRIOU RAMON NOVARO (Mr.
        Ramon Novaro's Ghost) 7–96 2nd edn. (Athens: Kedros,
        1982).

MT 3   3. I KIRIA PAPADIMITRAKOPOULOU-GAGANOPOULOU
        STO PARKO (Mrs Papadimitrakopoulou-Gaganopoulou in
        the Park), in MIKRO-ASTIKO DIKEO (Petty Bourgeoisie
        Law), 9–22 (Athens: Kedros, 1984).

MT 4   4. O EPIKIDIOS (The Funeral Oration), in MIKRO-ASTIKO
        DIKEO (Petty Bourgeoisie Law), 23–34 (Athens: Kedros,
        1984).

MT 5   5. TO MELON INE MONO DIKO MAS (The Future Is Only
        Ours), in MIKRO-ASTIKO DIKEO (Petty Bourgeoisie Law),
        35–47 (Athens: Kedros, 1984).

MT 6   6. ANDONA (Andona), in MIKRO-ASTIKO DIKEO (Petty Bourgeoisie Law), 49–62 (Athens: Kedros, 1984).

MT 7   7. SAKOULA APO BOUTIK GALIKI (Carrier Bag from a French Boutique), in MIKRO-ASTIKO DIKEO (Petty Bourgeoisie Law), 63–71 (Athens: Kedros, 1984).

MT 8   8. TO FTERO (The Feather), in MIKRO-ASTIKO DIKEO (Petty Bourgeoisie Law), 73–94 (Athens: Kedros, 1984).

PONDIKAS, MARIOS

P 1   1. THEATES (The Audience), 9–67, 2nd edn. (Athens: Kedros, 1985).

P 2   2. ESOTERIKE IDISIS (Domestic News), 21–104 (Athens: Gnosi, 1981).

SKOURTIS, GEORGE

S 1   1. DADADES (The Nannies), Theatro 2: 7–80 (Athens: Ermis, 1982). Translated by Philip Ramp (unpublished).

S 2   2. O FANDAROS (The Soldier), in KOMATIA KE THRIPSALA (Pieces and Fragments), 9–24, 5th edn. (Athens: Kedros, 1976).

S 3   3. ISTERIA (Hysteria), in KOMATIA KE THRIPSALA (Pieces and Fragments), 25–34, 5th edn. (Athens: Kedros, 1976).

S 4   4. O ANERGOS (Out of Work), in KOMATIA KE THRIPSALA (Pieces and Fragments), 35–47, 5th edn. (Athens: Kedros, 1976).

S 5   5. THRIPSALA (Fragments), in KOMATIA KE THRIPSALA (Pieces and Fragments), 49–63, 5th edn. (Athens: Kedros, 1976).

S 6   6. KOMATIA (Pieces), in KOMATIA KE THRIPSALA (Pieces and Fragments), 65–76, 5th edn. (Athens: Kedros, 1976).

S 7   7. TO DANIO (The Loan), in KOMATIA KE THRIPSALA (Pieces and Fragments), 77–86, 5th edn. (Athens: Kedros, 1976).

S 8   8. O APERGOSPASTIS (Scum), in KOMATIA KE THRIPSALA (Pieces and Fragments), 87–96, 5th edn. (Athens: Kedros, 1976).

S 9   9. I PALI (The Struggle), in KOMATIA KE THRIPSALA (Pieces and Fragments), 97–111, 5th edn. (Athens: Kedros, 1976).

ZIOGAS, VASILIS

Z 1   1. PASCHALINA PECHNIDIA (Easter Games), 9–135, 2nd edn. (Athens: Kedros, 1971).

Z 2   2. CHROMATISTES GINEKES (Scarlet Women), 5–52 (Athens: Ermis, 1985).

Z 3   3. TO PROXENIO TIS ANTIGONIS (A Match for Antigoni), 7–38 (Athens: Ermis, 1980).

Z 4   4. I KOMODIA TIS MIGAS (The Comedy of the Fly), 40–79
       (Athens: Ermis, 1980).

B. ENGLISH PLAYS

AYCKBOURN, ALAN

A 1   1. ABSURD PERSON SINGULAR, in *Three Plays*, 11–101
       (Harmondsworth: Penguin Books, 1976).

A 2   2. ABSENT FRIENDS, in *Three Plays* 103–70 (Harmondsworth:
       Penguin Books, 1976).

A 3   3. BEDROOM FARCE, in *Three Plays*, 171–251 (Harmonds-
       worth: Penguin Books, 1976).

BOND, EDWARD

B 1   1. SUMMER, 1–54 (London: Methuen, 1982).

B 2   2. SAVED, in *Plays: One*, 21–133 (London: Eyre Methuen,
       1977).

ORTON, JOE

OR 1   1. THE RUFFIAN ON THE STAIR, in *The Complete Plays*, 29–
        61 (London: Eyre Methuen, 1976).

OR 2   2. ENTERTAINING MR SLOANE, in *The Complete Plays*, 63–
        149 (London: Eyre Methuen, 1976).

OR 3   3. THE GOOD AND FAITHFUL SERVANT, in *The Complete
        Plays*, 151–92 (London: Eyre Methuen, 1976).

OR 4   4. LOOT, in *The Complete Plays*, 193–275 (London: Eyre
        Methuen, 1976).

OR 5   5. THE ERPINGHAM CAMP, in *The Complete Plays*, 277–320
        (London: Eyre Methuen, 1976).

OR 6   6. FUNERAL GAMES, in *The Complete Plays*, 321–60 (London:
        Eyre Methuen, 1976).

OR 7   7. WHAT THE BUTLER SAW, in *The Complete Plays*, 361–
        448 (London: Eyre Methuen, 1976).

OSBORNE, JOHN

OS 1   1. LOOK BACK IN ANGER, 6–96 (London: Faber and Faber,
        1957).

PAGE, LOUISE

PG 1   1. GOLDEN GIRLS, 1–108 (London, 1985).

Poliakoff, Stephen
PL 1   1. RUNNERS, 5–63 (London: Methuen, 1984).
PL 2   2. SOFT TARGETS, 65–117 (London: Methuen, 1984).

Pinter, Harold
PN 1   1. OLD TIMES, in *Plays: Four*, 1–71 (London: Eyre Methuen, 1981).
PN 2   2. NO MAN'S LAND, in *Plays: Four*, 73–153 (London: Eyre Methuen, 1981).
PN 3   3. BETRAYAL, in *Plays: Four*, 155–268 (London: Eyre Methuen, 1981).
PN 4   4. FAMILY VOICES, in *Plays: Four*, 279–296 (London: Eyre Methuen, 1981).

Russell, Willy
R 1   1. EDUCATING RITA, 1–96 (Harlow: Longman Study Texts, 1985).

Stoppard, Tom
ST 1   1. NIGHT AND DAY, 9–95 (London: Faber and Faber, 1978).

Storey, David
SR 1   1. EARLY DAYS, 7–53 (Harmondsworth: Penguin Books, 1980).
SR 2   2. SISTERS, 55–148 (Harmondsworth: Penguin Books, 1980).

APPENDIX II

Questionnaires

1. QUESTIONNAIRE ON THE DEFINITION OF POLITENESS

I would very much appreciate your help with my research. Could you please fill in the blanks or put an X in the appropriate box in the following. PLEASE PRINT OR WRITE CLEARLY.

Age: 18–25 ☐   26–40 ☐   41–60 ☐
Sex: F ☐   M ☐
Place of birth: —————————————————————————
Place of residence: ————————————————————————
How many years have you lived there?
        Up to 2 ☐   3–10 ☐   Over 10 ☐

Education: Elementary School: Yes ☐   No ☐
        High School: Yes ☐   No ☐
        University: Yes ☐   No ☐
Occupation/Profession: ————————————————————
Foreign languages you know very well: ——————————————

Education Elementary School: Yes ☐   No ☐
of mother: High School: Yes ☐   No ☐
        University: Yes ☐   No ☐
Mother's occupation/profession: ———————————————
Education Elementary School: Yes ☐   No ☐
of father: High School: Yes ☐   No ☐
        University: Yes ☐   No ☐
Father's occupation/profession: ———————————————

1. Could you please write in the space provided below what the word 'politeness' means to you, and what you consider to be the characteristics of a polite person.

———————————————————————————————————
———————————————————————————————————
———————————————————————————————————

2. Please give an example of behaviour which impresses you as being polite.

———————————————————————————————————
———————————————————————————————————
———————————————————————————————————

3. Please give an example of behaviour which impresses you as being impolite.

_____
_____
_____
_____

4. How could you characterise English people[1] in general? (Please tick the answer which for you is the most appropriate.)
   a. very polite ——————
   b. fairly polite ——————
   c. not polite   ——————

5. Add any comments you consider relevant to this questionnaire.

_____
_____
_____
_____
_____

Thank you for being frank and helpful.

[1] In the Greek version informants were asked to characterize Greek people.

2. QUESTIONNAIRE ON REQUESTS

I would very much appreciate your help with my research. Could you please fill in the blanks or put an X in the appropriate box in the following. PLEASE PRINT OR WRITE CLEARLY.

Age: 18–25 ☐   26–40 ☐   41–60 ☐
Sex: F ☐   M ☐
Place of birth: ————————————————————————————————
Place of residence: ————————————————————————————
How many years have you lived there?
         Up to 2 ☐   3–10 ☐   Over 10 ☐

Education: Elementary School: Yes ☐   No ☐
            High School: Yes ☐   No ☐
            University: Yes ☐   No ☐
Occupation/Profession: —————————————————————————
Foreign languages you know very well: ——————————————

Education	Elementary School:	Yes ☐	No ☐
of mother:	High School:	Yes ☐	No ☐
	University:	Yes ☐	No ☐

Mother's occupation/profession: —————————————

Education	Elementary School:	Yes ☐	No ☐
of father:	High School:	Yes ☐	No ☐
	University:	Yes ☐	No ☐

Father's occupation/profession: —————————————

Would you now read the following situations carefully and then fill in the missing parts of the dialogues. The length of the answers is not important; what is important is to be natural, where possible using responses you have employed in relevant, real-life situations. If you have any comments or wish to make additional qualifications, would you please write them in the space provided on the last page.

1. You are at a close friend's house. You did not have lunch and you feel very hungry.

You: You know something Kate, I didn't have time to have lunch;——
_____

_____

Kate: Oh, yes, there's still some food left over. What would you like?

2. You need a book and you know that one of your superiors (e.g. boss, manager, teacher) has got it, so you decide to go to his office and ask for it.

You: Excuse me, but I need the book you had here the other day;——
_____

_____

Superior: Yes, of course, but I shall be needing it myself next week.

3. You are flying off on holiday tomorrow and you haven't got your ticket from the travel agent. You are desperate, but you are unable to pick up the ticket yourself, so you ask a friend to do it.

        John, I've got so much work to do that I can't go and get my ticket from the travel agent; ——————————————
_____

_____

John: That's all right, I can go and get it this afternoon.

4. Your mother is about to go shopping. You would like her to pick up for you two magazines that have just come out.

You: I tried to get 'Private Eye' and 'TV Times' this morning, but they don't come out till this afternoon; ——————————
_____

Mother: Yes, and is there anything else you want?

5. You are going to a party and decide to borrow your sister's/brother's very nice new blouse/shirt.

You: I don't have anything that matches my new skirt/trousers; ——
_____
_____

S/he: Yes, you can have it.

6. You are at your office. You would like a packet of cigarettes/some stamps, but you can't go out. One of your subordinates (e.g. student, assistant) is just about to go out to get some for him/herself.
You: I haven't really got time to go out; ————————————
_____
_____

S/he: Yes, sure.

Please feel free to add any comments and information you consider relevant to this questionnaire.

_____
_____
_____
_____
_____
_____

Thank you very much for your help and co-operation.

3. QUESTIONNAIRE ON INDIRECTNESS

I would very much appreciate your help with my research. Would you please fill in the blanks or put an X in the appropriate box in the following.

Age: 18–22 ☐   23–32 ☐   33–42 ☐   43–60 ☐
Sex: F ☐   M ☐
Place of birth: ——————————————————————
Place of residence: ——————————————————————
How many years have you lived there?
            Up to 2 ☐   3–10 ☐   Over 10 ☐

Education: Elementary School: Yes ☐   No ☐
             High School: Yes ☐   No ☐
             Higher Education: Yes ☐   No ☐

University: Yes ☐   No ☐

Occupation/Profession: ————————————————————

Foreign languages you know very well: ——————————————

Education	Elementary School:	Yes ☐	No ☐
of mother:	High School:	Yes ☐	No ☐
	Higher Education:	Yes ☐	No ☐
	University:	Yes ☐	No ☐

Mother's occupation/profession: —————————————————

Education	Elementary School:	Yes ☐	No ☐
of father:	High School:	Yes ☐	No ☐
	Higher Education:	Yes ☐	No ☐
	University:	Yes ☐	No ☐

Father's occupation/profession: —————————————————

Would you now read the following four situations carefully and put an X in the box next to the utterance which you think best indicates the speaker's intention and seems to you the most natural in such situations.

If you have any comments or wish to make additional qualifications would you please write them in the space provided on the next page.

1. Two colleagues (A and B) are talking. A usually (but not always) gives B a lift to the university. In the course of their conversation B says:

B: Are you going to the university tomorrow?

a. B is asking just out of friendly interest.   ☐

b. B is asking because she wants to be given a lift.   ☐

2. A couple had the following exchange:

Wife: John's having a party. Would you like to go?

Husband: OK.

The husband thinks:

a. My wife is asking if I want to go to the party. I feel like going, so I'll say yes.   ☐

b. My wife wants to go to the party. I'll go to make her happy.   ☐

3. A mother is talking to her eleven year old son who is about to go out in the rain:

Mother: Where are your boots?

a. The mother is actually asking for the location of her son's boots.   ☐

b. The mother is asking because she wants her son to put on his boots before going out.   ☐

4. Between a couple:

Husband: Do you know where today's paper is?

a.   The husband wants to know where the newspaper was last seen.   ☐
b.   The husband is actually asking to be given the newspaper.   ☐

Add here any comments you consider relevant to this questionnaire.

_____

_____

_____

_____

_____

_____

Thank you for your help.

REFERENCES

AL-ISSA, J., and DENNIS, W. (1970) (eds.), *Cross-cultural studies of behavior* (New York: Holt, Rinehart, and Winston).

ANTONOPOULOU, E. (1991), *Agent-defocusing mechanisms in spoken English*, Paroouia Monograph Series 16 (Athens: University of Athens).

APPLEGATE, R. B. (1975), 'The language teacher and the rules of speaking', *TESOL Quarterly*, 9: 271–81.

ARMENIS, G. (1985), 'To theatro ke o logos', *I Lexi* 46: 594–5.

ARNDT, H., and JANNEY, R. W. (1985), 'Politeness revisited: cross-modal supportive strategies', *IRAL* 23/4: 281–300.

ATKINSON, J. M. (1982), 'Understanding formality: the categorization and production of "formal" interaction', *British Journal of Sociology*, 33: 86–117.

AUSTIN, J. L. (1962), *How to do things with words*, Harvard University, William James Lectures 1955 (Oxford: Oxford University Press).

BACH, E., and HARMS, R. T. (1968) (eds.), *Universals in linguistic theory* (New York: Holt, Rinehart, and Winston).

BACH, K., and HARNISH, R. M. (1982), *Linguistic communication and speech acts* (Cambridge, Mass.: MIT Press).

BARNLUND, D. C. (1975), 'Communicative styles in two cultures: Japan and the United States', in Kendon, Harris and Key (1975), 427–56.

BATES, E. (1976), *Language and context: the acquisition of Pragmatics* (New York: Academic Press).

—— and BENIGNI, L. (1975), 'Rules of address in Italy: a sociological survey', *Language in Society*, 4: 271–88.

—— CAMAIONI, L., and VOLTERRA, V. (1976), 'Sensorimotor performatives', in Bates (1976), 49–71.

BAUMAN, R., and SHERZER, J. (1974) (eds.), *Explorations in the ethnography of speaking* (Cambridge: Cambridge University Press).

BAXTER, L. A. (1984), 'An investigation of compliance-gaining as politeness', *Human Communication Research*, 10: 427–56.

BENTAHILA, A., and DAVIES, E. (1989), 'Culture and language use: a problem for foreign language teaching', *IRAL* 27/2: 99–112.

BETTEN, A. (1982), 'Language in modern drama as compared with authentic spoken discourse', *Proceedings of the XIIIth International Congress of Linguists*, 1077–81 (Tokyo).

BEVER, T. G., KATZ, J. J., and LANGENDOEN, D. T. (1976) (eds.), *An integrated theory of linguistic ability* (New York: Thomas Y. Crowell).

BLUM-KULKA, S. (1982), 'Learning to say what you mean in a second language: a study of the speech act performance of learners of Hebrew as a second language', *Applied Linguistics*, 3: 29–59.

—— (1983), 'Interpreting and performing speech acts in a second language: a cross-cultural study of Hebrew and English', in Wolfson and Judd (1983), 36–55.

—— (1987), 'Indirectness and politeness in requests: same or different?', *Journal of Pragmatics*, 11: 131–46.

—— (1990), 'You don't touch lettuce with your fingers: parental politeness in family discourse', *Journal of Pragmatics*, 14: 259–88.

—— HOUSE, J., AND KASPER, G. (1989) (eds.), *Cross-cultural pragmatics: requests and apologies* (Norwood, NJ: Ablex).

—— and OLSHTAIN, E. (1984), 'Requests and apologies: a cross-cultural study of speech act realization patterns (CCSARP)', *Applied Linguistics*, 5: 196–213.

BOLINGER, D. L. (1967), 'The imperatives in English', in *To Honour Roman Jakobson*, i. 335–62 (The Hague: Mouton).

—— (1981), *Aspects of language*, 3rd edn. (New York: Harcourt Brace Jovanovich, Inc.).

BRIGHT, W. (1966) (ed.), *Sociolinguistics: Proceedings of the UCLA Sociolinguistics Conference* (The Hague: Mouton).

BROWN, G., and YULE, G. (1983), *Discourse analysis* (Cambridge: Cambridge University Press).

BROWN, P. (1976), 'Women and politeness: a new perspective on language and society', *Reviews in Anthropology*, 3: 240–9.

—— (1980), 'How and why are women more polite: some evidence from a Mayan community', in McConnell-Ginet, Borker, and Furman (1980), 111–36.

—— and FRASER, C. (1979), 'Speech as a marker of situation', in Scherer and Giles (1979), 33–62.

—— and LEVINSON, S. (1978), 'Universals in language usage: politeness phenomena', in Goody (1978a), 56–310.

—— —— (1979), 'Social structure, groups and interaction', in Scherer and Giles (1979), 291–341.

—— —— (1987), *Politeness: some universals in language usage*, Studies in Interactional Sociolinguistics 4 (Cambridge: Cambridge University Press).

BROWN, R., and FORD, M. (1964), 'Address in American English', in Hymes (1964), 234–44.

—— and GILMAN, A. (1960), 'The pronouns of power and solidarity', in Giglioli (1972), 252–82.

—— —— (1989), 'Politeness theory and Shakespeare's four major tragedies', *Language in Society*, 18: 159–212.

BURTON, D. (1980), *Dialogue and discourse: a sociolinguistic approach to modern drama dialogue and naturally occurring conversation* (London: Routledge and Kegan Paul).

CAMPBELL, J. K. (1975), 'The honour of the Greeks', *The Times Literary Supplement*, 3 (Nov. 1975), 844.

CATTELL, R. (1973), 'Negative transportation and tag questions', *Language*, 49: 612–39.

CHAIKA, E. (1982), *Language: the social mirror* (Rowley, Mass.: Newbury House Publishers, Inc.).

CHERRY, R. D. (1988), 'Politeness in written persuasion', *Journal of Pragmatics*, 12: 63–81.

CLARK, H. H., and CARLSON, T. B. (1982), 'Hearers and speech acts', *Language*, 58: 332–73.

—— and LUCY, P. (1975), 'Understanding what is meant from what is said: a study in conversationally conveyed requests', *Journal of Verbal Learning and Verbal Behavior*, 14: 56–72.

—— and SCHUNK, D. H. (1980), 'Polite responses to polite requests', *Cognition*, 8: 111–43.

CLYNE, M. (1987a), 'Discourse structures and discourse expectations: implications for Anglo-German academic communication in English', in Smith (1987a), 73–83.

—— (1987b), 'Cultural differences in the organization of academic texts', *Journal of Pragmatics*, 11: 211–41.

COLE, P. (1978) (ed.), *Syntax and semantics 9: pragmatics* (New York: Academic Press).

—— and MORGAN, J. L. (1975) (eds.), *Syntax and semantics 3: speech acts* (New York: Academic Press).

—— and SADOCK, J. (1977) (eds.), *Syntax and semantics 8: grammatical relations* (New York: Academic Press).

COMRIE, B. (1975), 'Polite plurals and predicate agreement', *Language*, 51: 406–18.

—— (1977), 'In defense of spontaneous demotion: the impersonal passive', in Cole and Sadock (1977), 47–58.

COULMAS, F. (1979), 'On the sociolinguistic relevance of routine formulae', *Journal of Pragmatics*, 3: 239–66.

—— (1981a) (ed.), *Conversational routine: explorations in standardized communication situations and prepatterned speech* (The Hague: Mouton).

—— (1981b), ' "Poison to your soul" thanks and apologies contrastively viewed', in Coulmas (1981a), 69–91.

CRAIG, R. T., TRACY, K., and SPISAK, F. (1986), 'The discourse of requests: assessment of a politeness approach', *Human Communication Research*, 12: 437–68.

CULICOVER, P., WASOW, T., and AKMAJIAN, A. (1977) (eds.), *Formal syntax* (New York: Academic Press).

DAVISON, A. (1975), 'Indirect speech acts and what to do with them', in Cole and Morgan (1975), 143–85.

—— (1979), 'On the semantics of speech acts', *Journal of Pragmatics*, 3: 413–29.

DENDRINOS, V. (1985), *Teacher guide: for the teacher of English as a foreign language* (in Greek) (Athens: OEDV).

—— (1986), 'Cross-cultural issues in conversation', *Journal of Applied Linguistics*, 2: 37–50 (Thessaloniki: Greek Applied Linguistics Association).

—— (1988), *Views on EFL teaching and learning* (Athens: University of Athens).

DE SILVA, S. M. W. (1976), 'Verbal aspects of politeness expression in Sinhalese with reference to asking, telling, requesting and ordering', *Anthropological Linguistics*, 18: 360–70.

DIL, A. S. (1978) (ed.), *Language, culture and history: essays by Mary R. Haas* (Stanford, Calif.: Stanford University Press).

DIXON, R. M. W. (1980), *The languages of Australia*, Cambridge Language Surveys (Cambridge: Cambridge University Press).

DONALDSON, S. K. (1984), 'Some constraints of consideration on conversation: interactions of politeness and relevance with Grice's second maxim of quantity', unpublished Ph.D. dissertation (University of Illinois at Urbana-Champaign).

DOWNES, W. (1977), 'The imperative and pragmatics', *Journal of Linguistics*, 13: 77–97.

DRAZDAUSKIENE, M. L. (1981), 'On stereotypes in conversation, their meaning and significance', in Coulmas (1981a), 55–68.

DUBOIS, B. L., and CROUCH, I. (1975), 'The question of tag questions in women's speech: they don't really use more of them, do they? ↓ ' *Language in Society*, 4: 289–94.

DURANTI, A. (1985), 'Sociocultural dimensions of discourse', in van Dijk (1985a), 193–230.

DURRELL, L. (1978), *The Greek islands* (London: Faber and Faber).

EADES, D. (1982), 'You gotta know how to talk . . .: information seeking in South-East Queensland Aboriginal society', *Australian Journal of Linguistics*, 2: 61–82.

EDMONDSON, W. (1981), *Spoken discourse: a model for analysis* (London: Longman).

EDWARDS, V. K., TRUDGILL, P., and WELTENS, B. (1984), *The grammar of English dialect: a survey of research*, a Report to the ESRC Education and Human Development Committee, London.

ERVIN-TRIPP, S. (1972a), 'Sociolinguistic rules of address', in Pride and Holmes (1972), 225–40.

—— (1972*b*), 'On sociolinguistic rules: alternation and co-occurrence', in Gumperz and Hymes (1972), 213–50.

—— (1976), 'Is Sybil there? The structure of some American English directives', *Language in Society*, 5: 25–66.

—— (1981), 'How to make and understand a request', in Parret, Sbisà, and Verschueren (1981), 195–209.

—— GUO, J., and LAMPERT, M. (1990), 'Politeness and persuasion in children's control acts', *Journal of Pragmatics*, 14: 301–31.

FAERCH, C., and KASPER, G. (1984), 'Pragmatic knowledge: rules and procedures', *Applied Linguistics*, 5: 214–25.

FANG, H., and HENG, J. H. (1983), 'Social changes and changing address norms in China', *Language in Society*, 12: 495–507.

FERGUSON, C. A. (1959), 'Diglossia', in Giglioli (1972), 232–51.

—— (1981), 'The structure and use of politeness formulas', in Coulmas (1981*a*), 21–35.

FISHMAN, J. A. (1968) (ed.), *Readings in the sociology of language* (The Hague: Mouton).

FLEISCHMAN, S. (1989), 'Temporal distance: a basic linguistic metaphor', *Studies in Language*, 13: 1–50.

FOTION, N. (1981), 'Review of Searle: expression and meaning: Studies in the theory of speech acts', *Language in Society*, 10: 114–20.

FRASER, B. (1978), 'Acquiring social competence in a second language', *RELC Journal*, 9: 1–26.

—— (1990), 'Perspectives on politeness', *Journal of Pragmatics*, 14: 219–36.

—— and NOLEN, W. (1981), 'The association of deference with linguistic form', *International Journal of the Sociology of Language*, 27: 93–109.

—— RINTELL, E., and WALTERS, J. (1980), 'An approach to conducting research on the acquisition of pragmatic competence in a second language', in Larsen-Freeman (1980), 75–91.

FRIEDRICH, P. (1966), 'Structural implications of Russian pronominal usage', in Bright (1966), 214–59.

—— (1972), 'Social context and semantic feature: the Russian pronominal usage', in Gumperz and Hymes (1972), 270–300.

GARNICA, O. K. (1977), 'Rules of verbal interaction and literary analysis', *Poetics*, 6: 155–67.

GEERTZ, C. (1968), 'Linguistic etiquette', in Fishman (1968), 282–95.

GIBBS, R. W. (1979), 'Contextual effects in understanding indirect requests', *Discourse Processes*, 2: 1–10.

GIGLIOLI, P. P. (1972) (ed.), *Language and social context* (Harmondsworth: Penguin Books).

GIVÓN, T. (1978), 'Negation in language: pragmatics, function, ontology', in Cole (1978), 69–112.

GLEASON, J. B., and WEINTRAUB, S. (1976), 'The acquisition of routines in child language', *Language in Society*, 5: 129–36.

GODARD, D. (1977), 'Same setting, different norms: phone call beginnings in France and the United States', *Language in Society*, 6: 209–19.

GOFFMAN, E. (1956), 'The nature of deference and demeanor', *American Anthropologist*, 58: 473–502.

—— (1967), *Interaction ritual: essays on face-to-face behavior* (Garden City, NY: Anchor Books).

—— (1972), 'On face-work: an analysis of ritual elements in social interaction', in Laver and Hutcheson (1972), 319–46.

—— (1981), *Forms of talk* (Oxford: Blackwell).

GOODY, E. N. (1978a) (ed.), *Questions and politeness: strategies in social interaction* (Cambridge: Cambridge University Press).

—— (1978b), 'Towards a theory of questions', in Goody (1978a), 17–43.

GORDON, D., and LAKOFF, G. (1975), 'Conversational postulates', in Cole and Morgan (1975), 83–106.

GRADDOL, D., CHESHIRE, J., and SWANN, J. (1987), *Describing language* (Milton Keynes: Open University Press).

GREEN, G. M. (1975), 'How to get people to do things with words: the whimperative question', in Cole and Morgan (1975), 107–41.

GREENBERG, J. H. (1963) (ed.), *Universals of language* (Cambridge, Mass.: MIT Press).

—— OSGOOD, C. E., and JENKINS, J. J. (1963), 'Memorandum concerning language universals', in Greenberg (1963), 255–64.

GREIF, E. B., and GLEASON, J. B. (1980), 'Hi, thanks and good bye: more routine information', *Language in Society*, 9: 159–66.

GRICE, H. P. (1975), 'Logic and conversation', in Cole and Morgan (1975), 41–58.

GU, Y. (1990), 'Politeness phenomena in Modern Chinese', *Journal of Pragmatics*, 14: 237–57.

GUMPERZ, J. J. (1970), 'Sociolinguistics and communication in small groups', in Pride and Holmes (1972), 203–24.

—— (1982a), *Discourse strategies*, Studies in Interactional Sociolinguistics 1 (Cambridge: Cambridge University Press).

—— (1982b) (ed.), *Language and social identity*, Studies in Interactional Sociolinguistics 2 (Cambridge: Cambridge University Press).

—— and HYMES, D. H. (eds.) (1972), *Directions in sociolinguistics: the ethnography of communication* (New York: Holt, Rinehart, and Winston).

HAAS, M. (1978), 'The expression of the diminutive', in Dil (1978), 82–7.

HACKMAN, D. J. (1977), 'Patterns in purported speech acts', *Journal of Pragmatics*, 1: 143–54.

HALL, E. T. (1966), *The hidden dimension* (New York: Doubleday).

HARNISH, R. M. (1976), 'Logical form and implicature', in Bever, Katz, and Langendoen (1976), 313–92.

HARRIS, R. M. (1984), 'Truth and politeness: a study in the pragmatics of Egyptian Arabic conversation', unpublished Ph.D. dissertation, University of Cambridge.

HATCH, E., and LONG, M. H. (1980), 'Discourse analysis, what's that?', in Larsen-Freeman (1980), 1–40.

HAUGEN, E. (1975), 'Pronominal address in Icelandic: from you-two to you-all', *Language in Society*, 4: 323–39.

HAVERKATE, H. (1988), 'Politeness strategies in verbal interaction: an analysis of directness and indirectness in speech acts', *Semiotica*, 71: 59–71.

HENLEY, N. M. (1973), 'Status and sex: some touching observations', *Bulletin of the Psychonometry Society*, 2: 91–3.

HERBERT, R. K., and STRAIGHT, H. S. (1989), 'Compliment-rejection versus compliment-avoidance: listener-based versus speaker-based pragmatic strategies', *Language & Communication*, 9: 35–47.

HERINGER, J. (1972), 'Some grammatical correlates of felicity conditions and presuppositions', *Working Papers in Linguistics*, 11: 1–110 (Columbus, Oh.: Ohio State University, Department of Linguistics).

HERZFELD, M. (1980), 'Honour and shame: problems in the comparative analysis of moral systems', *Man*, NS 15: 339–51.

—— (1983), 'Looking both ways: the ethnographer in the text', *Semiotica*, 46: 151–66.

—— (1984), 'The significance of the insignificant: blasphemy as ideology', *Man*, NS 19: 653–64.

HILL, B., IDE, S., IKUTA, S., KAWASAKI, A., and OGINO, T. (1986), 'Universals of linguistic politeness', *Journal of Pragmatics*, 10: 347–71.

HINDS, J. (1976), *Aspects of Japanese disourse structure* (Tokyo: Kaita-kusha).

HOLLOS, M., and BEEMAN, W. (1978), 'The development of directives among Norwegian and Hungarian children: an example of communicative style in culture', *Language in Society*, 7: 345–55.

HOLMES J. (1986), 'Functions of *you know* in women's and men's speech', *Language in Society*, 15: 1–22.

HOLTGRAVES, T. (1986), 'Language structure in social interaction: perceptions of direct and indirect speech acts and interactants who use them', *Journal of Personality and Social Psychology*, 51: 305–14.

HOOK, D. D. (1974), 'Sexism in English pronouns and forms of address', *General Linguistics*, 14: 86–96.

—— (1984), 'First names and titles as solidarity and power semantics in English', *IRAL* 22/3: 183–9.

HOUSE, J. (1989), 'Politeness in English and German: the function of *Please* and *Bitte*', in Blum-Kulka, House, and Kasper (1989), 96–119.

—— and KASPER, G. (1981), 'Politeness markers in English and German', in Coulmas (1981*a*), 157–85.

HOWELL, R. (1965), 'Linguistic status markers in Korean', *Kroeber Anthropological Papers*, 33: 91–7.

HUDSON, R. A. (1980), *Sociolinguistics* (Cambridge: Cambridge University Press).

HURFORD, J. R., and HEASLEY, B. (1983), *Semantics: A coursebook* (Cambridge: Cambridge University Press).

HWANG, J. (1990), ' "Deference" versus "politeness" in Korean speech', *International Journal of the Sociology of Language*, 82: 41–55.

HYMES, D. H. (1964) (ed.), *Language in culture and society: a reader in Linguistics and Anthropology* (New York: Harper and Row).

—— (1966), 'Two types of linguistic relativity (with examples from Amerindian ethnography)', in Bright (1966), 114–67.

—— (1968*a*), 'Opening remarks: current frontiers in linguistic anthropology', *Proceedings of the 8th International Congress of Anthropological and Ethnological Sciences 3: Ethnology and Archeology*, 405–6 (Tokyo: Science Council of Japan).

—— (1968*b*), 'The ethnography of speaking', in Fishman (1968), 99–138.

—— (1972*a*), 'The scope of sociolinguistics', in Shuy (1972), 313–33.

—— (1972*b*), 'Editorial introduction', *Language in Society*, 1: 1–14.

—— (1972*c*), 'Models of the interaction of language and social life', in Gumperz and Hymes (1972), 35–71.

—— (1985), 'Toward linguistic competence', *AILA Review* 2: 9–23 (Association Internationale de Linguistique Appliquée).

—— (1986), 'Discourse: scope without depth', *International Journal of the Sociology of Language*, 57: 49–89.

IDE, S. (1989), 'Formal forms and discernment: two neglected aspects of universals of linguistic politeness', *Multilingua*, 8: 223–48.

IRVINE, J. T. (1979), 'Formality and informality in communicative events', *American Anthropologist*, 81: 773–90.

JANNEY, R. W., and ARNDT, H. (1993), 'Universality and relativity in cross-cultural research: a historical perspective', *Multilingua*, 12/1.

JOSEPH, B. D., and PHILIPPAKI-WARBURTON, I. (1987), *Modern Greek* (London: Croom Helm).

KACHRU, Y. (1987), 'Cross-cultural texts, discourse strategies and discourse interpretation', in Smith (1987*a*), 87–100.

KASPER, G. (1979), 'Errors in speech act realization and use of gambits', *Canadian Modern Language Review*, 35: 395–406.

—— (1990), 'Linguistic politeness: current research issues', *Journal of Pragmatics*, 14: 193–218.

KATO, K. (1986), 'Another look at ellipsis: non-native recoverability of ellipsis and its implications for linguistic competence', *Journal of Pragmatics*, 10: 415–34.

KATZ, J. J., and POSTAL, P. M. (1964), *An integrated theory of linguistic descriptions* (Cambridge, Mass.: MIT Press).

KEENAN, E. (1974), 'Norm-makers, norm-breakers: uses of speech by men and women in a Malagasy community', in Bauman and Sherzer (1974), 125–43.

—— (1976), 'The universality of conversational postulates', *Language in Society*, 5: 67–80.

KEESING, R. M. (1979), 'Lingustic knowledge and cultural knowledge: some doubts and speculations', *American Anthropologist*, 81: 14–36.

KEMPF, R. (1985), 'Pronouns and terms of address in Neues Deutschland', *Language in Society*, 14: 223–37.

KENDON, A. (1981) (ed.), *Nonverbal communication, interaction, and gesture* (The Hague: Mouton).

—— HARRIS, R. M., and KEY, M. R. (1975) (eds.), *Organisation of behavior in face-to-face interaction* (The Hague: Mouton).

KESHAVARZ, M. H. (1988), 'Forms of address in post-revolutionary Iranian Persian: a sociolinguistic analysis', *Language in Society*, 17: 565–75.

KIM, S. (1968), 'An expansion structure of the polite form in Korean', *Proceedings of the 8th International Congress of Anthropological and Ethnological Sciences 3: Ethnology and Archeology*, 419–22 (Tokyo: Science Council of Japan).

KRAMER, C. (1975), 'Sex-related differences in address systems', *Anthropological Linguistics*, 17: 198–210.

LABOV, W. (1966), *The Social stratification of English in New York City* (Washington, DC: Center for Applied Linguistics).

—— (1972a), *Sociolinguistic patterns* (Philadelphia: University of Pennsylvania Press).

—— (1972b), 'Some principles of linguistic methodology', *Language in Society*, 1: 97–120.

—— and FANSHEL, D. (1977), *Therapeutic discourse: psychotherapy as conversation* (New York: Academic Press).

LAKOFF, R. (1969), 'A syntactic argument for negative transportation', *Papers from the Fifth Regional Meeting of the Chicago Linguistic Society*, 140–7 (Chicago).

—— (1972), 'Language in context', *Language*, 48: 907–27.

—— (1973), 'The logic of politeness; or, minding your p's and q's', *Papers from the Ninth Regional Meeting of the Chicago Linguistic Society*, 292–305 (Chicago).

—— (1975), *Language and woman's place* (New York: Harper and Row).

—— (1977), 'What you can do with words: politeness, pragmatics, and performatives', in A. Rogers, B. Wall, and J. P. Murphy (eds.), *Proceedings of the Texas Conference on Performatives, Presuppositions and Implicatures*, 79–105 (Washington, DC: Center for Applied Linguistics).

LARKIN, D., and O'MALLEY, M. H. (1973), 'Declarative sentences and the rule-of-conversation hypothesis', *Papers from the Ninth Regional Meeting of the Chicago Linguistic Society*, 306–19 (Chicago).

LARSEN-FREEMAN, D. (1980) (ed.), *Discourse analysis in second language research* (Rowley, Mass.: Newbury House).

LASCARATOU, C. (1984), 'The passive voice in Modern Greek', unpublished Ph.D. thesis, Reading University.

—— and PHILIPPAKI-WARBURTON, I. (1981), 'The use of passive constructions in Modern Greek', *Mandatoforos*, 17: 53–64.

—— (1983–4), 'Lexical versus transformational passives in Modern Greek', *Glossologia*, 2–3: 99–109.

LAVER, J., and HUTCHESON, S. (1972) (eds.), *Communication in face-to-face interaction* (Harmondsworth: Penguin).

LEECH, G. N. (1980), *Language and tact*, Pragmatics and Beyond Series (Amsterdam: Benjamins).

—— (1983), *Principles of pragmatics* (London: Longman).

LEVINSON, S. C. (1978), 'Sociolinguistic universals', unpublished paper, Department of Linguistics, University of Cambridge.

—— (1983), *Pragmatics* (Cambridge: Cambridge University Press).

LIGHTFOOT, D. (1979), *Principles of diachronic syntax* (Cambridge: Cambridge University Press).

LOCASTRO, V. (1987), '*Aizuchi*: a Japanese conversational routine', in Smith (1987*a*), 101–13.

LOVEDAY, L. (1982), *The sociolinguistics of learning and using a non-native language* (Oxford: Pergamon Press).

—— (1983), 'Rhetoric patterns in conflict: the socio-cultural relativity of discourse-organizing processes', *Journal of Pragmatics*, 9: 169–90.

LYONS, J. (1968), *Introduction to theoretical linguistics* (Cambridge: Cambridge University Press).

—— (1981*a*), *Language and linguistics: an introduction* (Cambridge: Cambridge University Press).

—— (1981*b*), *Language, meaning and context* (London: Fontana Paperbacks).

MCCAWLEY, J. D. (1968), 'The role and semantics in a grammar', in Bach and Harms (1968), 124–69.

MCCONNELL-GINET, S., BORKER, R., and FURMAN, N. (1980) (eds.), *Women and language in literature and society* (New York: Praeger).

MACKRIDGE, P. (1985), *The modern Greek language* (Oxford: Oxford University Press).

MAKRI-TSILIPAKOU, M. (1983), 'Apopira perigrafis tis neoellinikis prosfonisis', *Studies in Greek Linguistics: Proceedings of the Fourth Annual*

Meeting of the Department of Linguistics, Faculty of Philosophy, Aristotelian University of Thessaloniki, 219–39.

MALTZ, D. N., and BORKER, R. A. (1982), 'A cultural approach to male–female miscommunication', in Gumperz (1982*b*), 196–216.

MANES, J., and WOLFSON, N. (1981), 'The compliment formula', in Coulmas (1981*a*), 115–32.

MARKEL, N. (1975), 'Coverbal behavior associated with conversation turns', in Kendon, Harris, and Key (1975), 189–97.

MARMARIDOU, A. S. A. (1987), 'Semantic and pragmatic parameters of meaning: on the interface between contrastive text analysis and the production of translated texts', *Journal of Pragmatics*, 11: 721–36.

MATSUMOTO, Y. (1988), 'Reexamination of the universality of face: politeness phenomena in Japanese', *Journal of Pragmatics*, 12: 403–26.

—— (1989), 'Politeness and conversational universals: observations from Japanese', *Multilingua*, 8: 207–21.

MORAIN, G. G. (1986), 'Kinesics and cross-cultural understanding', in Valdes (1986), 64–76.

MORGAN, J. L. (1978), 'Two types of convention in indirect speech acts', in Cole (1978), 261–80.

MYERS, G. (1989), 'The pragmatics of politeness in scientific articles', *Applied Linguistics*, 10: 1–35.

NEUSTUPNÝ, J. V. (1968), 'Politeness patterns in the system of communication', *Proceedings of the Eighth Congress of Anthropological and Ethnological Sciences*, 412–19 (Tokyo and Kyoto).

—— (1978), *Post-structural approaches to language: language theory in a Japanese context* (Tokyo: University of Tokyo Press).

NIDA, E. (1964), 'Linguistics and ethnology in translation problems', in Hymes (1964), 90–100.

NIPPOLD, M. A., LEONARD, L. B., and ANASTOPOULOS, A. (1982), 'Development in the use and understanding of polite forms in children', *Journal of Speech and Hearing Research*, 25: 193–202.

OLSHTAIN, E., and COHEN, A. D. (1983), 'Apology: a speech act set', in Wolfson and Judd (1983), 18–35.

PAPAEFTHYMIOU-LYTRA, S. (1987*a*), *Language, language awareness and foreign language learning* (Athens: University of Athens).

—— (1987*b*), 'Classroom interaction: the L1 in the foreign language classroom', *ERIC ED 289–359* (Center for Applied Linguistics, Washington, DC).

—— (1990), *Explorations in foreign language classroom discourse*, Parousia Monograph Series 10 (Athens: University of Athens).

PARRET, H., SBISÀ, M., and VERSCHUEREN, J. (1981) (eds.), *Possibilities and limitations of pragmatics: Proceedings of the Conference on Pragmatics at Urbino, July 8–14 1979* (Amsterdam: Benjamins).

PAULSTON, C. B. (1976), 'Pronouns of address in Swedish: social class semantics and a changing system', *Language in Society*, 5: 359–86.

PAVLIDOU, T. (1984), 'Paratirisis sta thilika epagelmatika', *Studies in Greek Linguistics: Proceedings of the Fifth Annual Meeting of the Department of Linguistics, Faculty of Philosophy, Aristotelian University of Thessaloniki*, 201–17.

—— (1986), ' "Na rotiso kati?' erotisis se ipotaktiki', *Studies in Greek Linguistics: Proceedings of the Seventh Annual Meeting of the Department of Linguistics, Faculty of Philosophy, Aristotelian University of Thessaloniki*, 233–49.

PERLMUTTER, D., and POSTAL, P. (1977), 'Toward a universal characterization of passivization', *Proceedings of the Third Annual Meeting of the Berkeley Linguistics Society*, 394–417.

PERSSON, G. (1974), *Repetition in English. Part 1: sequential repetition*, Uppsala, Acta Universitatis Upsaliensis 21.

PHILIPPAKI-WARBURTON, I., and VELOUDIS, I. (1984), 'I ipotaktiki stis simpliromatikes protasis', *Studies in Greek Linguistics*, 5: 149–67 (Faculty of Philosophy, Aristotelian University of Thessaloniki).

PHILIPS, S. U. (1976), 'Some sources of cultural variability in the regulation of talk', *Language in Society*, 5: 81–95.

POSTAL, P. M. (1964), 'Underlying and superficial linguistic structure', in Reibel and Schane (1964), 19–37.

PRIDE, J. B., and HOLMES, J. (1972) (eds.), *Sociolinguistics: selected readings* (Harmondsworth: Penguin Books).

PSASTHAS, G. (1979) (ed.), *Everyday language: studies in ethnomethodology* (New York: Irvington Publishers, Inc.).

QUIRK, R., GREENBAUM, S., LEECH, G., and SVARTVIK, J. (1972), *A grammar of contemporary English* (London: Longman).

RASKIN, V. (1979), 'Literal meanings in speech acts', *Journal of Pragmatics*, 3: 489–95.

REIBEL, D., and SCHANE, S. (1964) (eds.), *Modern studies in English* (Englewood Cliffs, NJ: Prentice-Hall).

RIBEIRO-PEDRO, E. (1981), *Social stratification and classroom discourse: a sociolinguistic analysis of classroom practice* (Stockholm: CWK Gleerup Liber Laromedel Lund).

RICHARDS, J. R., and SCHMIDT, R. W. (1983) (eds.), *Language and communication* (London: Longman).

RINTELL, E. (1981), 'Sociolinguistic variation and pragmatic ability: a look at learners', *International Journal of the Sociology of Language*, 27: 11–34.

ROBINSON, W. P. (1972), *Language and social behaviour* (Harmondsworth: Penguin Books).

ROSALDO, M. Z. (1982), 'The things we do with words: Ilongot speech acts and speech act theory in philosophy', *Language in Society*, 11: 203–37.

SADOCK, J. (1974), *Towards a linguistic theory of speech acts* (New York: Academic Press).

SAVILLE-TROIKE, M. (1982), *The ethnography of communication: an introduction*, Language in Society 3 (Oxford: Blackwell).

SCHEFLEN, A. E. (1975), 'Micro-territories in human interaction', in Kendon, Harris, and Key (1975), 159–73.

SCHEGLOFF, E. A. (1979), 'Identification and recognition in telephone conversation openings', in Psathas (1979), 23–78.

SCHERER, K. R., and GILES, H. (1979) (eds.), *Social markers in speech* (Cambridge: Cambridge University Press).

SCHIFFRIN, D. (1981), 'Handwork as ceremony: the case of the handshake', in Kendon (1981), 237–50.

SCOLLON, R., and SCOLLON, S. B. K. (1981), *Narrative literacy and face in interethnic communication* (Norwood, NJ: Ablex).

—— —— (1983), 'Face in inter ethnic communication', in Richards and Schmidt (1983), 156–88.

SCOTTON, C. M., and WANJIN, Z. (1983), '*Tóngzhì* in China: language change and its conversational consequences', *Language in Society*, 12: 477–94.

SEARLE, J. R. (1975), 'Indirect speech acts', in Cole and Morgan (1975), 59–82.

—— (1979), *Expression and meaning: studies in the theory of speech acts* (Cambridge: Cambridge University Press).

SHIBATANI, M. (1985), 'Passives and related constructions: a prototype analysis', *Language*, 61: 821–48.

SHUY, R. (1972) (ed.), *Monograph series on language and linguistics* (Washington, DC: Georgetown University Press).

SIFIANOU, M. (1989), 'On the telephone again! Differences in telephone behaviour: England versus Greece', *Language in Society*, 18: 527–44.

—— (1992), 'The use of diminutives in expressing politeness: Modern Greek versus English', *Journal of Pragmatics*, 17: 155–73.

—— (1993), 'Off-record indirectness and the notion of imposition', *Multilingua*, 12/1.

SINCLAIR, J., and COULTHARD, R. M. (1978), *Towards an analysis of discourse: the English used by teachers and pupils* (Oxford: Oxford University Press).

SINGH, R., LELE, J., and MARTOHARDJONO, G. (1988), 'Communication in a multilingual community: some missed opportunities', *Language in Society*, 17: 43–59.

SMITH, L. E. (1987a) (ed.), *Discourse across cultures: strategies in world Englishes* (New York: Prentice Hall).

SMITH, L. E. (1987*b*), 'Introduction: discourse strategies and cross-cultural communication', in Smith (1987*a*), 1–6.

SNOW, C. E. PERLMANN, P. Y., GLEASON, J. B., and HOOSHYAR, N. (1990), 'Developmental perspectives on politeness: sources of children's knowledge', *Journal of Pragmatics*, 14: 289–305.

STUBBS, M. (1983), *Discourse analysis: the sociolinguistic analysis of natural language*, Language in Society 4 (Oxford: Blackwell).

TANNEN, D. (1980), 'Implications of the oral/literate continuum for cross-cultural communication', in J. E. Alatis (ed.), *Current issues in bilingual education*, 326–47 (Washington, DC: Georgetown University Press).

—— (1981), 'The machine-gun question: an example of conversational style', *Journal of Pragmatics*, 5: 383–97.

—— (1982), 'Ethnic style in male–female conversation', in Gumperz (1982*b*), 217–31.

—— (1983), ' "I take out the rock-dok!": how Greek women tell about being molested (and create involvement)', *Anthropological Linguistics*, 25: 359–73.

—— (1984*a*), *Conversational style: analyzing talk among friends* (Norwood, NJ: Ablex Publishing Corporation).

—— (1984*b*), 'Cross-cultural communication', *CATESOL Occasional Papers*, 10: 1–16.

—— (1985), 'Cross-cultural communication', in van Dijk (1985*b*), 203–15.

—— (1986), *That's not what I meant: how conversational style makes or breaks your relations with others* (New York: W. Morrow and Company, Inc.).

—— (1990), *You just don't understand: women and men in conversation* (New York: W. Morrow and Company, Inc.).

—— and OZTEK, P. C. (1981), 'Health to our mouths: formulaic expressions in Turkish and Greek', in Coulmas (1981*a*), 37–54.

THOMAS, J. (1983), 'Cross-cultural pragmatic failure', *Applied Linguistics*, 4: 91–112.

THORNE, B., and HENLEY, N. (1975) (eds.), *Language and sex: difference and dominance* (Rowley, Mass.: Newbury House Publishers).

TRIANDIS, H. C. (1972) (ed.), *The analysis of subjective culture*, Comparative Studies in Behavioral Science (New York: Wiley).

—— KILTY, K. M., SHANMUGAM, A. V., TANAKA, Y., and VASSILIOU, V. (1972), 'Cognitive structures and the analysis of values', in Triandis (1972), 181–261.

—— and TRIANDIS, L. M. (1970), 'Social distance among Greek and United States college students', in Al-Issa and Dennis (1970), 175–95.

—— and VASSILIOU, V. (1972), 'A comparative analysis of subjective culture', in Triandis (1972), 299–335.

TRIANDAFILLIDES, M. (1978), *Neolliniki grammatiki (tis dimotikis)*, rev. edn. (Aristotelio Panepistimio Thessalonikis).

TRUDGILL, P. (1974), *Sociolinguistics: an introduction to language and society* (Harmondsworth: Penguin Books).

—— (1975a), *Accent, dialect and the school* (London: Edward Arnold).

—— (1975b), 'Sex, covert prestige, and linguistic change in the urban British English of Norwich', in Thorne and Henley (1975), 88–104.

TSOCHATZIDES, S. L. (1986), 'I pragmatologia tu "nde" ', *Studies in Greek Linguistics: Proceedings of the Seventh Annual Meeting of the Department of Linguistics, Faculty of Philosophy, Aristotelian University of Thessaloniki*, 223–31.

VALDES, J. M. (1986) (ed.), *Culture bound: bridging the cultural gap in language teaching* (Cambridge: Cambridge University Press).

VAN DIJK, T. (1985a) (ed.), *Handbook of discourse analysis 1: disciplines of discourse* (London: Academic Press).

—— (1985b) (ed.), *Handbook of discourse analysis 4: discourse analysis in society* (London: Academic Press).

VASSILIOU, V., TRIANDIS, H. C., VASSILIOU, G., and McGUIRE, H. (1972), 'Interpersonal contact and stereotyping', in Triandis (1972), 89–115.

VELOUDIS, I. (1987), ' "*Mi fiɣo, mi fiɣis, *mi fiɣi . . ./na mi fiɣo, na mi fiɣis, na mi fiɣi . . . i gramatikopiisi tis amesotitas stin Elliniki glosa', *Studies in Greek Linguistics: Proceedings of the Eighth Annual Meeting of the Department of Linguistics, Faculty of Philosophy, Aristotelian University of Thessaloniki*, 293–309.

—— and PHILIPPAKI-WARBURTON, I. (1983), 'I ipotaktiki sta Nea Ellinika', *Studies in Greek Linguistics: Proceedings of the Fourth Annual Meeting of the Department of Linguistics, Faculty of Philosophy, Aristotelian University of Thessaloniki*, 151–68.

VERSCHUEREN, J. (1981), 'The semantics of forgotten routines', in Coulmas (1981a), 133–53.

VINE, J. (1975), 'Territoriality and the spatial regulation of interaction', in Kendon, Harris, and Key (1975), 357–87.

WADMAN, K. L. (1983), ' "Private ejaculations": politeness strategies and George Herbert's poems directed to God', *Language and Style*, 16: 87–106.

WARBURTON, I. (1975), 'The passive in English and Greek', *Foundations of Language*, 13: 563–78.

WARDHAUGH, R. (1985), *How conversation works* (Oxford: Blackwell).

—— (1986), *An introduction to sociolinguistics* (Oxford: Blackwell).

WASOW, T. (1977), 'Transformations and the lexicon', in Culicover, Wasow, and Akmajian (eds.), 327–60.

WERTH, P. (1981) (ed.), *Conversation and discourse: structure and interpretation* (London: Croom Helm).

WETZEL, P. J. (1988), 'Are "powerless" communication strategies the Japanese norm?', *Language in Society*, 17: 555–64.

WIERZBICKA, A. (1979), 'Ethno-syntax and the philosophy of language', *Studies in Language*, 3: 313–83.

—— (1984), 'Diminutives and depreciatives: semantic representation for derivational categories', *Quaderni di Semantica*, 5: 123–30.

—— (1985a), 'Different cultures, different languages, different speech acts: Polish vs. English', *Journal of Pragmatics*, 9: 145–78.

—— (1985b), 'A semantic metalanguage for a cross-cultural comparison of speech acts and speech genres', *Language in Society*, 14: 491–513.

—— (1986), 'Does language reflect culture? Evidence from Australian English', *Language in Society*, 15: 349–73.

WILSON, D., and SPERBER, D. (1981), 'On Grice's theory of conversation', in Werth (1981), 155–78.

WOLFSON, N. (1976), 'Speech events and natural speech: some implications for sociolinguistic methodology', *Language in Society*, 5: 189–209.

—— (1981), 'Compliments in cross-cultural perspective', *TESOL Quarterly*, 15: 117–24.

—— (1983), 'An empirically based analysis of complimenting in American English', in Wolfson and Judd (1983), 82–95.

—— D'AMICO-REISNER, L., and HUBER, L. (1983), 'How to arrange for social commitments in American English: the invitation', in Wolfson and Judd (1983), 116–28.

—— and JUDD, E. (1983) (eds.), *Sociolinguistics and language acquisition*, Series on issues in second language research (Rowley, Mass.: Newbury House Publishers).

—— and MANES, J. (1980), ' "Don't 'dear' me!" ', in McConnell-Ginet, Borker, and Furman (1980), 79–92.

YAMANASHI, M. (1974), 'On minding your p's and q's in Japanese: a case study from honorifics', *Papers from the Tenth Regional Meeting of the Chicago Linguistic Society*, 760–71 (Chicago).

YALDEN, J. (1983), *The communicative syllabus: evolution, design and implementation* (Oxford: Pergamon Press).

YOUNG, L. W. L. (1982), 'Inscrutability revisited', in Gumperz (1982b), 72–84.

ZIMIN, S. (1981), 'Sex and politeness: factors in first- and second-language use', *International Journal of the Sociology of Language*, 27: 35–58.

INDEX